INTO THE CLOSET

Cross-Dressing and the Gendered Body
in Children's Literature and Film

Victoria Flanagan

Children's Literature and Culture
Jack Zipes, *Series Editor*

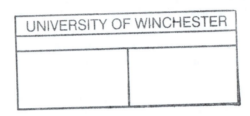

Routledge
Taylor & Francis Group
711 Third Avenue
New York, NY 10017

Routledge
Taylor & Francis Group
2 Park Square
Milton Park, Abingdon
Oxfordshire OX14 4RN

© 2008 by Taylor & Francis Group, LLC
Routledge is an imprint of Taylor & Francis Group, an Informa business

First published in paperback 2011

ISBN13: 978-0-415-98008-1 (hbk)
ISBN13: 978-0-415-80904-7 (pbk)

Library of Congress Cataloging-in-Publication Data

Flanagan, Victoria, 1976-
   Into the closet : cross-dressing and the gendered body in children's literature and film / by Victoria Flanagan.
      p. cm. -- (Children's literature and culture ; 47)
   Includes bibliographical references and index.
   ISBN 978-0-415-98008-1 (hardback : alk. paper)
   1. Children's literature--History and criticism. 2. Sex role in literature. 3. Sex role in motion pictures. 4. Transvestism in literature. 5. Transvestism in motion pictures. I. Title.

PN1009.5.S48F53 2007
809'.89282--dc22   2007004913

Visit the Taylor & Francis Web site at
http://www.taylorandfrancis.com

and the Routledge Web site at
http://www.routledge.com

For Riku and Sirke

Identifying with a gender under contemporary regimes of power involves identifying with a set of norms that are and are not realizable, and whose power and status precede the identifications by which they are insistently approximated. This "being a man" and this "being a woman" are internally unstable affairs.

Judith Butler

Bodies That Matter

CONTENTS

SERIES EDITOR'S FOREWORD

Dedicated to furthering original research in children's literature and culture, the Children's Literature and Culture series includes monographs on individual authors and illustrators, historical examinations of different periods, literary analyses of genres, and comparative studies on literature and the mass media. The series is international in scope and is intended to encourage innovative research in children's literature with a focus on interdisciplinary methodology.

Children's literature and culture are understood in the broadest sense of the term "children" to encompass the period of childhood through adolescence. Owing to the fact that the notion of childhood has changed so much since the origination of children's literature, this Routledge series is particularly concerned with transformations in children's culture and how they have affected the representation and socialization of children. While the emphasis of the series is on children's literature, all types of studies that deal with children's radio, film, television, and art are included in an endeavor to grasp the aesthetics and values of children's culture. Not only have there been momentous changes in children's culture in the last fifty years, but there have also been radical shifts in the scholarship that deals with these changes. In this regard, the goal of the Children's Literature and Culture series is to enhance research in this field and, at the same time, point to new directions that bring together the best scholarly work throughout the world.

Jack Zipes

ACKNOWLEDGMENTS

This book, which began its life as my doctoral thesis, would never have had a beginning, middle, or end without Professor John Stephens. I am forever indebted to him for his unwavering support, guidance, and friendship. He also provided me with a delightful English translation of *Min Syster är en Ängel* (Stark 1996), a Swedish picture book which soon became my favorite text. For me, it is the definitive example of cross-dressing's transformative and intersubjective potential. Without his generous assistance, I would not have been able to include *Min Syster är en Ängel* in this project. It is impossible to thank him enough.

I extend my heartfelt thanks to my parents for the numerous ways in which they assisted, supported, and tolerated(!) me during the completion of this project. Having children is what inadvertently thwarted my father's own attempts at a doctorate, so this project is dedicated to him in gratitude for what he relinquished for us. My mother, Carol, whose lively passion for literature and wonderfully argumentative nature inspired me to begin writing in the first place, was nothing short of angelic in the way that she devoted her energies to helping me in the final stages of this project. Her expert editorial skills, generously applied to my entire manuscript despite an excessively busy life, will always be remembered. (The exhortation "Shorten your sentences!" will probably haunt me to my grave.) She also gave me comfort when I needed it most, proffering a shoulder to cry on whenever I felt despondent. She was simultaneously my biggest critic and my greatest ally.

My thanks would not be complete without mentioning Damien MacRae. Damien graciously read one of my chapters and made incisive comments about it. However, I am most indebted to him for the unlimited enthusiasm he has always had for my work. He is a truly fabulous friend, and I hope that one day I can repay him for all the kindness he has shown me over the many years of our friendship. Last, but not least, I express my deepest gratitude to Riku Miekk-oja. He wasn't there at the beginning of this project, but he showed his love and support in countless ways toward the end—which is where it counts most.

INTRODUCTION

In the introduction to *Vested Interests,* an examination of Western culture's fascination with the subject of cross-dressing, Marjorie Garber writes, "It is curious to note how many literary and cultural critics have recently studied the phenomenon of cross-dressing in literature from the Renaissance to high modernism" ([1992] 1993, 9). Perhaps even more curious, then, is that despite its abundance in children's literature and film, very little critical attention has been paid to the significance of cross-dressing representations in media directed at child or adolescent audiences. Clothing is a potent cultural symbol of gender and sexual difference, and the wearing of the clothes deemed socially appropriate for the opposite sex is generally considered to be a transgressive and provocative act. Aside from being a sign of social rebellion, the appeal of cross-dressing, explains Garber, "is clearly related to its status as a sign of the constructedness of gender categories" (9). Central to the children's cross-dressing narrative is a preoccupation with the relationship between gender and sex, particularly in the context of how gender is socially inscribed upon the human body. Literature and film for children typically offer a nonsexualized and temporary construction of cross-dressing which focuses on the cross-dresser's potential to destabilize normative gender categories through the simulation of a differently gendered subjectivity.

The figure of the cross-dresser features prominently within Judith Butler's significant treatise, *Gender Trouble,* as an illustration of how gender is performatively constituted through the "stylized repetition of acts" that approximate rather than express a stable and fixed gender identity ([1990] 1999, 179). Butler's theory is germane to the construction of female-to-male cross-dressing in children's literature, which similarly embraces the notion of gender as illusory and performative. Although cross-dressing is popularly perceived to be a male activity, the predominant type of cross-dressing behavior in children's literature is female-to-male. One of the more remarkable aspects of female-to-male cross-dressing representations in children's literature is their lack of homogeneity with regard to genre and sociocultural context. Narratives which feature female cross-dressing characters are consistently dissimilar in terms of setting, use of generic conventions, and cultural origin. Notwithstanding this extensive diversity, these narratives cohesively employ cross-dressing as a unique and effective strategy through which to interrogate gender stereotypes. The cross-dressing heroine's ability to master an authentic masculine performance is celebrated and validated as a legitimate response to prescriptive definitions of masculinity and femininity. Stories of female cross-dressers demonstrate the limitations that normative gender categories can impose upon individuals. They use the cross-dresser's masculine success to promote a more liberatory and fluid conceptualization of gender.

Children's retellings of the story of Joan of Arc comprise an exception to the characteristic representation of female-to-male cross-dressing. Joan of Arc's refusal to abandon her masculine costume, and her subsequent execution, are an intrinsic part of her legend. However, children's texts are generally wary of emphasizing her transgressive gender behavior. Unlike other cross-dressing heroines of children's literature, who easily subvert gender stereotypes and negotiate an individualistic gender identity for themselves, Joan of Arc's cross-dressing is less effective as a form of gender protest. Authors and illustrators alike demonstrate an unwillingness to fictionalize the subjectivity of this celebrated historical figure, employing a range of narrative and pictorial techniques to situate her at one remove from the viewer/reader. Her subjectivity is therefore constructed in limited terms, concealed rather than explored. The significance of Joan of Arc's cross-dressing is consequently diminished. Her perception of it is obscured by narrative and visual strategies which prevent the viewer/reader from accessing the emotional complexity of her interior character. Retellings of Joan of Arc's life contradict the usual association of female cross-dressing with agency in children's literature, illustrative of the way in which representational strategies can compromise the operation of cross-dressing as a strategy for gender criticism.

Due to the pervasiveness of female cross-dressing, it is not possible to examine every occurrence of it here. For this reason I have tried to include a variety of archetypal examples, from different genres and cultural contexts, to demonstrate how female cross-dressing operates as a motif in children's literature. Retellings of the Joan of Arc legend provide a constructive contrast to the general representation of female cross-dressing, but I have also chosen to examine a selection of other texts which similarly feature less effective female cross-dressing performances. These representations of female cross-dressing are compromised for a variety of reasons, such as prevailing patriarchal conceptualizations of masculinity or a propensity to use limited focalization strategies that restrict the realization of the female cross-dressing character as a multidimensional, agential character. Nevertheless, the masculine disguise of these female characters still enables them to excel at masculine social roles, implicitly facilitating reframing of masculinity that accentuates the constructedness of traditional gender norms, or, in the case of Joan of Arc, valorize female cross-dressing as legitimate behavior.

Paradoxically, male-to-female cross-dressers in children's literature and film are much less successful at interrogating gender stereotypes. Male cross-dressing, like female cross-dressing, is dissociated from the adult concepts of transvestism and transsexualism when depicted in children's literature. Yet, unlike cross-dressing heroines, the male-to-female cross-dressing characters who occasionally appear in children's literature are incapable of similarly using cross-dressing to reflect upon the machinations of socially constructed gender categories.

Male cross-dressers are usually prepubescent and their cross-dressing is unwillingly forced upon them. Although their cross-dressing is not of their own volition, the specter of "deviant" sexuality looms with foreboding above the idea of an effective performance of femininity by a male cross-dresser. Children's narratives rely on the male cross-dresser's complete inability to give an authentic performance of femininity, and his dismay at being forced against his will to do so, to distance his cross-dressing from an adult context. (To be convincingly feminine would draw comparisons with drag.) This performative failure is presented in carnivalesque terms, as the conventional gender hierarchy is comically inverted when a masculine subject suddenly finds himself forced to inhabit a feminine subjectivity. The subversive potential offered by cross-dressing and the carnivalesque is relinquished, however, by a resolution which affirms patriarchal gender ideologies. Instead of questioning the concept of gender in order to make a critical statement about its application to individuals, male-to-female cross-dressing narratives are rarely able to construct cross-dressing as anything other than a short-lived, comic gesture which is used to reinforce the superiority of patriarchal masculinity.

Cross-dressing films for child and adolescent audiences add a fascinating dimension to a discussion on how depictions of cross-dressing influence the ideological construction of gender within children's narratives. Films which contain cross-dressing are generally aimed at teenage, rather than child, viewers and almost exclusively feature male cross-dressing. These films generally conform to the pattern of male cross-dressing established in children's literature, but because of the older age of the implied viewer, the distinction between the innocent and nonsexualized form of cross-dressing which conventionally occurs in children's literature and the contemporary, adult-oriented concept of cross-dressing is blurred. Yet, the visibility of sexuality in such films for teenagers does not coincide with a more liberal representation of cross-dressing as a valid form of gender experimentation. For the most part,

male cross-dressing films are more conservative and misogynistic than portrayals of male cross-dressing in literature. Cross-dressing is generally associated in film with deviant sexuality (that is, homosexuality), and is presented to viewers as a departure from the prescribed norms of patriarchal masculinity that can have calamitous consequences. Cross-dressing films seek to naturalize the relationship between sex and gender, explicitly negating any form of sexual identity other than heterosexuality.

The conservative representation of cross-dressing in adolescent cinema is substantively challenged by a select number of recently published young adult (YA) novels which explicitly address the traditional cultural marginalization of the transgendered subject. Sexual identity, an issue rarely broached in cross-dressing literature (or else handled in hysterical or reactionary terms, as happens in film), is directly confronted within this group of texts. These novels also address with sensitivity the social stigmatization that frequently accompanies transgressive gender or sexual behavior. The outcomes of this form of cross-dressing portrayal are diverse, as, ironically, the situation with regard to more traditional, nonsexualized cross-dressing representations is reversed. Male transgendered characters are more successful at challenging and destabilizing gender/sexual identity categories than their transgendered sisters, often resulting in a queered construction of gender and sexuality that defies categorization. Notwithstanding these differences, this small subset of novels shares an emerging tolerance toward transgendered individuals who violate socially dictated gender and sexual norms.

Representations of cross-dressing are both abundant and diverse in children's literature and film, occurring in a wide range of forms and contexts. The deceptively simple act of wearing the clothes socially prescribed for the opposite sex has far-reaching implications for the ideological construction of gender. Depictions of cross-dressing invite a range of interpretive possibilities concerning gender, encompassing the theoretical breadth of Judith Butler, Mikhail Bakhtin, and Queer Theory. While not all instances of cross-dressing in children's literature and film are successful at re-evaluating gender stereotypes, cross-dressing characters ingeniously reveal how the discourses of femininity and masculinity operate in children's texts, and thus provide a valuable means through which the regulatory regimes of gender and sexual politics can be made visible and effectively challenged.

1

CHILDREN'S LITERATURE AND THE
CULTURAL DISCOURSE OF CROSS-DRESSING

Real gender freedom begins with fun.

Kate Bornstein
Gender Outlaw

If transvestism offers a critique of binary sex and gender distinctions, it is not because it simply makes such distinctions reversible
but because it denaturalises, destabilizes and defamiliarises sex
and gender signs.

Marjorie Garber
Vested Interests

INTRODUCTION

"Responding from my transvestic state of mind, I admitted that I wasn't
even sure what masculinity and femininity were, let alone truth. My
admission was so out of the context of their question that it confused
them." So begins the final chapter of J. J. Allen's poignant and personal
analysis of cross-dressing, *The Man in the Red Velvet Dress* (1996, 191).
His statement, prompted by the arrival of two Jehovah's Witnesses at
his door who had questioned him about "truth," is indicative of popular
responses to the concept of cross-dressing. Cross-dressing is something
about which society knows very little. On a superficial level, it is prepared to "accept" cross-dressing as the preserve of the eccentric and

1

the perverse. It is encouraged to do so by the popular media—which often present humorous portrayals of cross-dressing (think *Some Like It Hot* [1959]) or *Tootsie* [1982]) without delving into the areas of motivation; eroticism; social stigmatization and vilification; connections to homosexuality; or the challenge to constructed gender identity which cross-dressing presents.

Cross-dressing is frequently depicted in film, television, and literature, and habitually misunderstood. Cultural criticism of the twentieth and twenty-first centuries has sought to destabilize the difference between the sexes, and to establish that gender identity is socially constructed. The resulting debate has placed the cross-dressed or transgendered subject in an awkward position: understood by some elements of the academic fraternity; misunderstood by the public, within the context of which the transgendered individual is an "othered" member. Children's literature and film make a unique contribution to this ongoing conceptual dilemma. Contrary to popular expectation, cross-dressing is not unusual in literature produced for children. There are three distinctive models—the male-to-female, which is often used for comedic purposes, drawing inspiration from "drag"; the female-to-male, the most common paradigm, which generally facilitates a critique of gender through the protagonist's ability to give a successful performance of masculinity; and the transgender model, which occurs only rarely and offers the closest approximation to the contemporary adult transgender experience. The result of these varying representations is that children's literature engages with a multiplicity of cross-dressing discourses, ranging from a limited and often negative construction of cross-dressing as a deviant behavioral practice, to a more progressive and liberal appreciation of cross-dressing as a unique strategy for deconstructing normative gender categories.

RESPONDING TO THE PROBLEM OF CROSS-DRESSING TERMINOLOGY

Rather than discussing the operation and effect of these divergent cross-dressing constructions any further, my primary intention in this chapter is to deal with the issue of terminology and to identify the various discourses of cross-dressing that are relevant to literature produced for children and adolescents. Terminology is always a perplexing issue when discussing behavioral and cultural practices that involve wearing clothes considered socially appropriate for the opposite sex. A range of different terms can be used to characterize this type of behavior and the individuals who practice it, applicable in differing contexts and situations. The most widely recognized of these terms are "transvestism" and "transsexualism." "Transvestism" is a condition that was first coined by the sexologist Magnus Hirschfeld and characterized by the "irresistible tendency to dress in the clothing of the opposite sex" (Dekker and van de Pol 1989, 54). "Transvestism," in particular, is a concept imbricated with issues of sexuality and eroticism. It is viewed as an adult behavioral fetish, a means of procuring sexual gratification. "Transsexualism" is the name given to the behavior of individuals who "identify with the opposite sex and may seek to live as a member of this sex" (*Merriam-Webster Online Dictionary 2007*. http://www.m-w.com ((2 Jan 2007))). "Transsexualism" is understood to be a psychological condition (or even illness, in some contexts), and its association with surgical intervention and hormone replacement therapy likewise consigns it to adulthood. Both terms originated in the nineteenth and twentieth centuries and came to be used by the medical profession to designate conditions of psychological illness and sexual perversion. In some circumstances children's literature alludes to the adult-oriented concepts of transvestism and transsexualism in relation to cross-dressing characters, but these instances are rare. Such concepts are largely incompatible with the majority of gender-bending characters in children's fiction. This is because of the absence of issues pertaining to sexuality or sexual identity in most children's fiction, which I would argue play a significant role in constructing contemporary transvestite and transsexual subjectivities.

The unsuitability of these terms to describe the phenomenon of cross-dressing children's literature is similarly problematic in a historical context. Examples of what might be characterized in accordance with the contemporary frameworks of transvestism and transsexualism have been practiced and well documented in a range of societies and cultures since the beginning of recorded history. Sabrina Ramet remarks that "Many societies in the past institutionalised procedures for permanent or temporary gender reversal or gender change" (1996, xvii). However, the problem associated with applying modern terminology to age-old cultural practices is that it is not always easily transferable or entirely applicable. This is particularly so when discussing gender-bending practices that were socially acceptable and practiced openly, unlike transvestite and transsexual behaviors, which have traditionally been subject to social stigmatization and medical and state interference in Western society. The histories of transvestism and transsexualism are therefore largely entwined within the broader cultural history of cross-dressing, as the distinction between the two is a phenomenon of the twentieth century.

Cross-dressing practices have played a diverse role within a variety of different non-Western cultures that have openly accepted (or even valorized) experimental gender behavior. Vern and Bonnie Bullough report that cross-dressing played a prominent role in "many non-Western religious traditions and exists in the mythologies of many peoples" (1993, 6). For example, they explain that cross-dressing practices are evident in Hinduism, where androgyny is idealized and highly valued, and similarly have a place in Islamic culture, where Muslim dervishes exhibited a form of "psychic transvestism" that greatly influenced Sufi philosophy (13). In Myanmar, cross-dressing behavior is interpreted in light of "animistic beliefs still ingrained in Burmese Buddhism" (15). Further examples of cross-dressing behavior abound in Masai, Indian, Papua New Guinean, Madagascan, and Tahitian cultures. A particularly notable example of cross-dressing practices can be found in the history of North America, where "white explorers and missionaries in the seventeenth and eighteenth centuries found that many Native American tribal cultures recognized multiple genders, including 'women-men' and 'men-women' who took on cross-gender roles, often involving cross-dressing" (Beemyn 2004).

Responding to the problem of terminology, Sabrina Ramet uses the expression "gender reversal" in her cultural history of what could arguably be classified as varying forms of transvestite and transsexual practices. Ramet uses this label as an alternative for the terms "transvestism" and "transsexual," as the contemporary meanings of these medicalized words fail to accord with historical and anthropological accounts of situations in which biological females and males adopted the clothing and gender identity of the opposite sex. "Gender reversal," however, is also limiting as terminology. It gives the impression of only two gendered possibilities—as if motion can be made only by going "to" and "from" a masculine or feminine identity. This notion does not recognize/acknowledge that in many cultures cross-gendered persons were perceived as "other" to the conventional categories of man and woman. They were often considered to belong to a "third" sex, and in some cultures, such as North American Indian, were awarded their own gender terminology. The appropriation of this terminology to a non-Western context would be both inaccurate and inadequate, however, as these cultural phenomena differ substantially from the contemporary concepts of transvestism and transsexualism.

Another term that is regularly used within contemporary situations to describe gender-bending behavior is "drag." Drag is primarily associated with female impersonation and homosexuality in a contemporary cultural context (although "drag kings" has recently gained popularity as an expression for male impersonators). Kris Kirk and Ed Heath, authors of *Men in Frocks* (1984), argue that drag is "widely assumed to be theatre- and performance based" (8). Indeed, drag is regularly conceptualized within a theatrical framework of legitimate artistic expression within the gay community, as opposed to the psychological context within which transvestite behavior is often pathologized. Bullough and Bullough suggest that the difference between drag and cross-dressing is not always distinct, as "the admission by at least some gay queens that they regard cross-dressing as a way of expressing their feminine selves is similar to the statements of some heterosexual cross-dressers" (1993, 249). However, due to the heavily gendered manner in which drag is popularly perceived to be a male, homosexual activity, it is a term that I have preferred to abandon when examining texts produced for children and adolescents—given that the predominant form of gender disguise within these narratives is female-to-male and lacks any direct connection with sexuality.

Although I occasionally use the terms "gender disguise" and "gender-bending" to describe situations in which females disguise themselves as men or vice versa, for the purposes of this discussion the term that I have chosen to rely on principally is "cross-dressing." "Cross-dressing" is a relatively neutral term that allows for multiple interpretive possibilities, because (if dissociated from the popular presumption that it is inherently entwined with the issue of sexual, rather than just gender, identity) it linguistically marks a very simple act—the crossing of cultural boundaries related to the wearing of various articles of gender-specific clothing. The plethora of motivations behind the act of cross-dressing, and the issue of whether such motivations can be categorized as either transvestite or transsexual (or otherwise), are left "veiled" if such behavior is not prescriptively labeled and defined: endowed with potential, but not confirmation. My choice of "cross-dressing" as the most appropriate term to use within the context of children's literature is therefore deliberate, as it has enabled me to investigate representations of subversive gender behavior in an open-ended manner that engages with the gender confusion which cross-dressing behavior regularly elicits.

While I have predominantly used the generalized term "cross-dressing" throughout this discussion, a second term that I have found useful to employ is "transgender." I have used "transgender" in accordance with the definition favored by gender theorists such as Leslie Feinberg and Susan Stryker, both of whom use "transgender" as an "umbrella term that refers to all identities or practices that cross-over, cut across, move between, or otherwise queer socially constructed sex/gender boundaries" (Stryker 2004). Stryker also emphasizes the political aspect of the term, arguing that "Perhaps the most significant aspect of the recent and rapid development of transgender is the role the term has played in giving voice to a wide range of people whose experiences and understandings of gender, embodiment, and sexuality previously had not entered into broader discussions and decision-making processes" (2004). "Transgender" is therefore an inappropriate term for characterizing the majority of cross-dressing representations in children's literature because, in most, the political agenda to which Stryker refers is absent. As a general rule, the cross-dressing undertaken by both male and female characters is temporary and brief, enacted out of necessity rather than nonconformity with (or alienation from) normative gender categories. In instances of female cross-dressing, an inability to conform with conventionally defined femininity can indeed be an aspect of a character's motivation in adopting a masculine disguise. However, this lack of feminine identification is generally the result of patriarchal social structures which limit feminine behavior, and it is thus a logical response to a situation where femininity is equated with passivity and inactivity. Female cross-dressers also return to their former gender position with relative ease after their cross-dressing ceases, suggesting that their gender identities are not situated outside or on the margins of socially constructed femininity. (This is in spite of the fact that their cross-dressing temporarily shifts and redefines the meanings of masculinity and femininity within the narrative.)

Male cross-dressing representations are analogous, as, rather than enabling a critique of gender stereotypes, they more often than not use cross-dressing to reassert conventional gender boundaries. However, a small subgroup of cross-dressing literature, produced mainly for adolescent consumption, provides representations of cross-dressing behavior that reflect the contemporary definition of "transgender." These texts use cross-dressing within a politicized context to denote individual subjectivities that move across and breach conventional gender boundaries, and commonly face political and social oppression for doing so. Depictions of transgendered subjectivity encompass transvestite, transsexual, and gay possibilities (in their modern and adult-oriented senses), as well as addressing queer subjectivity, which problematizes traditional binarisms such as man/woman or gay/straight. Hence sexuality is constructed as a significant issue within each text's thematic exploration of transgendered subjectivity.

Depictions of transgendered subjectivity in adolescent fiction address the critical opportunities provided by cross-dressing behavior, but at the same time acknowledge the contemporary reality of transgender experience. This convergence of cross-dressing representations (i.e., cross-dressing as critical strategy and cross-dressing as social reality) produces a rich and complex construction of cross-dressing subjectivity that addresses both the theoretical and the practical consequences of gender non-conformity. The resulting portrayal of cross-dressing identity embodies the transgressive principles of contemporary transgender discourse and warrants the use of comparable terminology, which is why I have chosen to incorporate the term "transgender" into my discussion, specifically as it relates to this unique group of texts. With the exception of this particular group, however, the term "cross-dressing" will be applied to all other instances of gender disguise. Unless otherwise stated, my use of the term "cross-dressing" will always be a reference to the ways in which cross-dressing occurs in children's literature, rather than its broader cultural application.

EXISTING SCHOLARSHIP ON CROSS-DRESSING REPRESENTATION IN CHILDREN'S LITERATURE AND FILM

As is apparent from this discussion of the problems associated with terminology, cross-dressing occurs in an array of forms and contexts within narratives produced for pre-adult audiences. Cross-dressing is also used for divergent purposes in children's literature, ranging from the conservative reinscription of normative gender boundaries to the advocation of a new, more fluid category of gender that would replace the limitations and restrictions of traditional conceptions of masculinity and femininity. At the farthest end of the spectrum, a small number of innovative and progressive texts capably introduce the contemporary notion of transgender to child and adolescent audiences, using transgendered identity simultaneously to expose the artifice of socially constructed gender categories and to teach the reader/viewer of the importance of values such as tolerance and compassion. The many metamorphoses which occur to cross-dressing representations in children's literature similarly provide a multiplicity of interpretive possibilities—each with its own implications for gender construction. The issue of how gendered bodies and behaviors are represented in children's literature has garnered much critical scholarship, but although cross-dressing representations offer a unique and challenging perspective on this exact subject, only a limited amount of research has been conducted in the area.

When I first embarked upon this project, literature on the subject of cross-dressing representations in children's literature did not exist.

This provided an interesting challenge and allowed me a considerable amount of freedom in relation to how I could situate my work theoretically. I turned first to the work of gender theorists, such as Judith Butler, and cultural commentators on cross-dressing, like Marjorie Garber, applying their theories to the corpus of children's texts that I had assembled. Butler and Garber both assert that cross-dressing plays a highly significant role in belying the constructedness of socially prescribed gender categories, but of course their analyses only address cross-dressing in an adult cultural context. This enabled me to use their work selectively, as appropriate to the children's texts that comprised my corpus, and permitted me to encompass a larger and more dynamic theoretical framework that extended beyond gender theory to include the work of theorists like Mikhail Bakhtin.

Some time after I commenced writing, three articles concerning cross-dressing in children's literature were published, and it was informative to compare their approaches with my own. Lisa Brocklebank (2000), Etsuko Taketani (1999), and Jody Norton (1999) each tackle the subject of cross-dressing and its representation in children's narratives, but confine their analyses to either one specific type of cross-dressing or to a single literary genre. Their articles consequently provide an analysis of cross-dressing representations that is insightful but limited because of its narrow application. Brocklebank's article, "Rebellious Voices: The Unofficial Discourse of Cross-Dressing in d'Aulnoy, de Murat and Perrault," (2000), parallels my own application of Judith Butler's theory of performativity to cross-dressing. Brocklebank's summation of the cross-dressed character as "a touchstone to contest official order and socially constructed representations of power" (127) aptly describes the function of the female cross-dresser within the broad range of texts that I have included in my own examination of female cross-dressing representations, but her analysis of cross-dressing constructions is restricted to a very specific context—fairy tales of the seventeenth century. Brocklebank's arguments about the destabilizing effects of cross-dressing are focused not only on the hierarchical gender structures of this period, but also on the sociopolitical contexts of textual production and reception, which in the case of her chosen fairy tales were "reliant upon the stylistic construction and representation of the Sun-King" (127).

Due to the specificity of Brocklebank's analysis, her arguments in relation to cross-dressing do not address the broader tradition of cross-dressing in children's literature, which cuts across a multiplicity of genres and sociocultural contexts. This is particularly relevant to Brocklebank's discussion of "The Counterfeit Marquise," a tale co-authored by Charles Perrault and the Abbé de Choisy (a renowned cross-dresser). It is the story of Marianne, who was born a male but whose mother raises her as girl in order to avoid the fate of her father, a soldier killed in battle. Marianne lives happily and successfully as a woman, wooed by many suitors until she finally chooses a man to be her husband. On their wedding night, Marianne discovers that her lover is in fact a woman disguised as a man. Marianne then reveals her true sex to him, and both decide to maintain their adopted gender identities and live happily ever after. Brocklebank comments that Perrault and de Choisy choose to assume a female narrative persona within the story, which "positions itself on the margins from where it can challenge the status quo. It mocks socio-political conventions, representations, and images, suggesting that they are just as artificial as 'she' [Marianne] is" (130). Brocklebank's comment that "the tale emphasises the fact that gender behavior, far from being innate, results rather from learning and acculturation" (130) is applicable almost verbatim to the presentation of female cross-dressing in a broad spectrum of children's narratives which similarly use cross-dressing to accentuate the constructedness of normative gender categories.

"The Counterfeit Marquise," however, is an atypical example of male-to-female cross-dressing. This French fairy tale originated in a context of adult readers and tellers, rather than of children, and was intended to be a subversive critique of gender politics during a specific period in French history (Brocklebank, 127). One of the story's authors, the Abbé de Choisy, was an "infamous transvestite" himself (130), in an era when masculine privilege (de Choisy was a "libertine priest, courtier, historian, deputy Ambassador to Siam" [130]) afforded de Choisy a degree of social tolerance, if not acceptance, for his unconventional behavior. Unsurprisingly, then, "The Counterfeit Marquise" is a sympathetic portrayal of transgendered subjectivity which advocates social tolerance for those individuals whose sex conflicts with their gender identity—particularly heterosexual transvestites. Brocklebank's primary interest lies in the sociohistorical context of seventeenth-century French literary salons: the subversive motifs and coded language employed by writers; the political discourses which informed the fairy tales; and the subject positions developed in salon conversation. As a result, her examination does not distinguish between male and female cross-dressing. Brocklebank's definition of "cross-dressing" is also extremely broad, including fairy tales where characters "cross-dress" by disguising their political rank and class. For these reasons, Brocklebank's narrower focus makes it difficult to translate her ideas to more generalized examples of children's cross-dressing literature. Her evaluation of cross-dressing is specific to one sociocultural context and literary genre, and is therefore unsuited to my own more wide-ranging approach. (A more detailed discussion of "The Counterfeit Marquise" appears in Chapters 2 and 7.)

Etsuko Taketani's discussion of child cross-dressing, entitled "Spectacular Child Bodies: The Sexual Politics of Cross-Dressing and Calisthenics in the Writings of Eliza Leslie and Catharine Beecher," is comparable to Brocklebank's because of its sociocultural specificity. Taketani focuses on a period of American history, the antebellum period of the 1830s, 1840s, and 1850s, for the purpose of analyzing how cross-dressing behavior in children's stories of this time "confirms and reaffirms children's heteronormativity in the service of reproducing the heterosexual/homosocial national economy" (367).

The two children's stories on which Taketani focuses, "Lucy Nelson; Or, The Boy Girl" (1831) and "Billy Bedlow; Or, The Girl Boy" (1832), which were both written by Eliza Leslie, present children who adopt an unconventional gender identity which involves a preference for wearing the clothes decreed appropriate for the opposite sex. Both Lucy and Billy also exhibit the behaviors and attributes conventionally associated with the opposite sex: Lucy preferring activities such as "flying a kite, walking on stilts or riding a horse without a saddle" and Billy, a "typical sissy boy who likes to make pincushions and purses with his sisters, and above all 'dress' their dolls" (Taketani, 359). Taketani argues that cross-dressing is constructed very differently in each story. In Lucy's case, she suggests that her cross-dressing belies a genuine "gender-identity disorder" (358). Billy, on the other hand, "does not cross-dress to pass for a woman" (361), but instead displays effeminate behavior because of his homosexuality. Leslie's stories, according to Taketani, are both cautionary and moralistic tales about the dangers of gender and sexual nonconformity, which "ultimately denounce blurred genders...and sanction binary sex distinctions" (363). Taketani, however, does not directly address the differences between male and female cross-dressing, but uses her texts as general evidence of the way in which American literature produced for children during the antebellum period employed cross-dressing as a strategy to curtail "devious" gender experimentation. The use of cross-dressing to reinscribe conventional gender categories in books for children is in fact widespread, particularly in relation to the depiction of male cross-dressing. Nevertheless, Taketani's analysis of cross-dressing, like Brocklebank's, is limited in application to other texts because it does not take into account the widespread tradition of both female and male cross-dressing representations in children's literature. This tradition encompasses a variety of paradigmatic constructions, and while in some instances cross-dressing is used to reaffirm gender heteronormativity in accordance with Taketani's contentions (generally in relation to representations of male cross-dressing), in many others cross-dressing is successfully used as a strategy to challenge and critique traditional gender norms.

Jody Norton's analysis of cross-dressing is distinctive because it is not restricted to a particular historical period. It draws upon a range of cross-dressing texts (a short story by Mark Twain; a contemporary film) and is therefore more reflective of the manner in which cross-dressing as a phenomenon in children's literature bridges a multiplicity of genres and sociohistorical contexts. Norton acutely articulates the type of cross-dressing representation which is the focus of her discussion: "transchildren," or depictions of children with transgendered subjectivities. Rather than examining how children's narratives of a certain sociohistorical era used cross-dressing as a strategy either to confirm or critique normative gender categories, Norton is more concerned with exploring how transgendered subjectivity is constructed. Hence the scope of her discussion does not include representations of cross-dressing where characters adopt the clothing of the opposite sex for the purposes of temporary disguise, out of dire necessity, or because they are forced against their will (a representative strategy which features in numerous texts that depict male cross-dressing). Norton instead limits her argument to children's literature which features characters "whose experience and sense of their gender does not allow them to fit their sexed bodies into seamless accord with a congruent, conventional gender identity" (415–416), and are thus "transgendered" in the contemporary sense of the word. Norton's definition of "transchildren" can be applied to a number of characters which feature in the cross-dressing texts discussed by both Brocklebank and Taketani. However, her ideological approach is very different in its quest to uncover the social reality of transgendered experience. Norton introduces her subject matter by describing the "historical desire to deny, by one means or another, the reality of alternative forms of sex and gender" (416). She proceeds to argue that the acknowledgment of transgendered subjectivities is needed to prevent the widespread denial of transgendered existence (in the face of growing psychological, medical, and social research that emphatically proves the reality of the phenomenon). Norton remarks that the literary validation of transgendered characters performs the equally important function of educating other children to treat transgendered individuals with respect and understanding (416–417).

Norton's work on the subject of transchildren complements my own hypotheses on the depiction of transgendered subjectivity in children's literature, particularly in regard to her recognition of transchildren as an identifiable group of individuals that has been traditionally disenfranchised and oppressed by a regulatory gender system. This political oppression, a significant aspect of transgenderism according to theorists such as Stryker (2004) and Fienberg (1996), plays a crucial role in representations of transgendered cross-dressing children's texts. Norton's arguments about this oppression (and the need for its elimination) have provided a preliminary point for my own examination of transgendered subjectivity. For the purposes of my discussion I have utilized Norton's definition of "transchildren" as characters "whose experience and sense of their gender does not allow them to fit their sexed bodies into seamless accord with a congruent, conventional gender identity" (415–416). But rather than applying it only to children who exhibit transvestite or transsexual tendencies (as Norton does), I have adopted Stryker's more flexible definition of "transgender" as referring to identities which "cross-over, cut across, move between, or otherwise queer socially constructed sex/gender boundaries" (Stryker 1994, 251). Extending Norton's definition has allowed my discussion to engage with a larger expanse of cross-dressing practices and identities that constitute the contemporary concept of transgenderism—such as drag queens, drag kings, transsexuals, transvestites, bisexuals, homosexuals, and queer cross-dressing identities. Adopting Stryker's definition has also allowed me to establish the importance of sexual identity to the construction of trangendered subjectivity (an issue which Norton does not explore). A more detailed examination of transgendered cross-dressing can be found in Chapter 7.

Brocklebank, Taketani, and Norton's scholarship on the subject of cross-dressing poses a series of initial questions about how the depiction of cross-dressed bodies offers a revelatory glimpse at the ideological construction of gender. However, each of their analyses covers only a small area of either children's literature or cross-dressing types. My intention here is to provide a more comprehensive survey of cross-dressing that makes a distinction between female-to-male, male-to-female, and transgendered cross-dressing and which also attempts to theorize the distinctive models of gender construction produced by each of these cross-dressing paradigms.

THE CROSS-DRESSED FIGURE IN GENDER THEORY

Cross-dressing is responsible for producing a remarkable array of gender constructions in literature produced for children and adolescents, a phenomenon indicated by the different functions attributed to cross-dressing in the work of Brocklebank, Taketani, and Norton. Whether it is used to confirm or to interrogate conventional gender boundaries, it is clear that cross-dressing is a subject that incontrovertibly raises questions about gender. The cross-dressed body confounds the supposedly natural order between gender and natal sex, inviting questions about masculinity and femininity that necessarily destabilize these categories and reveal their constructed nature. (Even a male-to-female cross-dresser whose performance of femininity is nothing but an exaggerated caricature is still forced to become conscious of what it is that constitutes femininity.)

The figure of the cross-dresser is not new to gender theory and criticism, having been popularized by Judith Butler's use of drag to illustrate the performative nature of gender in her highly influential book *Gender Trouble* ([1990] 1999). Butler suggested here that if gender is "the cultural meanings that the sexed body assumes," then it cannot automatically be assumed that "gender will follow from sex in any one way" (10). Instead, she argued that gender should not be viewed as a secure or established identity, but rather as something created and produced over time, naturalized but not natural: "Gender is always a doing, though not a doing by a subject who might be said to pre-exist the deed....There is no gender identity behind the expressions of gender; that identity is performatively constituted by the very 'expressions' that are said to be its results" (33). Butler's characterization of gender as performative, a "stylised repetition of acts" (179), is where the figure of the cross-dresser comes into play. Drag performances, according to Butler, epitomize the disjunction that exists between sex and gender:

> The performance of drag plays upon the distinction between the anatomy of the performer and the gender that is being performed. But we are actually in the presence of three contingent dimensions of significant corporeality: anatomical sex, gender identity and gender performance. If the anatomy of the performer is already distinct from the gender of the performer, and both of those are distinct from the gender of the performance, then the performance suggests a dissonance not only between sex and performance, but sex and gender, and gender and performance....In imitating gender, drag implicitly reveals the imitative structure of gender itself—as well as its contingency. (175)

Butler's comments on the deconstructive nature of drag are equally applicable to cross-dressing performances in children's books, particularly in relation to heroines who disguise themselves as men. These young women replicate masculinity so successfully that their cross-dressing performances necessarily call gender itself into question.

After witnessing a triumphant gender performance emerge from the body of an individual belonging to the opposite sex, the reader/viewer is prompted to ask, "What, exactly, *is* masculinity or femininity?" Female cross-dressing narratives expose gender as a social construct, using the heroine's cross-dressing performance to show that gender is not unequivocally attached to a particularly sexed body, but something more fluid and flexible. Butler subsequently thought that *Gender Trouble* had been misunderstood and misinterpreted, and wrote *Bodies That Matter* (1993) as a corrective. In the preface to *Bodies That Matter*, her rejoinder to the ways in which she felt that gender performativity had been (mis)understood was expressed accordingly:

> For if I were to argue that genders are performative, that could mean that I thought that one woke in the morning, perused the closet or some more open space for the gender of choice, donned that gender for the day, and then restored the garment to its place at night. Such a wilful and instrumental subject, one who decides on its gender, is clearly not its gender from the start and fails to realize that its existence is already decided by gender. Certainly such a theory would restore a figure of a choosing subject....

> **(Preface, x)**

In children's literature, female cross-dressing narratives often construct masculinity and femininity as options which the cross-dresser is able to adopt and disregard at will, in a sense conforming to Butler's disdainful rejection of the notion that gender can actually be chosen for a day, and "then restored...to its place at night" (x). Butler recognizes that the ability to choose one's gender would restore a humanist concept of the subject—a notion which poststructuralist theories of the twentieth century sought to eradicate in their conception of subjectivity as fragmented and insubstantial, and which militates against Butler's concept of gender as something constructed. However, female cross-dressing narratives revolve around the concept of a humanist subject capable of agency, entailing that the construction of gender in these texts accords with this (mis)interpretation of Butler's work. Female cross-dressers in children's literature occupy subjugated feminine positions, their capacity for agency limited by pervading patriarchal practices. Through cross-dressing, however, this situation is remedied. The societal norms that generally govern feminine behavior are temporarily displaced by the masculine disguise, allowing the subjectivities of these heroines to evolve through a dialogic exchange between masculine and feminine subject positions.

The relative ease (there is always some initial period of difficulty) with which cross-dressing heroines negotiate a masculine performance is often improbable, in a realistic social sense, but achievable nonetheless within a symbolic narrative context. Children's literature, particularly that which can be classified as belonging to the fantasy genre, is never a direct transcription of reality. Female cross-dressers are generally situated within an environment or setting which is greatly removed from contemporary consensus reality (even if located within a historical reality). This enables them to use cross-dressing in a metaphoric or strategic way that comments upon the constructedness of gender in the real world occupied by the readers or viewers, as opposed to directly reflecting or re-creating this condition. This is not to say that the crossing of gender boundaries is presented as either natural or socially acceptable behavior in female cross-dressing texts. Children's literature does engage with Western culture's conventional prohibition of cross-dressing practices, portraying such behavior as potentially dangerous if discovered. However, it ultimately disregards this cross-dressing taboo (and some of the practical realities of cross-dressing, such as the issue of visually "passing" for the assumed gender, which is rendered insignificant in many texts) in the pursuit of a more symbolic form of gender deconstruction. Consequently, my application of Butler's gender paradigm to female cross-dressing narratives is only partial, due to inherent differences in the conceptualization of subjectivity and the disjunction between literature and reality, a fissure which enables cross-dressing to be used in a figurative rather than a literal sense.

Butler's gender theories, like the concepts of Brocklebank, Taketani, and Norton, are not appropriate for each form of cross-dressing representation in children's literature. Female-to-male cross-dressing narratives adopt a performative gender model that shares a number of ideological similarities with the work of Butler, but applying Butler's concept of gender to male-to-female cross-dressing is much more difficult and far from satisfactory. Unlike the type of drag performances that Butler refers to, which play "upon the distinction between the anatomy of the performer and the gender that is being performed" ([1990] 1999, 175), most instances of male cross-dressing in children's texts contain no element of feminine performance. In contrast to their female counterparts, who willingly cross-dress to flee an oppressive gender regime, male characters usually cross-dress against their will and better judgment. They are unable to discard their masculine subjectivity in favor of a feminine one and are typically humiliated at the thought of doing so. These aspects of (straight) male cross-dressing have traditionally been rendered comic in Western popular culture, and continue to be constructed humorously in children's texts. Male cross-dressers in children's literature rarely attempt to modify their behavior (unlike their cross-dressing sisters), and their cross-dressing failure therefore necessitates that the correlation between male cross-dressing and "gender performance" is something of an anomaly. A more appropriate theoretical framework for the comic construction of male cross-dressing is Mikhail Bakhtin's work on the carnivalesque, which investigates the implications of a world turned "upside down." This is exactly what happens when males cross-dress and the conventional gender hierarchy is inverted, laughter ensuing as these boys or men wrestle inexpertly with feminine subjectivity.

Representations of transgendered subjectivity, a relatively new phenomenon in children's literature and films which occurs most frequently in texts produced for adolescent audiences, require a slightly different analytical model. Performativity is always a crucial issue to critical analyses of cross-dressed gender success (or failure), but constructions of transgendered subjectivity go one step further through their resistance of normative categories of gender and sexual identity. For this reason, Queer Theory presents the most viable analytic option due to its expansive field of investigation, which examines all forms of gender-bending and nonnormative behaviors in an attempt to destabilize traditional binaries such as man/woman and gay/straight. Originating in part from Butler's concept of performativity, which takes as a foundational principle that identity is not fixed or stable, Queer Theory questions the very concepts of gender and sexual identity. Transgendered cross-dressers in children's literature and film accord with this more politicized perspective of gender and sexual identity as their represented behavior and subjectivity similarly resist conventional definitions and categories. As characters, they are ambiguously gendered individuals whose sexual desires also defy normative identity paradigms. In addition to exposing the constructedness of conventional gender categories through their cross-dressing (and other instances of transgressive gender behavior), these characters are unique because they subvert and undermine the very question of what it means to be a man or a woman, or gay or straight.

Cross-dressing occurs in many forms within children's literature and films, and as a result can be approached from numerous theoretical standpoints. Cross-dressing likewise generates a variety of reactions in Western society which are also manifest in literature produced for children and adolescents. These range from genuine admiration for successful gender performances to fearful hysteria from those who seek to naturalize the sex/gender distinction and find the "radical discontinuity between sexed bodies and socially constructed genders" (Butler [1990] 1999, 10) which the cross-dresser symbolizes as abhorrent and shocking. Regardless of these distinctions, it is obvious that representations of cross-dressing are a potentially powerful tool in the hands of the author or filmmaker. For despite its varying constructions, cross-dressing is a simple and potent symbol for the exploration of one of the most fundamental and basic principles of human existence—gender. The real issue to be pondered is how this ideological tool is wielded within children's literature and film. The inherent social rebellion which cross-dressing behavior constitutes is always potentially transgressive, but this potential is utilized (or underutilized) by children's texts in a manner that deserves greater critical attention. Representations of cross-dressing provide unique insight into the often contrasting ideological messages about sex and gender that prevail in children's literature and film:

> Dress traditionally has been a ubiquitous symbol of sexual differences, emphasising social conceptions of masculinity and femininity. Cross-dressing, therefore, represents a symbolic incursion into territory that crosses gender boundaries.
>
> **(Bullough and Bullough, 1993)**

2

THREE MODELS OF GENDER DISGUISE

Hirschfeld coined the word transvestite in 1910 and wrote the germinal works on the subject. One of Hirschfeld's contributions was his conclusion, based on his research, that sex and gender expression were not automatically linked . . . .

Leslie Feinberg
Transgender Warriors

INTRODUCTION

Cross-dressing representations are not confined to a single or definitive type in children's literature and film. Nor is cross-dressing used by authors for a universal purpose or effect. Marjorie Garber describes the myriad possibilities that cross-dressing creates in this all-encompassing manner: "Cross-dressing is about gender confusion. Cross-dressing is about the phallus as constitutively veiled. Cross-dressing is about the power of women. Cross-dressing is about the emergence of gay identity. Cross-dressing is about the anxiety of economic or cultural dislocation, the anticipation or recognition of 'otherness' as loss" ([1992] 1993, 390). While this statement cannot be transferred in entirety to the domain of children's literature, it does effectively articulate the disruptive and diverse power of cross-dressing—a power that is clearly evident in the differing manifestations of cross-dressing that are evident in children's narratives.

Three paradigmatic models of cross-dressing can be identified in children's literature and film—the female-to-male, the male-to-female, and the transgender. This chapter examines the paradigmatic structure of each model, using a selection of texts to illustrate how the model operates and affects gender construction. Because female cross-dressing predominates, this model will be discussed most comprehensively. The male-to-female and transgender paradigms will be examined only briefly at this stage, as each of these models will be addressed more explicitly in later chapters.

Female-to-male cross-dressing is by far the most commonly occurring type of gender-bending behavior in children's literature, which may seem surprising, given that the concept of "cross-dressing" in our culture is popularly perceived as a male-to-female phenomenon. This is perhaps the exact reason for its abundance in children's narratives. By disengaging itself from the sexually oriented world of adult transvestism, the construction of female cross-dressing favored by children's texts allows them to reclaim it as their own, refashioning female cross-dressing into a clever strategy for the interrogation of traditional gender categories.

The female-to-male cross-dressing model typically features a young girl living in a patriarchal society which imposes limitations on the behavior of girls and women. In order to escape, she disguises herself as a boy—whereby she discovers a new world of freedom and individual autonomy, made available to her purely because of her assumed masculine gender. This cross-dressing model is the most removed from the adult-oriented concept of transvestism, primarily because the cross-dresser is biologically female. Female cross-dressing has a long and varied cultural history. Yet, despite this history, it remains culturally invisible. Bullough and Bullough (1993) address the "absence" of female cross-dressing in this way:

> Although cross-dressing as a historical phenomenon was much more common in women than in men, and women continue to cross-dress, they are not called transvestites because the male club movement and, consequently, the DSM-III-R [*Diagnostic and Statistical Manual*, revised third edition, of the American Psychiatric Association] does not include them. Prince's argument was that women cannot cross-dress because they can wear anything they want without stigma, while some scholars have said that women cannot be called transvestites because they do not find cross-dressing erotic.... (302–303)

This cultural reluctance to include women within the parameters of transgender discourse is used to great effect in children's literature. The use of a female cross-dressing protagonist effectively dissociates her gender-bending behavior from the implications of sexual fetishism and immorality that constitute the adult concept of transvestism. (Fairy tales which feature female cross-dressers often incorporate the idea of sexual attraction into their narratives, but it functions either to remind the reader of the cross-dresser's biological sex ((when a man is attracted to the cross-dressed woman)) or to emphasize her performative success ((when other women are attracted to the cross-dresser))). Moreover, female-to-male cross-dressing is distinct from the adult transgender arena because of its brevity. It is typically undertaken for a period of several weeks or months, but ceases when the cross-dresser is discovered, or chooses to reveal herself at an opportune moment. Her cross-dressing is rarely a lifestyle choice or behavioral practice that she undertakes on a regular and ongoing basis (as is the case with most adult transvestites). The female cross-dressing heroine is also distinctive because of her propensity to "become" male (for all intents and purposes) for a portion of the text with relative ease. She is then able to revert comfortably to her former feminine gender position. The female-to-male cross-dresser performs effectively as a male, but is equally capable of returning to her former gender position without needing any strategic reiteration of her femininity in order to render her an authentic woman once again. (The case with male-to-female cross-dressers is quite different.) She has nothing to lose—in terms of socially constructed gender status—by deciding to discard her femininity temporarily in favor of masculinity. Her cross-dressing enables her to improve her gender status (because masculinity is traditionally regarded as superior to femininity), and therefore does not pose a threat to her femininity. She ultimately resumes her original gender position as a heroine, having redoubtably proved herself as a hero. Her final victory is her ability to bridge the distinctive literary traditions of masculine and feminine success, ingeniously weaving them together in order to deconstruct and interrogate their modes of operation.

The most unique and remarkable feature of the female-to-male cross-dressing model is the way in which it subverts dominant gender paradigms. The female cross-dresser's ability to adopt a successful masculine persona occasions a unique perspective on gender. Female cross-dressing generally functions as a critique of traditional gender categories and stereotypes. The female characters who disguise themselves as males are able to perform masculinity not only as capably as their biologically male peers, but even more so—receiving accolades from all whom they encounter. The biological female protagonists of these texts are clearly capable of being "better" men than their male counterparts. Their cross-dressing behavior provokes a reevaluation of traditional masculinity and femininity based on the heroine's lack of conformity with such categorizations.

As a literary phenomenon, female-to-male cross-dressing traverses a broad spectrum of writing for children. It is used for a range of purposes that share much thematic commonality, despite the fact that the texts in which it occurs differ greatly from one another in terms of sociohistorical context and literary genre. Direct associations and parallels can thus be made between children's sword and sorcery fantasy (Pierce, *Alanna: The First Adventure*—book 1 of *The Song of the Lioness Quartet*, hereafter referred to as *Alanna*), historical Chinese legend (*Mulan*, Disney films), Russian folktale (Husain, "A Riddle for a King"), and seventeenth-century French salon tales (L'Héritier de Villandon, "The Subtle Princess"), indicative of a children's literary paradigm that is able to transcend genre-related limitations of meaning and thereby produce significance on a scale that supersedes the genre-imposed confines of the text itself. Children's texts step outside conventional frames of reference by featuring portrayals of nonsexual cross-dressing, practiced by women, which thematically interrogate dominant gender paradigms. Although dissociated from contemporary concepts of transvestism and transsexualism, female cross-dressing is still represented in children's literature as unconventional, and as an act of social rebellion. The ideological alliance between female cross-dressing and rebellion is important, because it explains why female cross-dressing is synonymous with agential subjectivity in children's literature. Cross-dressing heroines disrupt gender conventions by successfully adopting a gendered subjectivity which is different from their natal sex. This act of gender transformation, argues Westin, seeks "to reveal the construction of the sexes and deconstruct the established conceptions of them. To turn the tradition upside-down or inside-out, so to speak" (1999, 92). Female cross-dressers necessitate a rethinking of traditional gender concepts. Their successful performance of masculinity radically questions the concept of a natural gender identity and also highlights the contributory roles played by socializing forces in the constitution and maintenance of gendered identities. Regardless of much dissimilarity in plot, characterization, sociocultural context, and genre, female cross-dressing literature uses the figure of the cross-dresser to prompt a reevaluation of the relationship between sex and gender, to interrogate dominant gender paradigms, and to posit a more fluid concept of gender that embraces individuality and difference.

CROSS-DRESSING HEROINES

Female cross-dressing narratives question socially assumed under-standings in relation to gender by playfully exposing the redundancies of two polarized gendered identities and ridiculing the limitations that such a system imposes on supposedly autonomous individuals. These narratives begin their process of gender revaluation through the por-trayal of a female character to whom stereotypical constructions of femininity do not apply. In the sword and sorcery fantasy text *Alanna* (1983), the central character is a young girl who yearns for adventure and other traditionally masculine pursuits that are unattainable for women according to her society's gender codes. The story opens with a pronouncement from Alanna's father about her future which instantly positions her within a subordinate role, as both a child and a female, subject to her father's masculine authority: "That is my decision. We need not discuss it" ([1983] 1997, 1). Alanna and her twin brother, Thom, are equally distressed at the prospect of their gendered desti-nies, but it is Alanna who quickly realizes that her capacity for agency will be most compromised by her father's arrangements, and therefore hatches a plan to swap places with her twin brother. Their father origi-nally intends for her to be sent to a convent to learn magic; Thom is to be sent to the king's palace to train to be a knight. Both have non-traditional gender identities and deplore their father's choices: Alanna shines at traditionally masculine activities, while her brother is inept, preferring magic to swordsmanship.

> "Why do you get all the fun?" she complained. "I'll have to learn sewing and dancing. You'll study tilting, fencing—"
>
> "Do you think I *like* that stuff?" he yelled. "I *hate* falling down and whacking at things. *You're* the one who likes it, not me!" (2)

Alanna's plan to exchange places with her brother illustrates the privileged status of masculinity in their social context because even in the event of a swap, it will not be necessary for Thom to disguise his gender: as well as training girls at the convent, the priestesses also "train young boys in magic" (2). Alanna's orchestration of the plan indicates her resolve to escape the subordinated social role decreed appropriate for her gender. When Thom expresses concern about their father's reac-tion, Alanna asks him, "D'you want to be a sorcerer bad enough?…Will you have the guts for it?" (3). Her question implicitly articulates her own feelings, warning Thom that their plan will only succeed if both children are utterly committed to it. They each affirm their intentions to disobey their father's decree, and Alanna then becomes the focalizing character of the story, which details her experiences as a knight-in-training at the palace. Alanna's behavior is substantially more transgressive than her brother's, because in addition to deceiving her father, her cross-dressing disguise perpetuates a much greater deception. It allows her, as a feminine subject, to gain unprecedented access to masculine spaces and masculine privilege, permitting her to experience all that is usually forbidden to women because of their perceived inferiority.

In the Walt Disney film *Mulan* (1998)[1] a corresponding pattern emerges. Mulan is a dutiful daughter who simply cannot fulfill the requirements of traditional femininity. The film begins just prior to Mulan's culturally all-important encounter with the matchmaker, showing Mulan trying to cheat on this significant test of her femininity (which amounts to her prospects of finding a good husband) by painting the traditional attributes of femininity on her wrist. The words she writes are "quiet and demure...graceful, polite, delicate, refined, poised," and she thereby physically inscribes on her body what the conventionally feminine subject internalizes. Mulan's attempts are futile, however, as she performs dreadfully for the matchmaker, disgracing herself in the eyes of her parents and small village community. An opportunity for her to reinstate herself beckons when news of an imperial decree reaches her village, demanding that all families enlist their sons, or in the absence of a son, their father, in the imperial army. Mulan has no brother, so in order to prevent her elderly father from enlisting she disguises herself as a man and joins the army in his place.

Filial piety determines Mulan's transgressive decision, but the film constructs her cross-dressing as behavior that has agential possibilities. Mulan is constructed as an alienated feminine subject in the earliest part of the film, and her failure at the matchmaker's ceremony deepens her sense of social ostracism. The film conveys Mulan's isolation through song, a solo titled "Reflection." The song begins with soft, rather sad strings (reminiscent of the traditional Chinese plucked lute or zither), and its melancholy tune reflects Mulan's unhappiness as she considers her future within a society whose strict definitions of femininity she is unable to conform to. Mulan sings her solo to an image of herself reflected in a pool of water, a self-reflexive strategy which indicates that the song is a meditation on self and identity. This solo allows Mulan's interiority to be represented, its first-person narration voicing her fears about the prescriptive nature of traditional femininity. Cast outside its rigidly defined boundaries, Mulan's lyrics repeatedly refer to the distinction between her socially constructed feminine identity (which is interpellated by feminine discourses that render her a failure) and her "essential" humanist self. Mulan ideologically defines subjectivity in humanist terms as resistant to social determination and capable of agency (she claims in the lyrics that she "cannot hide" her true identity), but the song's structure—a series of unanswered questions about who she is—suggests that she is unable to find an alternative and more satisfactory mode of feminine development. In accordance with the patriarchal gender binary, the lyrics of Mulan's song make reference to the fact that women of her age are either "brides" or "daughters," their identities defined by their relationships with men. Mulan's inability to perform either of these roles entails that her subjectivity can only be constructed in terms of what it lacks. Musically, "Reflection" is a conventional type of ballad, the melody and music typical of Western musical films. The melody becomes more urgent and powerful as Mulan contemplates her situation, plaintively asking when her reflection will show who she truly is inside.

Mulan's musical lament for her alienated feminine subjectivity importantly foregrounds the film's construction of gender as performative. Her lyrics specifically refer to feminine social roles as "parts," albeit parts which Mulan cannot seem to play successfully. The notion of identity as fragmented is visually represented at the close of the song, when Mulan looks into the pool and sees the same image of herself replicated again and again. Positioned alongside Mulan, the viewer sees as she does: the entire screen is filled with multiple copies of her face, a visual strategy which symbolizes the socially constructed (and therefore fragmented and multiple) nature of identity.

Mulan's allusion to gender as a social construct in her lyrics, a series of learned instead of natural behaviors, is sustained by the following scenes, in which Mulan learns of her father's conscription and then steals his armor and sword so that she can take his place. The juxtaposition of Mulan's musical solo with these scenes which introduce her cross-dressing directs viewers to interpret her cross-dressing behavior within the context of her continued failure to be feminine. In contrast to her father, whom she has previously watched drop his sword when attempting to practice with it, the cross-dressed Mulan handles the sword adeptly. Her father's feeble and elderly male body fails to meet the conventional standards of masculinity, but Mulan's agility with the weapon suggests that, at last, she has found a "part" that she can finally play. Although the consequences of her cross-dressing are not yet clear at this stage, the film draws attention to its exciting possibilities.

The feisty heroines of the fairy tale "The Subtle Princess" and the folktale "A Riddle for a King" are also situated outside conventional femininity. Vasilisa, the vodka-swilling heroine of "A Riddle for a King" who loves to dress as a man and to hunt, delights in the gender confusion she provokes in the king. (The tale's structure is very simple. Intrigued by the young man whose hunting ability he admires, the king invites him to dine with him several times. The king is confused by conflicting information he has received about Vasilisa's sex, but because of her successful masculine performance he is never able to prove that she is a woman—until she finally tells him herself.) Finessa, who is the "subtle princess" of her tale's title,[2] does not transgress feminine behavioral codes as explicitly as Vasilisa, Alanna, or Mulan. She is an unusual female cross-dresser because she performs femininity exceptionally well, but she also accommodates masculine attributes and skills into her gender repertoire which ensure that she is perceived as "different" from traditionally feminine subjects. Finessa clearly fulfills a model of feminine perfection—evident in her talents for music, sewing, and dancing—but she also embodies qualities that elude feminine categorization, particularly due to their conventionally masculine orientation: her intelligence, perspicacity, and aptitude for political negotiation and diplomacy.

Alanna, *Mulan*, "The Subtle Princess," and "A Riddle for a King" all assume a preliminary position in which gender is the primary concern, because the represented female characters do not accord with traditional definitions of femininity. Once the physical act of changing clothes has taken place (this event is given little focus), the more important aspect of behavior becomes the text's primary concern. The female cross-dresser soon realizes that physical appearance is but one small component of gender. Eager to acquire knowledge of masculine behavior, she embarks upon a learning process that quickly debunks the myth that gendered behavioral attributes are "natural" or inherent: initiative, strong powers of observation, and a few training sessions are all that stand between her and a successful masculine performance. In representing this experience, gender becomes the crucial focal point, regardless of textual variances in plot and genre. Notwithstanding a wide discrepancy in genre, sociohistorical context, and narrative mode, the essential core of these stories is an analysis and fundamental questioning of gender itself.

THE VISUAL VIABILITY OF THE FEMALE CROSS-DRESSER

Underlying most female-to-male cross-dressing narratives is an appreciation of gender as a performance rather than as an inherent aspect of biological identity. Gender is presented within these narratives as an amalgam of socially prescribed behaviors that must be learned and acquired, or temporarily adopted, as opposed to existing naturally. The performative nature of gender becomes the most significant denotation of gender identity in these narratives, and is far more critical than the outward, physical characteristics which are usually perceived to construct a subject's sex. One obvious reason for this is that literature is not based on visual images, but on language.

The dilemma of most contemporary adult cross-dressers—that of visually "passing" for a gender not aligned with their natal sex—is absent in children's literature. While clothing and appearance are important, they are not solely responsible for creating the illusion of gender. The issue of visually passing for a man is often not raised, as once the female character assumes a masculine gender identity, there is a general textual acceptance of this fact. The reader is not plagued with questions of "Does this girl really look like a boy?" or "Does she look 'masculine' enough to be convincing?" Instead, it is assumed that the female character does look convincing, and the narrative proceeds from this point. The majority of children's texts that feature a female cross-dressing theme spend little or no time describing the newly adopted attire of the cross-dressing character. Their central concern is whether the character can act like a boy. When she has proved that she can, the remainder of the story focuses on how long she can maintain the performance without detection. That the character can be assumed to look authentic is facilitated by the fact that physical gender divisions are not as clearly articulated in children as in adults. The defining physical characteristics of gender—breast and hip development in women; facial and body hair in men—do not distinguish prepubescent children. In *Alanna*, for example, the physical differences between Alanna and her male twin are minimal:

> Thom and Alanna Trebond were twins, both with red hair and purple eyes. The only difference between them—as far as most people could tell—was the length of their hair. In face and body shape, dressed alike, they would have looked alike. (1)

Children's female cross-dressing narratives assume that the visual presentation of the cross-dressed character will immediately be accepted as convincing by the reader or viewer. This phenomenon is most acutely realized in the animated film *Mulan*, where the feminine Mulan who appears in the first portion of the film is replaced by a significantly different and more visually masculine character when cross-dressed. When the viewer first sees Mulan, her long hair, shapely eyebrows, wide eyes, and rose-tinted lips conform to conventional notions of feminine beauty. When she is cross-dressed, however, a number of changes occur in her visual presentation: her eyebrows are thicker and lower; her jaw becomes squarer, her eyes are noticeably smaller, and her lips lose their fullness.

These changes eradicate the possibility of cross-dressing failure based purely on visual appearance. Mulan undeniably looks the part of a man, allowing the film to concentrate specifically on the supposedly natural behaviors and gestures attributed to traditional gender categories.

Alanna, however, is one of the few female cross-dressing narratives that attempt to deal specifically with the issue of physicality. Pierce refers, on more than one occasion, to the way that Alanna binds her breasts, in order to conceal them. These same curves eventually lead to her public disclosure at the end of book 2 (*In the Hand of the Goddess*), when her corset is slashed and her breasts show through her shirt (Pierce [1984] 1998, 225). Alanna's first experience of menstruation is also mentioned: "Alanna awoke at dawn, ready for another session with Coram's big sword. She got out of bed—and gasped in horror to find her thighs and sheets smeared with blood" ([1983] 1997, 132). This interlude is relatively exceptional among other examples of female cross-dressing, most of which choose to ignore the phsyical realities of a girl masquerading as a boy and the pubescent difficulties such a situation presents. The incident also prefigures a development from childhood, where successful cross-dressing can occur with ease because of the physical similarities between boys and girls, to adulthood, where the many dilemmas of contemporary adult transvestism and transsexualism begin to encroach on an otherwise simple and straightforward story of gender disguise. Pierce adeptly handles the challenge by bringing the issue of puberty and the gendered physical changes it entails to the forefront of her narrative. Alanna is also provided with certain friends who can sensitively aid her through her gendered rites of passage without giving away the secret of her identity. The result is an illuminating and socially realistic examination of the physical difficulties associated with successful cross-dressing.

Pierce's approach to the relationship between sex and gender is not overtly radical. She does not try to suggest that Alanna's affinity with masculinity should be read in accordance with the contemporary concept of transsexualism. However, she does play with the relationship between sex and gender. When Alanna goes to see Mistress Cooper, the mother of her friend George, for advice about menstruation, she is horrified to learn of the biological processes attached to being female. Reacting to her dismay, Mistress Cooper sternly tells her, "You're a female, child, no matter what clothing you wear. You must become accustomed to that" (137). Mistress Cooper's words draw attention to Alanna's natal sex, but Pierce instantly disrupts the presumed relationship between sex and gender. When asked what she knows about sex, Alanna reveals that she "know[s] the man's side of it" (138) and then expresses little interest in learning about pregnancy. Alanna's response inverts patriarchal constructions of femininity because her disregard for the consequences of sexual behavior, like childbirth, mimics masculine attitudes toward sex. A short time later, when George joins the discussion, Alanna voices her regret at deceiving her friends at the palace by cross-dressing:

> "But I'm a girl," she cried. "I'm *lying* to them. I'm doing men's things—" "And you do them better than most young men," George replied firmly. "Hush yourself. Think of them hatin' you *if* it comes to be. And don't worry. Your secret is safe with us." (139)

George's reply is pertinent because, first, he is able to view Alanna's masterful performance of masculinity within the context of his own masculine subject position. Like everyone else, he is fooled by her convincing masculine presentation. He is assured that Alanna is male, only becoming aware of her female sex after she chooses to disclose it to him. Second, George uses her successful masculine performance as a reason for persisting with her cross-dressing disguise. His mother may have chastised Alanna about not being able to change her sex, but Alanna's unconsciously masculine behavior and George's perception of her success together demonstrate that she is perfectly capable of changing her gender. She has internalized the attributes and behaviors associated with masculinity and is perceived by others as having a masculine identity. Pierce chooses to emphasize this behavioral aspect of gender, and the focus throughout the narrative remains firmly fixed on Alanna's conduct rather than on her appearance. Alanna's success as a young man depends on such a focus.

PERFORMING MASCULINITY

Judith Butler's analysis of gender in *Gender Trouble* (1990) offers an insightful theoretical tool for examining female cross-dressing narratives. Jonathan Culler writes that Butler's *Gender Trouble* took issue "with the notion, common in American feminist writing, that a feminist politics requires a notion of feminine identity, of essential features which women share as women and which give them common interests and goals" (1997, 102). Butler instead called for a radical reappreciation of gender as a kind of "improvisational theatre, a space where bodies can be more or less freely adopted and explored at will" (Osborne and Segal 1994), and her work has been greatly influential within the sphere of contemporary gender criticism. Butler's self-professed purpose (as she indicates in the preface to *Gender Trouble*) is "to trace the way in which gender fables establish and circulate the misnomer of natural facts" (xiii). It is precisely against these gender fables that the cross-dressing heroines of children's literature react, debunking traditional myths regarding the essential and so-called "innate" attributes of masculine and feminine gender identities. This challenges the dominant cultural assumption that gender is a defining characteristic of an individual's identity. Children's cross-dressing narratives challenge this assumption by showing that it is indeed possible to change one's gender identity, in this case through cross-dressing. These texts take an ideological position which views gender as an artificial construct or, as David Gauntlett suggests, they use cross-dressing to demonstrate that "rather than being a fixed attribute in a person, gender should be seen as a fluid variable which shifts and changes in different contexts and at different times" (1998).

Butler's problematization of identity, which she argues is not stable and fixed, but rather free-floating, and her concept of gender performativity—whereby she contends that "gender reality is performative which means, quite simply, that it is real only to the extent that it is performed" (1999 [1990], 278)—are readily applicable to female cross-dressing representations. Gender is invariably presented as a behavioral construct imposed by cultural conditioning in these narratives. The physical realities of cross-dressing (i.e., how to make a girl look convincingly masculine) are rendered insignificant in the context of the primary importance of behavioral transformation. The key to the female cross-dresser's masculine success is her ability to walk, talk, and act like a man. She incorporates both masculine and feminine behaviors into her gender performance, alternating between them according to the demands of the situation she finds herself in. A person's gender, as these children's books and films demonstrate, is principally based on how that person behaves rather than who he or she is inside (Culler 1997, 103). Female cross-dressing narratives bring an imaginatively fictionalized dimension to Butler's gender thesis, because while Butler argues that gender is naturalized over time through the repetition of particular behaviors and actions (giving the appearance of authenticity), these texts take the liberty of allowing their heroines to effect a flawless masculine performance with only minimal practice.

The issue of performance is crucial to cross-dressing texts such as *Alanna* and *Mulan*. In both, a similar paradigm emerges. A young woman, unable to satisfy the dictates of conventional femininity, cross-dresses to gain entrance to a military pursuit or endeavor available only to men. The challenge presented to her is not only to "look" like a man in terms of dress, but also to "act" like a man. Alanna and Mulan must learn to wield a weapon with ease, as well as to assume the traditionally masculine attributes of aggression and self-sufficiency. Alanna and Mulan both give triumphant performances of masculinity, despite some initial hiccups in their "opening scenes." They perform more successfully than their male peers, who have a biological advantage but fail to achieve the performative success of their cross-dressed female friends. Jonathan, the king's son, chooses Alanna as his personal page, considered a great honor by the other male pages. Mulan, with her strategic battle tactics, is single-handedly responsible for saving both her captain and the emperor from the invading Hun army.

The central tenet of female cross-dressing narratives strikes at the foundations of the perceived relationship between sex and gender. The female cross-dresser's successful performance of masculinity disrupts the presumption that gender is biologically decreed by dissecting masculinity into a series of behaviors and gestures that can be learned by a female subject just as easily. These narratives use female cross-dressing to expose the frailty of socially manipulated gender classifications, holding them up for worldly inspection—often with a great deal of good-natured humor. To use Butler's reasoning, these stories of female cross-dressing present gender as "a kind of persistent impersonation that passes as real" ([1990] 1999, x).

A significant element of female cross-dressing success is that by disguising themselves as men, these heroines gain an imaginary penis and the cultural status and significance traditionally attached to it. They gain a phallus, so to speak. In Lacanian terms the phallus is constituted by the relationship between the signifier of hegemonic male attributes (the penis) and the signified, meaning the sociocultural concept of "masculinity." According to Lacan, the phallus therefore is, and at the same time is not, the penis. (The penis comes to signify the phallus because it is endowed with such vital sexual and social importance; however, it is only the signifier—notwithstanding Lacan's reference to it as the "privileged signifier"—rather than the signified.) Lacan writes that the signifier "has an active function in determining certain effects in which the signifiable appears as submitting to its mark, by becoming through that passion the signified" (1977, 284). Thus for Lacan, gender and sexual difference are determined by either "having" or "being" a phallus. Men "have" the phallus symbolically, but women can "be" the phallus by virtue of their connection with the natural and instinctive order of the real. The determining factors of this system of gender difference are possession, or lack and absence, of a phallus. Lacan envisions femininity as a subject position characterized primarily by lack, but female cross-dressing heroines victoriously claim the cultural signifier of masculinity as their own while disguised as men. These feisty cross-dressed girls manage to transfer ownership, or possession, of the phallus to their own subjectivity while cross-dressed, thus gaining the privileges and social status usually reserved for men.

Lacan's relegation of women to a subordinated position within the gender hierarchy because of this perceived lack is an issue which Judith Butler revisited in *Bodies That Matter* (1993). She argues there that the phallus is "fundamentally transferable" (82–83), specifically in relation to the way that it can be applied to lesbian sexuality. Butler's contentions regarding the phallus as "conveyable" resonate with the construction of female cross-dressing, because the heroines of these texts similarly "acquire" a phallus when they disguise themselves as men and performatively enact a masculine gender identity.

Butler distinguishes the phallus from the penis by referring to the process of symbolization, suggesting that symbolization essentially "depletes that which is symbolized of its ontological connection with itself" (84). She then proceeds to question the assumption "that the phallus requires that particular body part to symbolize," asking readers to consider "why it could not operate through symbolizing other body parts" (84). Butler's conclusion is that the phallus *can* be transferred to women, and it is through the process of transference (and act of possession) that women can transgress and subvert its signifying power. She explains, "Precisely *because* it is an idealization, one which no body can adequately approximate, the phallus is a transferable phantasm, and its naturalized link to masculine morphology can be called into question through an aggressive reterritorialization" (86). A reterritorialization of masculinity, to use Butler's own expression, is an accurate characterization of what cross-dressing heroines like Alanna and Mulan achieve by disguising themselves as men. Their masculine performances are extremely effective, successfully exposing the constructed nature of patriarchal masculinity, but at the same time, each cross-dressed character subverts this category of gender identity by subtly reworking it. Her masculine performance is perceived as authentic, yet its difference (which usually occurs when the cross-dresser integrates elements of femininity into her assumed masculine subjectivity) is what singles her out as extraordinary, causing others to notice and celebrate her unique behavioral achievements.

Michaela Grey, however, points out that a significant issue arises when Butler's thesis regarding the lesbian phallus is applied to female-to-male transsexual identity—specifically because Butler uses queer subjectivity to illustrate the possibility of a feminine phallus. Grey suggests that "Lesbians have their own relationship to the phallus which operates in an almost diametric opposition to that of FTMs [female-to-male transsexuals]" (2002). Whereas lesbians define themselves against the patriarchal order, Grey argues that "FTMs embrace, rather than discard, the phallic identification." The same could be said of female cross-dressers in literature and film, each of whom willingly seeks to approximate a masculine subjectivity. Nevertheless, in spite of these theoretical distinctions, Butler's concept of the lesbian phallus, which "is and is not a masculinist figure of power" (Butler 1993, 89), offers a useful theoretical standpoint from which to consider female cross-dressing in children's literature and film. Female cross-dressers achieve subjective agency through their adoption of a masculine subjectivity (thus they "have" a phallus), but this agency is a simultaneous affirmation and subversion of patriarchal masculinity's privileged social status.

Before addressing the issue of how female cross-dressers gain status and agency through performing masculinity in further detail, it is necessary to return to the concept of gender performativity. Butler famously used the example of a drag performance to illustrate her theory of performativity, arguing that the figure of the drag artist usefully highlights "the very distinctions between the natural and the artificial, depth and surface, inner and outer through which discourse about genders almost always operates" ([1990] 1999, xxviii). Butler's reference to drag suggests that her theoretical framework is instantly applicable to female cross-dressing representations in children's literature and film, but a significant distinction is that children's texts rarely parody gender performances as overtly as drag. *Mulan* is an obvious exception. When Mulan first arrives at the army camp, she is appalled at the exaggeratedly crass masculine behavior she sees the other recruits display. *Mulan* is also unusual among female cross-dressing stories because it invokes an adult cross-dressing discourse. Female cross-dressing behavior is rarely referred to as "cross-dressing" in children's literature, because "cross-dressing" is a culturally loaded term often connected with deviant sexuality. *Mulan*, however, makes a number of self-conscious references to contemporary transvestism. The ancestral spirits of Mulan's family overtly refer to her as a "cross-dresser" in a squabble that erupts among them prior to her departure for the army, while Mushu, the miniature dragon who accompanies Mulan on her adventures, comments upon her "taking her drag show on the road."

Such explicit associations are generally absent from female cross-dressing representations, but both drag and female cross-dressers in children's literature have a similar critical purpose: to expose the many constructs of the sex-gender relationship. Female cross-dressing narratives thematize the concept of performance, repeatedly blurring the demarcation between what is assumed to be the heroine's natural or genuine female sex and her gender identity, which subverts social expectations by easily accommodating masculinity. Alanna problematizes the relationship between sex and gender particularly effectively, because her skillful masculine performance exposes the way in which cultural practices regulate gendered behavior: once she has assumed a masculine subjectivity, it is difficult for her to remember how to be feminine again. Secretly trying on a dress for the first time in years, she is amazed at how unsuitable it looks:

> "It's going to be as hard to learn to be a girl as it was to learn to be a boy."
>
> "Harder," the woman said, putting the tea on.
>
> "Most girls don't have to unlearn being a boy."
>
> ### (*In the Hand of the Goddess*, 125–126)

The difficulty Alanna experiences when attempting to resume a feminine subjectivity shifts the narrative's focus from the discourse of masculinity (and the potential feminist theme of women's ability) back to femininity, exposing the constructedness of both genders. Pierce's novels self-reflexively refute the supposition that sex and gender are the same, drawing the reader's attention to the ways in which gender is a series of "learned" behaviors and gestures.

Mulan approaches the issue of performativity somewhat differently, but is equally successful in exposing the cultural practices that impose prescribed roles (gender and otherwise) on individual bodies. Mulan's successful masculine performance, during which she carefully imitates the behavior and speech traditionally associated with hegemonic masculinity, effectively deconstructs masculinity to reveal how it is constituted and naturalized by the repetition and reiteration of certain behaviors and actions. The film is carefully structured around scenes of performance, each of which blurs the distinction between what is natural and what is artificial (or "theatrical"). Mulan's cross-dressing performance is the most crucial, but it is complemented by several others: Mushu also performs a role other than the one officially bestowed upon him. He was once a family guardian, but Mulan's ancestral spirits reveal that he has been disgraced due to poor performance in the past. Mushu has since been demoted, his current role involving only the awakening of the spirits at times of crisis when they are needed. Directed to awaken the "Great Stone Dragon" (who has been entrusted with ensuring Mulan's safe return), Mushu accidentally destroys him. Unbeknownst to the ancestors, Mushu takes the Great Stone Dragon's place. He is an unlikely substitute for a wise "guardian" because of his miniature size and irreverent manner (Mushu is voiced by comedian Eddie Murphy, whose cultural visibility as a black actor is contingent upon his comic subversion of Hollywood's dominant (i.e., white) racial discourses. Murphy's flippant and antiauthoritarian brand of humor is well suited to Mushu's character, whose panic at finding himself in an unfamiliar situation is complemented by Murphy's chaotic and impertinent verbal style.) Mushu's fear of failure is unwarranted, however, as he triumphantly fulfills the role of guardian by virtue of Mulan's success.

Mushu's unauthorized role switch is analogous to Mulan's, the relationship between the two made explicit by Mushu's comment to her, "The truth is, we're both frauds." Yet, the film's constant references to nature and authenticity assist in undermining this dichotomy, especially in the context of each performer's success in his or her assumed (and therefore supposedly unnatural) role. The climactic scene in which Mulan and her fellow soldiers rescue the emperor from the Huns refocuses the theme of performance on gender, as the men gain entry to the palace by cross-dressing as concubines. This double cross-dressing motif (which is not entirely successful, as the Huns immediately notice the cross-dressed men's visual failure, referring to them as "ugly concubines") highlights the inadequacy of the supposed sex-gender relationship by drawing attention to the way in which Mulan's behavior is comparable to the cross-dressed soldiers. The scene commences by showing the soldiers attacking the Huns (without Mulan, who is not on screen). Each man is attired in a brightly colored, feminine robe and his face has been gaudily painted with cosmetics. The scene is an incongruous display of gendered appearance and behavior: although attired like women, the soldiers' combative behavior is definitively masculine. A short time later, Mulan comes into view—also dressed in feminine clothing, but her masculine fighting skills look just as inappropriate when performed by a conventionally pretty feminine subject. As with the soldiers, there is a gap between Mulan's feminine appearance and masculine behavior which subverts the correlation between natal sex and gender identity.

This is not to say that it is easy for the female cross-dresser to subvert the gender identity she acquired at birth. In these children's texts, "changing" one's gender is difficult and requires considerable effort and perseverance. The scenes in which Mulan practices her swaggering masculine stance and tries unsuccessfully to spit like a man (her saliva remains embarrassingly stuck to her bottom lip) are amusing examples of this. The fact that female cross-dressers experience difficulty in assuming a gender role different from the one they are accustomed to playing illustrates the seemingly insurmountable divisions between "masculinity" and "femininity," but the characters' successful transformation from one gender to another vividly highlights the socially constructed nature of gender categories and conceptualizes behavior as their chief determinant. If the female cross-dresser can approach masculinity as an actor does a demanding new role, she can successfully "perform" it without her natal sex being detected. "Sex" becomes simply a biological feature like any other, rather than the determining characteristic of a body. Armed with the necessary social information, that is, which behaviors are considered to be masculine or feminine, and hence which behaviors should be either adopted or discarded, each female-to-male cross-dresser gives a spectacularly good performance of masculinity—to the extent that she often "outperforms" male subjects who would appear to have an advantage over her because their gender is more closely aligned with their sex.

GENDER AS "OUTPERFORMANCE"

One way of rationalizing this "outperformance" is to consider it in terms of the characters performing in a realm that is, in a sense, beyond conventional gender categories. Each of these cross-dressing women consciously performs masculinity at the expense of her feminine subjectivity, but she also unconsciously brings elements of both genders to the role. The female cross-dressing subject is able to operate outside the patriarchal gender binary. Her masculine performance is regarded as exceptional precisely because it is more than just a performance of traditional masculinity. Her behavior draws on elements of both masculinity *and* femininity, alternating between the two and benefiting from her knowledge of each. This achievement lies in the amalgamation of "positive" masculine and feminine gender attributes. Alanna, for example, is highly skilled in swordsmanship, but also a great healer (or witch). She combines sensitivity and acute perception (traditional feminine attributes) with the masculine values of strength, courage, and determination. When confronted by situations that seem to demand one form of gendered behavior over another—that is, her feminine gift of healing or her masculine prowess with a sword—Alanna draws on her knowledge of femininity and masculinity. When she is called to heal Jonathan, the king's son, who has a mysterious illness, Alanna's closely focalized narration reveals that she is able to harness her magical powers by applying a masculine discourse of authority and control to them:

Something inside her rebelled. She clenched her fists and fought the pain. She ground her teeth together. *She* would ride this tiger. Her body had never given the orders before— she could not let it start now. *Am I a silly child?* she thought angrily. *Or am I a warrior?* (101)

Alanna had previously been afraid of her magical gifts, but her ability to conquer her fears in this instance is implicitly related to her assumed masculine subjectivity. She refers to herself as a "warrior," a term that is traditionally masculine in orientation, which is indicative of the way that Alanna's behavior cuts across and through established gender boundaries. Although female, she is also a warrior; she is gifted in the use of a sword but also an expert healer and channeler of spirits. Alanna's successful integration of differently gendered attributes and behaviors is not merely a matter of reader perception—her difference is noticed and favorably commented upon by the other boys as well (Alan is the masculine name Alanna adopts):

Raoul frowned. "I hadn't meant to say anything, but since I have the chance—Alan, you seem to think we won't like you unless you do things just like everyone else. Have you ever thought we might like you because you're different?" (109)

Mulan also proves herself to be different. She plays a pivotal role in defeating the Hun army by twice coming up with ingenious plans to thwart Shan Yu's attempted invasion of China. Mulan's "difference" is first observed during her preliminary military training session. Shang shoots an arrow high up into a pole that is situated in the middle of the training camp, saying to Yao:

Shang: Yao. Thank you for volunteering. Retrieve the arrow.

Yao: I'll get that arrow, pretty boy, and I'll do it with my shirt on.

Shang: One moment, you seem to be missing something. [Shang takes two huge medallions out of a box.] This represents discipline. And this represents strength. You need both to reach the arrow.

Shang ties both medallions to Yao's hands, but despite Yao's bravado, neither he nor any of the other men is able to reach the arrow. Shang then breaks into the song "I'll Make a Man Out of You," a playful parody of conventional masculinity that self-consciously refers to gender as socially fashioned, "made" instead of "natural." The song's allusion to the constructed nature of gender is complemented by the ensuing scene, which directly suggests that Shang's efforts to "make men" out of his trainees has been most successful in relation to Mulan's reconstruction as a masculine subject. The next scene shows the empty campground at night, with Mulan slowly coming into view as she slowly climbs the pole to retrieve the forgotten arrow. She does indeed reach the arrow and pass Shang's test of masculinity, but does so by using an ingenuity that is based upon her ability to incorporate aspects of femininity into her masculine performance—in this case, creative thinking. Mulan achieves what the other men could not by inventively lacing the medallions together over her wrists, allowing her to use them as a grip while she proceeds up the pole.

Mulan's ability to think creatively is repeatedly marked as feminine, distinguishing her from the other male soldiers. She is superior on the battlefield because she combines the technical proficiency of warfare (a masculine ability) with lateral thinking (which the film suggests is a feminine skill). When Shan Yu makes a surprise attack on Shang's men, it is Mulan who cleverly shoots the snow-covered cap off a mountain, causing an avalanche that averts the Huns' attack. Mushu's response to her action demonstrates why Mulan's cross-dressed performance of masculinity is always more successful than that of her male peers— because, unlike them, she is able to interweave masculine and feminine behaviors advantageously. Seeing her strike the mountain cap with the cannonball, Mushu bewilderedly shouts, "You missed! How could you miss?! He was three feet in front of you!" Mushu's berating tone quickly changes when he sees the eventual effect of Mulan's strategic shot, but his initial (masculine) incomprehension is a useful example of how individuals are conditioned to behave and act according to the requirements of one particular gender category, making it impossible to perceive any type of behavioral alternative (unless, of course, you are a cross-dresser like Mulan). The film's climax confirms Mulan's unique abilities, constructing her victory against Shan Yu as a permutation of masculine and feminine behaviors. Mulan's ability to think laterally is plainly evident, illustrated by her plan of cross-dressing the soldiers as concubines and also in the way that she purposefully positions Shan Yu above a tower filled with fireworks, so that when Mushu shoots a rocket into him, knocking him off balance into the tower, it explodes on impact. Yet, Mulan's victory over Shan Yu is equally dependent on her ability to give a conventionally masculine performance. It is her skillful swordsmanship that enables her to maneuver Shan Yu into the correct position above the fireworks tower, reinstating the traditionally masculine significance of physical aggression and conquest in her triumph over the Huns' leader.

The female cross-dressing characters of the fairy tale "The Subtle Princess" and the folktale "A Riddle for a King" also "outperform" the masculine and feminine subjects around them, but their "outperformance" is of a different nature than Alanna's and Mulan's. Fairy tales and folktales are usually brief in form, driven by plot rather than character development, and reliant on character archetypes—generic conventions which produce a type of cross-dressing representation that is distinct from the closely focalized and personal experiences of Alanna and Mulan. The construction of gender as performative is implicit rather than explicit, implied by the heroine's actions and the responses that her subversive behavior engenders in others. These fairy tale/folktale female cross-dressers give superlatively successful masculine performances, and their abilities are proudly acknowledged—in "The Subtle Princess" by a subversive narrator who extols Finessa's virtues and in "A Riddle for a King" by the immense frustration that Vasilisa's authentically masculine behavior causes the "wily" King Barakat. Finessa's and Vasilisa's transgressive gender identities are privileged over characters that conform to gender stereotypes—particularly male characters that represent traditional patriarchal values. Most of these are subtly humiliated. Richcraft, the villain of "The Subtle Princess," so named because of his calculating and manipulative disposition, is consistently duped by the fast-thinking and even quicker-acting Finessa. "A Riddle for a King" is told from Vasilisa's point of view, a strategy which ensures that King Barakat is mocked for going to such improbable lengths to expose her as a male fraud. The folktale's closure resists the patriarchal resolution common to most folktales, which validates feminine passivity and invariably involves a romantic union between the hero and heroine, instead accentuating Vasilisa's individuality and independence. Vasilisa's words resolve the tale, in the form of a note that she directs her servant to deliver to the king. The note eloquently unravels the mystery of Vasilisa's identity and chides the king for his ridiculous behavior:

> "You're a wily old raven, King Barakat," the message read, "but you could not get the better of the falcon in flight. It has never been my intention to create a mystery. I would have told you that I am Vasilisa Vasilyevna and not Vasily Vasilyevich. You had only to ask me." (9)

The thematic examination of gender constructs in these two tales of female cross-dressing far exceeds a simple call for feminine equality. In portraying cross-dressing heroines, each of whom engages in wondrous deeds and adventures, as the equals of the very sex systematically responsible for feminine oppression, these narratives question the culturally instigated and enforced codes that divide men from women. The conventional characteristics and behaviors attributed to masculinity and femininity are revealed to the reader as absurd and artificial. In the case of Finessa, these concerns are articulated by her ability to excel (to the point of perfection) at all manner of traditionally masculine and feminine tasks and behaviors:

> Her thoughts and hands were never idle. She was of a surprising vivacity and she applied it only to good use. She danced, sang and played music to perfection. She would finish, with quite wonderful skill, all of the finicky little tasks of the hand which are reputed to divert those of her sex.... (67–68)

The intrusive and opinionated narrator praises Finessa's performance of femininity, but it is also clear that the narrator holds stereotypical feminine values in contempt (this is also obvious in the construction of Finessa's traditionally gendered sisters, who are constantly derided for their feminine passivity). The narrator's disdainful reference to needlecraft in this passage, as one of the "finicky little tasks" that women were expected to delight in, attacks the patriarchal construction of women as easily distracted and intellectually inferior to men.

In addition to her mastery of feminine skills, Finessa is equally talented at operating within masculine discourses. The narrator refrains from criticizing traditional masculinity as vehemently as femininity, but Finessa's behavior reveals that she plays a leading role in palace diplomacy, outperforming those males (the king and his appointed ministers) in whose hands this responsibility is presumed to lie:

> Young as she was, for instance, she had cleverly discovered, in a treaty that was just about to be signed, that a perfidious foreign ambassador had laid a cunning trap for the king her father.... In like fashion, she exposed a vile roguery that a certain minister had a mind to play on the king; and, by the advice she gave her father, matters were arranged so that the traitor's villainy would fall on his own head. (68)

Although Finessa cross-dresses for only a minor portion of the text, her behavior throughout resists conventional gender classification. The fairy tale uses Finessa to advocate a concept of gender that is unrestricted and "changeable." She exhibits both feminine and masculine attributes and behaviors, alternating between them at her whim. She is ultimately constituted as belonging to a third realm of gender, fusing aspects of both the feminine and the masculine into her unique and individual performance. In the words of the tale's narrator, Finessa is—by means of her extraordinary behavior—a "paragon" (96).

Vasilisa, the heroine of "A Riddle for a King," is openly scornful of stereotypical gender constructions, asserting that they are meaningless to her. Hearing that the king is puzzled after seeing her from a distance, she says, "Am I a man? Am I a woman? If a woman, why do I wear breeches? Everyone wants an answer. Well, you know, I never even thought about it myself!" (2). Vasilisa's behavior, in contrast to Finessa's, is consistently masculine throughout the narrative. She wears trousers, has commendable hunting skills, "knocks back" vodka because "she loved that hot feeling of the drink as it chased down her gullet," detests "frivolous, girlish fripperies" (4), and disregards the social etiquette that characterizes conventionally feminine decorum: she enters rooms without knocking first (3), and expresses herself in "chuckles" (3) and "roars" (5). The "riddle" of the folktale is Vasilisa's sex, which the king perceives as male—but he has heard from others that he is wrong. In vain he tries to uncover her femininity, but Vasilisa's masculine presentation is so authentic that he can never find fault with it. The text introduces its gender theme by opening with the king's thoughts, "Vasily Vasilyevich? Vasilisa Vasilyevna? Is it a woman? Is it a man?" (1), which are then mirrored by Vasilisa's own open-ended application of these questions to herself. She is unrepentant about her willful gender rebellion, ignoring her father's admonition that "drinking vodka was not becoming to a woman" (2), and also scathing in her view of the paradoxical nature of patriarchal femininity. When she hears that the king has consulted a witch to determine her sex, she is furious: "He's so desperate he's asking old crones for advice now. And yet it's women they malign for their idle curiosity" (3).

"The Subtle Princess" and "A Riddle for a King" both use female cross-dressing characters to rework the phallocentric order typical of fairy tales and folktales. Finessa's and Vasilisa's recourse to trousers is a natural extension of their transgressive feminine identities. These cross-dressing heroines redress the traditional subordination of feminine characters by demonstrating their ability to perform masculinity as successfully as any biological male. Their superior masculine performances restore an unprecedented equilibrium between the sexes in the fairy tale and folktale environment, a rigidly constructed and divided context that conventionally prevents such gendered harmony. In spite of the repressive social and literary structures that seek to curtail the activities of feminine characters, Finessa and Vasilisa actively resist such passivity. Their cross-dressing behavior signifies a rebellious incursion of traditional gender boundaries, a refusal to be limited by the oppressive regimes of patriarchal gender constructions.

AGENCY AND CLOSURE: RECLAIMING GENDERED NARRATIVE TRADITIONS THROUGH FEMALE CROSS-DRESSING

Narrative closure is a contentious issue within stories of female cross-dressing because, in most cases, the equation of cross-dressing with feminine agency is seemingly undermined by the heroine's eventual return to a position of conventional femininity. This is best illustrated by texts such as *Mulan* and "The Subtle Princess," which conclude with the heroine's impending marriage and therefore reinstate her gender identity in accordance with a traditional paradigm of femininity. The concept of "agency" is similarly problematic here because an ideological distinction must be drawn between the humanist definition of agency, wherein people are viewed as individuals who have the capacity to act reflectively and purposively, and Butler's postmodern concept of agency, which is specifically located in actions that disrupt and vary the normally reiterative nature of gender performance.

Female cross-dressing narratives offer highly unusual constructions of subjectivity and gender, in that they can be productively read in accordance with both of these differing concepts of agency. The humanist discourse prevalent in traditional and contemporary children's fiction, which constructs a unified subject as a "unitary self capable of action outside ideological systems" (Stephens and McCallum 1998, 20), is unmistakably apparent in texts such as *Mulan* and *Alanna: The First Adventure*, each of which constructs cross-dressing as behavior which enables female protagonists to act independently, reflectively, and purposefully. Mulan's subjective development primarily occurs during the period she spends cross-dressed as a soldier within the Chinese army. This is an experience which removes her from the limited feminine subject position she previously occupied within the social sphere of her family and village, and allows her to develop into an independent, decisive, and self-determining subject. Her transformation into an agential subject is best exemplified after her cross-dressing ceases and she has been dismissed from the army by Captain Shang. Although she is no longer disguised as a man, Mulan's subjectivity has developed and evolved due to her cross-dressing experiences. Her subjective agency is manifested through cleverness, resourcefulness, and superior swordsmanship, all of which are displayed in the film's climactic penultimate scene when Mulan uses an ingenious combination of skill and strategy to save the emperor from the Hun ambush. A comparable humanist conceptualization of agency is evident in *Alanna: The First Adventure*, where Alanna's development into a self-defining and unified subject is achieved by the text's eventual positioning of her character outside (or independent) of the ideological forces which previously prescribed her subordinated feminine subjectivity. Alanna's mastery of the masculine activities expected of a page, combined with her tactical battle skills and intuitive gift for magic, eventually give her a sense of purpose and individual capability. This is best demonstrated in the book's final scene, when the time has come for Prince Jonathan to select his personal squire. He asks Alanna whom he should choose, and an emboldened Alanna bravely responds: "'Me,' she said at last. 'You should pick me'" (215).

Empowerment is a defining feature of humanist conceptualizations of agency. Stories of female cross-dressing characteristically equate cross-dressing with subjective agency, whereby gender transgression becomes a means through which a feminine subject can resist the interpellating discourses of traditional femininity and also, to a certain extent, those which define masculinity. Cross-dressing becomes the means through which women can achieve a self-determining and reflective identity. Butler, however, points out that identity is really the result of a performative gesture or behavior rather than being located in fixed and stable categories of the subject. She suggests that identity should be understood as "a practice, and as a signifying practice" ([1990] 1999, 184). Agency therefore becomes "reformulated as a question of how signification and resignification work" (184). In this context, heroines such as Alanna, Mulan, and Finessa acquire agency by varying the traditional discourses of masculinity and femininity in their cross-dressed performances. If, as Butler suggests, identity is located within practices of signification, and all signification takes place "within the orbit of the compulsion to repeat" (185), then these heroines gain an agential subjectivity by subverting the conventional practices of gender signification. Their behavior is a conglomeration of the gestures and actions which construct masculinity and femininity, and as such it transgresses the traditional demarcation between these behaviors. Agency, as Butler remarks, "is to be located within the possibility of a variation on that repetition [which constitutes either masculinity or femininity]" (185). The success of the female cross-dresser in children's literature and film is contingent upon her ability to differentiate herself from conventional masculinity (if she merely replicated traditional masculinity, she would be unnoticeable rather than achieving the type of public victory which occurs with Alanna and Mulan). She must be convincingly masculine but also subtly distinctive, which she achieves with an ingenious blend of gendered behaviors. Her performance highlights the constructedness of gender stereotypes, destabilizing masculinity and femininity as stable categories of identity.

Female cross-dressers consequently achieve agency within the type of model envisioned by Butler, by disrupting the ways in which our society naturalizes the relationship between sex and gender. Their cross-dressing disturbs the behavioral repetitions which comprise the conventional categories of masculinity and femininity, clearly drawing the reader's/viewer's attention to the distinction between the biology of the human body (sex) and gender as a social construct. At the same time, cross-dressers such as Mulan and Alanna exemplify a humanist conceptualization of agency by developing a self-determining subjectivity that is resistant to the ideological discourses which seek to constrain and prescribe it (i.e., traditional femininity). This seemingly unusual situation—wherein a particular story or stories can be read in accordance with two very different concepts of agency—is contingent upon the role that "resistance" plays in shaping the cross-dressing protagonists' subjectivity. Within a humanist model of subjectivity, agency is dependent upon the subject's ability to resist ideological pressure (Smith 1988, xxxv). The idea of resistance is also fundamental to Butler's theory of agency. Rejecting the notion of identity as something stable and preexisting, and conceptualizing it instead as a signifying practice, and thus an "effect" of signification, Butler argues that identity is created and naturalized through the process of repetitive signification. Resisting the compulsion to repeat the actions and gestures which constitute categories of identity such as masculinity and femininity—and therefore repeating these behaviors in a subversive manner—is what leads to subjective agency, as repeatedly demonstrated by female cross-dressers. Characters such as Alanna and Mulan initially seek only to perform traditional masculinity, but the reason for their cross-dressed success lies in the way that they each alter and transform the behavioral repetitions required for masculinity. Their eventual performance of masculinity is one that constantly contests the rigidly defined boundaries of patriarchal masculinity. Female cross-dressers generally perfect their performances of conventional masculinity, changing the ways in which they move, speak, and behave in order to conform to a patriarchal type of masculinity defined by strength, independence, competitiveness, and aggression. At the same time, however, these cross-dressed women vary their masculine gender performances, indiscernibly incorporating (at least to the other men in their peer group) attributes and behaviors deemed feminine in order to produce a unique gender performance that challenges the limiting boundaries of traditional masculinity and femininity.

Stories of female cross-dressing also seek to redress traditional gender imbalances by reclaiming parts of traditional fairy tales, myths, and historical legends. Femininity is reinstated by elevating it to a position of prominence, far removed from its traditionally peripheral construction. Rather than promoting the actual roles of women in this literary and historical realm, female-to-male cross-dressing narratives directly challenge the primacy of masculinity by positing the question "Could the men who produced this tradition actually have been women in disguise?" This approach serves to rewrite the role of the feminine in history, myth, and legend by transposing it over the deeply etched domain of masculinity. It substantiates the feminine by making it interchangeable with the masculine, resulting in a conception of gender that transgresses the conventions of masculinity and femininity and carves its own gender niche. *Mulan* is the perfect embodiment of this concept, as not only does it portray a cross-dressing heroine who valiantly saves all of China from the invading Huns with her resourceful military tactics, but also merges two differently gendered histories and traditions. *Mulan* ingeniously integrates two established Disney film genres, the classic "girl" and the classic "boy" film. In the "girl" film, a young woman strays from her father's domain in search of adventure. She finds adventure, and also romance, and the film usually concludes with a scene depicting marital bliss and domestic harmony—a cyclic return to the patriarchal domain (*Beauty and the Beast* [1991], *Snow White* [1937], *The Little Mermaid* [1989], *Cinderella* [1950]). In the "boy" film, a young male outcast discovers his potential for leadership, bravery, and other forms of heroism through a series of rites of passage (*Aladdin* [1992], *Tarzan* [1999]). *Mulan* is the product of both of these genres. The central character of the film is a young girl who joins the Chinese army disguised as a boy in order to protect her beloved father. Her initial experiences fall into the "adventurous" category of Disney girl movies, yet as the text progresses and Mulan successfully achieves a masculine subjectivity (in that she is accepted by the other male soldiers), the film mutates into the Disney boy genre, as Mulan plays the role of male military hero and leads the army to victory, saves the emperor, and narrowly escapes death herself. During this middle portion of the film, which focuses on Mulan's militaristic endeavors, her cross-dressing status is relegated to the fringe, confirming the transfer of genres that occurs. The film's conclusion reverts to the previous "girl" genre. Mulan is reunited with her parents, and an inevitable romance with Shang, the captain of the army, forms the closing scene.

The merger of gendered genres in *Mulan* can be viewed as compromising its feminist message (if Mulan returns to a life of marital domesticity, then what have her adventures in the army achieved?), but this fusion of masculine- and feminine-oriented narratives can also be interpreted in the context of the aforementioned transposing of gendered traditions, and in the construction of a "third" realm of gender. *Mulan* does not make a historical statement about the lives of traditional Chinese women, nor does it attempt to examine a particular society, using feminist analytical principles. (*Mulan* is a Disney concoction of various Westernized representations of the Orient, drawing inspiration from both Chinese and Japanese cultures. The film is guilty of transposing Western cultural norms to a Chinese setting, wherein Chinese customs such as arranged marriages are ridiculed for compromising feminine agency[3]). The film is, however, a text that unites two divergent, instantly recognizable gendered traditions so successfully that they become virtually interchangeable with each other. Mulan fails the test of conventional femininity at the film's outset, but correctly performs femininity in the film's closure by choosing romance and marriage. In between, she masters masculinity, moving imperceptibly between a fusion of conventional and unconventional gender roles. Mulan's behavior detracts from the simple classification of an individual as either masculine or feminine. Her gender identity moves from one gendered discourse to the other, alternately resisting and conforming to their structures, until the rigidity of the gender realms into which she ventures evolves to the point where they are rendered meaningless through a profusion of conflicting behaviors. In depicting the differences between the sexes as blatantly and conventionally as possible, and positioning Mulan as an object that oscillates between and around them, a third dimension of gender is constructed in her wake. Into this dimension fall those transgressive gender behaviors that appear in minor scenes, making a not inconsiderable contribution to the text's construction of gender as ambiguous and ambivalent. I refer here to the characterization of Shang's feminized political adviser, Chi Fu, who becomes distressed at the thought of wetting his shoes in the river; the appearance of imperial soldiers disguised as concubines in the film's climactic scene; and Mushu, who serves to relocate this traditional Chinese text in contemporary Western sexual politics through his reference to drag. *Mulan* thus travels beyond the notion of feminist empowerment, whose standards are neglected, it could be argued, by virtue of its conventionally feminine conclusion. The end result is an unusually self-conscious reflection on the very nature of gender itself, which admits to the frailty of hegemonic gender norms and questions the validity of their imposition on individuals who fail to fulfill their restrictive criteria.

"The Subtle Princess" also reworks gendered traditions. Its cross-dressing heroine, Finessa, is ultimately the hero and the heroine of this fairy tale, performing both the traditional masculine and feminine roles herself. As one of the king's daughters, she is placed at risk (according to fairy tale convention) by a treacherous male villain; is rescued in true fairy tale style; and eventually finds love and marital bliss in the arms of an honorable prince. The twist of the tale is that Finessa is responsible for her own "rescue" (and that of her kingdom) by virtue of her perspicacity, intelligence, and cross-dressing capabilities. Finessa embodies feminist principles in her proactive behavior, negating any notions of feminine inequality in this narrative through her truly remarkable (and remarked-upon) deeds. Importantly, Finessa also destabilizes conventional gender binaries. Unmistakably feminine in her talents for music, sewing, and dancing, she is also a signifier of masculinity—illustrated by her diplomatic skills; her practical and rational mind; her (almost militaristic in nature) survival skills, which come to the fore during her escape from Richcraft; her active and adventurous disposition; and even her tendency toward aggressive behavior: "Without giving her tormentor any time to know where he was, she deftly kicked him inside and started to roll the barrel down the mountain" (87).

Pierce combines and revises the gendered traditions of fantasy in her *Song of the Lioness* quartet, using the cross-dressed figure of Alanna to interlace the distinctive narrative paths of the feminine "good witch" figure (Stephens 2003) and the masculine sword hero. Alanna's "gift," characterized by her affinity with the natural and spirit worlds and her magical ability to heal the sick, is typical of the "good witch" motif in fantasy literature, which Stephens argues is based on the schema of a woman who is "in tune with the natural world and its cycles and with her own instinctual responses" (198). Supernatural power is not always constructed as a feminine attribute in fantasy literature, but Pierce frames Alanna's "gift" within a feminine discourse. Magic is consistently associated with femininity—for example, Alanna is first introduced to her special abilities by Maude, the village healer, and the feminine construction of magic is sustained by Alanna's relationship with "the goddess," a powerful and benign mystical force who protects and guides her. Alanna problematizes this schematic construction of feminine subjectivity, however, by her simultaneous adherence to the masculine sword hero's developmental path, wherein the hero's maturation is framed within a masculine model of rivalry, conflict, and physical victory over one's enemies.

The revelation of Alanna's female sex to Jonathan, the king's son, occasions a positive reaction that symbolically places Alanna outside conventional gender categories (reiterated in the conclusion of book 2, when Alanna leaves the palace, after her sex is publicly revealed, to pursue a self-determined life as a female knight). Jonathan's discovery of Alanna's sex does not affect his friendship with her, nor his desire for her to be his designated squire at the palace. He is happy to disregard her sex on the basis of his estimation of her performance, complementing the text's thematic exploration of oppressive gender stereotypes. To Jonathan, Alanna has already proved herself worthy of this honor, establishing herself as unique precisely because she brings both masculine (swordsmanship) and feminine (witchcraft) attributes to a role previously restricted to only one set of gendered behaviors. Alanna's oft-proved capabilities cement her superiority over traditionally gendered individuals, even if she herself is unaware of her success:

> "Before we left, I told him I wanted you for my squire. He didn't seem very surprised." Jonathan wriggled, trying to find a softer spot on the ground.
>
> "B-but," Alanna stuttered, "isn't it different? Now that you know—"
>
> "That you're a girl? No, not in the way you mean. Girl, boy or dancing bear, you're the finest squire-to-be at Court." (215–216)

Jonathan's words to Alanna, "Girl, boy or dancing bear," encapsulate a central theme in children's female cross-dressing narratives. Children's narratives employ female cross-dressing in a manner that effectively demonstrates the need for individuals to be judged for who they actually are, and by the unique qualities each possesses, rather than their ability to fulfill a prescribed social and/or gendered role into which they have had the ill fortune to be born. Transgressive and nonconformist gender behavior is examined and validated in female cross-dressing literature, specifically in relation to the issue of individual identity and the complex questions that can often surround a young subject's quest for autonomy and selfhood.

Children's literature and film use female cross-dressing to destabilize the perceived relationship between sex and gender. It regularly presents a slightly unbelievable model (in terms of the modern concept of transgender) in which young women dress themselves as boys, escape an oppressive regime, prove themselves the equals of their male counterparts, and then revert to their former feminine subject positions. Their rebellious transgression is only temporary. Cross-dressing heroines enjoy a brief flirtation with transvestism rather than an enduring love affair, but although the cross-dressing ceases on a visible and physical level, its ultimate effects are unquantifiable. Having experienced what it is to be considered masculine, can the character easily resume a feminine subject position? If they do so (as is usually the case), surely this subject position will differ from the subject positions of other females because of its inside knowledge of masculinity? Each of these questions is posed by the female cross-dressing characters, creating a unique forum for inquiries regarding the construction of gender categories. Cross-dressing becomes the means through which gender can be positively subverted and reappropriated by subjects to whom it does not holistically apply. Female-to-male cross-dressing narratives become a catalyst for a radical reevaluation of gender and the role it plays in the constitution of individual identity. *Alanna, Mulan,* "The Subtle Princess," and "A Riddle for a King" advocate a liberal and individualistic approach to the issue of gender. Each rejects the limitations imposed upon individuals by an inflexible, bipolar system of gender, expressing their dissatisfaction through the representation of a character who refuses to be categorized or defined according to convention. The cross-dressing subjects of these texts reclaim gender for themselves as they destabilize and rebel against traditional gender values. Their gender takes an ultimately unprecedented form. It becomes a unique third category, against which traditional constructions of masculinity and femininity are interwoven and dissected through the rituals of performance.

THE MALE CROSS-DRESSER

Although female-to-male cross-dressing constitutes the most popular form of cross-dressing found in literature for children, a smaller number of texts provide a variation on this model by featuring male characters who cross-dress. It is this model which reproduces popular (mis)understandings of adult cross-dressing most closely. The depiction of a male character who dresses in feminine clothing invites comparisons with adult cross-dressing because in Western culture, cross-dressing is popularly considered to be a masculine phenomenon. Male cross-dressing is perceived as inherently sexual in nature (either in a fetishistic sense or in a homosexual context). However, literature produced for young children rarely delves into the area of sexuality, so male cross-dressing texts are similar to female cross-dressing texts in their desire to avoid an association between cross-dressing and sexuality. This presents a peculiar challenge, due to the biological sex of the cross-dressing character. Hence, male cross-dressing is depicted in children's literature in the negative terms of what it isn't (i.e., it signifies neither homosexuality nor sexual perversion; it is not a warning of effeminacy) rather than actively setting its own parameters of meaning. The cultural discourse of adult-oriented cross-dressing is much harder for male cross-dressers to escape than it is for their female counterparts. Conscious of, and restrained by, this adult transgender discourse, male cross-dressing narratives provide a representation of gender that is surprisingly conservative in nature.

Male cross-dressing representations usually feature a biologically male protagonist who is forced against his will to wear women's clothing. In contrast to their cross-dressing sisters, males who cross-dress in children's literature rarely do so voluntarily. While he is cross-dressed, the male protagonist's biological sex is never adequately disguised to the extent that he could genuinely be considered a female, and his inability to give a convincing feminine performance is often constructed in a humorous, carnivalized fashion. His failure in this respect is supposed to be conceived by the reader/viewer as humiliating for him as a subject, but amusing for the reader as it unfolds. Although female cross-dressing characters achieve subjective agency, cross-dressing is responsible for destroying or limiting the agency of the male protagonist. The hostility that characterizes the attitudes of popular and mainstream Western culture to cross-dressing is similarly evident in male cross-dressing literature. Cross-dressing is used as a means through which the male protagonist is humorously divested of his masculinity, which in essence also robs him of his subjective agency.

Within the male cross-dressing model, the authentic masculinity of the cross-dressing male subject is rarely in any genuine doubt. The characters of these narratives are first and foremost "male," and their inherent masculinity permeates the cross-dressing context, even though they may appear outwardly female. The form of masculinity that these characters embody, in spite of their brief gender transgression, is characterized in terms of traditional gender values. It is defined against femininity and encompasses the range of specific behaviors (physical strength, aggression, self-sufficiency, control) that have become symbolic, through controlling social practices and popular representations, of "hegemonic masculinity." The term "hegemonic masculinity" was first used by R. W. Connell in the influential *Masculinities* (1995). Connell used the term to refer to the dominant form of masculinity within a particular culture, which, as Stephens and Romoren argue, "in most cases...does coincide with masculinities based in domination and/or violence" (2002, 233). "Hegemonic masculinity" has thus become an abbreviated term for "forms of masculinity grounded in domination, physical assertiveness, and egocentric individualism which still predominate in media images" (Stephens and Romoren, 217). Surprisingly, given the interest which has recently surfaced in contemporary adolescent literature about masculinity and how it is formed and culturally regulated (for a more comprehensive discussion of this issue, please refer to Stephens and Romoren 2002), children's literature and film which contain male cross-dressing rarely present any alternative to hegemonic masculinity.

The recently published picture book *Another Perfect Day*, by Ross MacDonald (2002), is a characteristic example of the male cross-dressing model. Illustrated in the style of comic books from the 1930s and 1940s, *Another Perfect Day* is the story of Jack, a beefy, muscle-bound hero modeled to resemble a superhero of the Clark Kent variety. The verbal text of this picture book is familiar and uncomplicated, simply stating that Jack "got up and looked out," "got dressed," "ate his breakfast," "exercised," "stopped to help out here and there," and then "caught the train to work." The visual text, however, tells a very different story. Jack is a hyperbolic embodiment of hegemonic (superhero-influenced) masculinity. *Another Perfect Day* employs the conventions of Bakhtin's theory of the carnival, collapsing the hierarchical boundaries between reality and fantasy within Jack's daily existence: He lives in a circus tent; he dive-bombs headfirst into his bowl of breakfast cereal; he wrestles with an alligator for his morning workout; he flies to work in an airplane; he catches a derailed train in his bare hands; and he saves the Earth from invading aliens on his way to work (where he is employed as the chief flavor tester of the World's Best Ice Cream Company). Jack is the perfect fantasy of patriarchal masculinity—he is handsome (blonde hair, chiseled features, and an impossibly proportioned physique), athletic, daring and courageous, self-sufficient, and a protector of people weaker than himself. And despite his hectic morning, he still manages to arrive at work looking immaculate. He is, in every sense of the words, a "super man."

After Jack leaves work, however, a strange thing happens. The verbal text articulates the disruption of his visually fantastic morning in this low-key way: "...just when he thought things couldn't possibly get any better...they didn't. In fact, things started to go a little funny." As with Jack's earlier exploits, the visual text on this double-page spread depicts a much more startling and extreme situation. Midway through bounding over the roofs of tall buildings on his walk home, Jack suddenly finds himself attired in a frilly pink tutu. His expression is one of distress as he looks down at his torso, and says with confusion (via speech bubble), "Huh?!" The right-hand side of this spread reveals the escalation of Jack's humiliation. He next finds himself wearing not only the tutu but also a lacy white baby's bonnet and overly large clown shoes, and in his hand there appears a big purple rattle. The words "poof!," "pop!," and "ping" appear in large, capital letters within the right-hand image, signifying the startling nature of Jack's transformation. Together, these alliterative and onomatopoeic words make an aural contribution to the instantaneous quality of Jack's changed appearance, suggestive of the idiom a magician uses when performing a trick designed to alter the physical reality of an object. The word "poof," which is repeated in both the left- and right-hand images, is a provocative and controversial inclusion. One meaning of "poof" is etymologically derived from the word "puff" (i.e., of smoke), a convention that is familiar to magic shows and fairy tales and which heralds physical transformation. However, "poof" is also an abusive term for gay men. Its appearance in relation to an image of a man wearing a dress knowingly alludes to the popular association of effeminate masculinity with homosexuality. The allusion to homosexuality is maintained in the presentation of the word itself, which is feminized: it appears in pink print and the interior section of the repeated letter "O" has been stylized into the shape of a star. The derogatory connotations of the word "poof" are further developed by the inclusion of a small bird which is positioned in the lower right-hand side of the left-hand image. It laughs scornfully at Jack, the words "ha ha" appearing next to its open beak. The bird's derision complements the disparaging nature of the word "poof"; together they encourage readers to adopt a subject position which ridicules Jack on the basis that his nonconformist masculine clothing has compromised his agential masculine subjectivity. He is no longer a figure of envy. The tutu has made him a figure of mockery.

The threat precipitated by the pink tutu, as a signifier of femininity, manifests itself in both the verbal and the visual texts on this spread, signifying a covert process of ideological cooperation between the two discourses that has hitherto been absent. The former subtlety of the verbal text is forsaken due to the appearance of the word "funny," an inclusion which sustains the homophobic reading of the word "poof." "Funny" is a term that denotes a peculiar departure from the ordinary, and in the past it was often applied to homosexuals to indicate the abnormality of their sexual and gender identities. The homophobic discourse present in both the visual and the verbal texts gives Jack's tutu a perilous significance. It compromises Jack's masculine subjectivity by feminizing him, rendering him passive, and in the process causes his now effeminate identity to be associated with homosexuality. Jack finally manages to escape his horrible predicament upon being told by a small boy that it is only a dream, from which he must wake himself. It becomes clear to the reader at this point that "Jack" is actually a small child who has been dreaming of his perfect self, and experiencing his own fantasy of what would constitute a "perfect day."

Another Perfect Day is a classic example of how male-to-female cross-dressing is negatively associated with homosexuality, often quite overtly. It also demonstrates how male cross-dressing signifies a loss of subjective agency and social status. While a picture book such as *Another Perfect Day* is aimed at very young readers, the crisis that occurs to Jack is very much an adult crisis of masculinity. When dressed in the tutu and baby bonnet, which act as potent signifiers of femininity and childhood, and hence passivity, Jack loses his agential power as a subject. (The powerful effect of this combination also serves to associate femininity with infantilism, thereby implying passivity and loss of agency.) More disaster ensues when Jack's plane turns into a tricycle, which provides little assistance as he tries to escape the mob of policemen and angry bystanders who chase after him. The text offers no reason for their pursuit, apart from the obvious—they are incensed by his appearance. (The depiction of a ferocious-looking policeman among the group implies that Jack's clothing is somehow criminal, which harkens back to biblical prohibitions of cross-dressing and past eras in which cross-dressing was considered a criminal offense.)

Another Perfect Day highlights a problem inherent within representations of male cross-dressing with respect to feminine readers and the reading position they are forced to adopt by the text. The implied reader of male cross-dressing texts is unequivocally masculine, as is clear from the manner in which feminine clothing is constructed as shameful attire, necessitating that readers who are girls or women must identify against themselves. Male cross-dressing protagonists generally fail to give anything resembling a convincing feminine performance, yet despite failing to conceal their masculinity particularly effectively, the very fact that they are associated with femininity by reason of their clothing is sufficient to make the cross-dressing experience mortifying.

The male cross-dressing model diverges, quite distinctly, from the female model in that the issue of gender performance is seldom raised as a serious concern. In fact, very little about male cross-dressing representations is serious, due to the comic mode typically used. Male cross-dressers are generally not interested in learning how to behave convincingly as a woman. Instead, they are fearful of feminine garments—as if they are imbued with such powerful signifiers that simply wearing the clothes socially designated as feminine is enough to cause irreparable damage to the wearer's masculinity (and it is this panic which is constructed as humorous; the implied masculine reader finds the situation comical because it is happening to the cross-dresser, rather than to him). This is clearly the case with the adult Jack. He does not look convincingly feminine in any sense. His large, muscular frame is clearly visible while he is wearing the tutu and is immediately identifiable as male. However, his appearance still causes him great panic. His salvation comes in the form of his younger self, who tells him that he must wake up in order to escape his terrible tutu predicament. Jack tries an assortment of different "wake-up" techniques, but none are successful. His younger self then directs him to think carefully about his normal morning ritual (the sun shining through his bedroom window, the smell of breakfast being made) and thereby facilitates his return to reality. Jack then awakens, and finds himself back in his bedroom.

The male cross-dressing paradigm deliberately constructs male cross-dressing as comic through the masculine subject's inability to disguise himself effectively as a female, proceeding to use this failure as a confirmation of the superiority and indestructibility of his inherent masculinity. The construction of male cross-dressing in children's literature points to a significant inconsistency in the gendering of cross-dressing representations for young readers: while female characters (and implied readers) are encouraged to experiment with gender, boys are actively discouraged from doing the same. Male cross-dressing narratives engage with the cultural hysteria which has traditionally surrounded the concept of transgressive gender behavior, accordingly demonizing nonconformist gender behavior and in the process validating an outdated and patriarchal form of gender binarism.

TRANSGENDERED CROSS-DRESSING

The third type of cross-dressing paradigm found in children's literature is the transgender paradigm, which is rare because it addresses the disjunction between the temporary, desexualized world of children's cross-dressing (as presented within the female and male cross-dressing paradigms) and the adult transgender arena, where sexual identity plays an integral role and nonnormative gender behavior can have potentially disastrous social and political consequences. The explicit introduction of issues pertaining to sexuality and the acknowledgment of the political and social oppression which transgendered people often suffer in contemporary society make this type of cross-dressing construction unusual in children's literature. It appears in only a handful of texts, most of which can be categorized as belonging to the young adult genre. Transgendered cross-dressing representations are also a lot more elusive than the more straightforward types of cross-dressing which occur within the female and male paradigms. They canvass a range of transgressive gender identities and behaviors—for example, homosexuality, transvestism, transsexualism, drag, queer, etc. Due to the diversity of behaviors and identities that can be identified as transgendered, the construction of cross-dressing within this paradigm also differs substantially from one text to another. However, there are a number of generally applicable features that distinguish this paradigm from the others.

First, both male-to-female and female-to-male cross-dressing can be classified as transgendered, but a reversal of sorts occurs within the transgender paradigm: whereas female-to-male cross-dressing typically provides a more enlightened critique of gender boundaries than male-to-female in the majority of children's narratives, within the transgender paradigm it is the construction of male-to-female cross-dressing which interrogates the traditional gender binary and actively promotes gender proliferation. Female cross-dressing is less successful in this paradigm, as the limited number of representations of female-to-male cross-dressing subject the female cross-dresser to immense social stigmatism for her gender transgressions, on one occasion causing her death (Pohl [1985] 1991).

Second, the social and political oppression conventionally associated with cross-dressing in Western society is discernible in children's literature from the lack of agency generally attributed to transgendered characters and the marginalization of their representation within the text, entailing that these characters typically occupy a peripheral position within the narrative and are generally denied focalization. There is evidence (particularly in relation to several recently published gay "coming of age" novels) that this aspect of the transgender novel is evolving and changing because the occurrence of first-person, focalizing characters with transgendered subjectivities is becoming increasingly common.

Third, the cross-dressing behavior of transgendered characters is not, on the whole, constructed as temporary, as it is in both the female and the male paradigms. Instead, cross-dressing is indicative of a subjectivity that falls outside or cuts across the conventional boundaries associated with masculinity and femininity, and thus the development and maturation of transgressive gender identities (often in the face of considerable social pressure to conform) is a key thematic significance of texts which offer representations of transgendered cross-dressing characters. The construction of transgendered subjectivity in relation to, and against, social and political institutions also entails that the narrative mode favored by texts within the transgender paradigm is realism. The use of only one literary genre thus creates parallels between a group of texts which otherwise depict quite different forms of transgressive gender behavior and narrative outcomes.

While the transgender paradigm is mostly confined to contemporary texts produced for adolescent readers/viewers, I would like to introduce the concept of transgendered cross-dressing by briefly discussing two fairy tales which present cross-dressing characters in a highly unprecedented fashion. Subverting the more common paradigmatic structures of both the female and the male cross-dressing models (and the presentation of gender typical in fairy tales and folktales), "The Mouse, the Thing and the Wand" (Husain 1995) and "The Counterfeit Marquise" (Perrault and de Choisy 1996 [1695]) reject the notion of either temporary or comical cross-dressing in favor of a progressive representation of gender deviance which accords more accurately with the contemporary concept of transgender.

"The Mouse, the Thing and the Wand," a Middle Eastern folktale, and "The Counterfeit Marquise," a seventeenth-century French fairy tale, are ostensibly texts which feature portrayals of transsexualism and transvestism (in the contemporary adult sense of these terms), but they engage with these complex social issues by locating their transgendered characters within a folktale/fairy tale fantasy context. The originating cross-dressing premise is explained to readers in great detail by the omniscient narrator typical of folktales and fairy tales. In both texts, cross-dressing is not the choice of the protagonist. Instead, it is culturally imposed, a decision made by mothers loath to subject their children to the cruelty they believe will befall them if they remain in their biological gendered state. "The Mouse, the Thing and the Wand" is the magical telling of the story of Rahat, a biological female who is raised as a boy by a mother unwilling for her to inherit the subordinate lifestyle preordained for women. Rahat falls in love with a princess; is "discovered" on her wedding night; and is forced to perform a series of impossible tasks that the king (father of the princess) believes will kill her. Rahat, however, fulfills the criteria of each task with the help of a bewitched black horse and her own ability to adopt the behaviors requisite for a male-gendered performance. While completing her final task, a spell is cast upon Rahat by an ogress which turns her into a biological male. Having proved herself worthy of masculine status in every other respect (through the love of a woman; a complete rejection of femininity; and the completion of a series of tasks whose achievement was thought to be impossible *even* for a man), Rahat is at last awarded the only thing missing from her otherwise authentic masculine gender identity: male genitalia.

In "The Counterfeit Marquise," the death of the marquise's father in battle results in his pregnant wife's determination that she will never subject her unborn child to a similar atrocity. She gives birth to a boy, but instantly disguises him as female. His sex is hidden from all, and he is brought up as a girl named Marianne. A testament to her gendered success is that she is pursued by many suitors, one of whom she eventually falls in love with. At this point her mother is compelled to reveal the truth about Marianne's biological sex, as Marianne herself is oblivious to it. Undeterred, Marianne weds her suitor, and discovers, to her delight, that he is actually a cross-dressed woman. The couple move to the country, where their marriage produces "a beautiful child" (147) and they continue to live happily as cross-dressers.

The biological sexes of Rahat and Marianne are female and male, respectively, a distinction that emphasizes the way in which the transgender paradigm embraces a plurality of transgressive gender behaviors and identities. To thwart the course of their "natural" gendered paths, the mothers of Rahat and Marianne raise their children from birth to believe in their cross-dressed gender identity. Rahat and Marianne are themselves initially oblivious of the incongruity between their gender and sex, each convinced that their gender identity is genuine rather than artificially imposed. The protagonists of the two tales play no part in the decision to cross-dress—it is imposed on them unawares. However, despite this lack of agency in the decision-making process, Rahat and Marianne exhibit authentic gender identities regardless of their oppositely sexed bodies.

"The Mouse, the Thing and the Wand" and "The Counterfeit Marquise" accentuate the constructedness of gender, using the cross-dresser to demonstrate that gender is socially acquired rather than naturally coherent with an individual's sex. Gender is revealed as a performance, as commented upon by Brocklebank in relation to "The Counterfeit Marquise": "The marquise teaches her daughter so well that no one, not even Marianne herself, suspects her identity. The tale thus emphasises the fact that gender behavior, far from being innate, results rather from learning and acculturation" (2000, 130). This performative construction of gender accords with the way in which the female-to-male paradigm represents cross-dressing, but there are noteworthy differences (aside from Marianne's sex) evident in "The Mouse, the Thing and the Wand" and "The Counterfeit Marquise." Most significantly, Rahat and Marianne have been cross-dressed since birth and have no knowledge of what it is like to have a gender identity that is aligned with their biological sex. Rather than occupying an alienated or abject form of feminine subjectivity, like other female cross-dressers who are socially marginalized because their gender identity does not conform with patriarchal femininity, Rahat and Marianne have been functional and integrated members of society since birth, and it is only the risk of discovery which threatens to destabilize their otherwise successful gender identities. (Both characters perform a highly stereotypical form of masculinity and of femininity while cross-dressed, but this does not detract from each text's representation of gender as a social construct.)

The relationship between gender identity and sexual identity is also addressed quite explicitly in each of these texts, closing the gap which often exists between representations of cross-dressing in children's literature and the contemporary, adult-oriented concept of cross-dressing. In "The Counterfeit Marquise," the blossoming romance between the cross-dressed Marianne and the Marquis de Bercour is highly sexualized, unmarred by Marianne's discovery of her sex (revealed to her by her mother for the purpose of discouraging the relationship):

> The marquis's presence, his charm, his caresses, obliterated from the marquise's mind everything her mother had told her....Pleasure triumphed over reflection. She lived as she had done before with her lover and felt her passion increase with such violence.... (142)

A sexualized construction of cross-dressing is maintained throughout, culminating in the bridal chamber on the wedding night, when the marquis confesses his own gender deceit by placing Marianne's hand on "the most beautiful bosom in the world" (146). Rather than repelling Marianne, this gesture awakens a deeper sexual passion: "Who could describe here the little marquise's surprise and delight? At this moment she had no doubt that she was a boy and, throwing herself into the arms of her beloved marquise, she gave him the same surprise, the same delight" (146). Unperturbed by the discrepancies between each other's gender identity and sex, Marianne and the marquis live happily ever after, even producing a child. The construction of these transgendered characters directly replicates the modern social reality of adult cross-dressing which is predominantly practiced by heterosexual (rather than homosexual) individuals (Bullough and Bullough 1993, 294).

Sexuality is equally significant in "The Mouse, the Thing and the Wand." The euphemistic terms "mouse," "thing," and "wand" refer to the male penis or, more specifically, Rahat's lack of one. Her female sex is revealed to her bride on their wedding night, when in the bridal chamber "they undress, stroking each other with increasing urgency" until Eshka, Rahat's bride, "lifts a torch out of its holder and brings it down to Rahat's body and the next moment she has discovered the truth" (1995, 132). The disaster that ensues is not remedied until the ogress casts her spell on Rahat:

> Rahat shifts on her mount; she squirms—is this a mouse she feels in her trousers? She can hardly allow herself to believe that the ogress's curse has taken effect. She wriggles and wiggles and finally she is convinced. She has a Thing! (142)

Rahat's sexuality therefore concurs with her masculine gender identity and plays an integral role in the construction of her subjectivity, signifying that although she feels masculine she (and others) believe that she can never truly be male because she is lacking the primary signifier of maleness, a penis. The sexualized construction of cross-dressing in "The Mouse, the Thing and the Wand" directly contrasts with the typically desexualized manner in which cross-dressing is presented within the female paradigm, where any suggestion of deviant sexuality is rebuffed (the female cross-dresser's heterosexuality confirmed with a conventional romance upon narrative closure). The introduction of a more sexualized form of cross-dressing in "The Mouse, the Thing and the Wand," while according more accurately with the contemporary concepts of transgender cross-dressing, ultimately compromises the story's representation of gender as a social construct. The text suggests a causal connection between sex and gender (Rahat's desire for a penis and the obvious differences in behavior which occur after she receives one—indicated by the change in pronoun from "she" to "he" and the newly acquired "swagger about him, and a grin and squareness to his shoulders that commands larger amounts of space around his body than ever before" [142–143]). Rahat's physical change undermines the performative nature of her assumed masculine identity by proposing that a genuine masculine subjectivity requires a biological male body. This dilemma highlights the often precarious representation of transgendered subjectivity in children's literature, where transgendered characters are often rendered abject for their gender nonconformity. The potentially dangerous consequences of cross-dressing are never made explicit in "The Counterfeit Marquise," but they are implied in the couple's decision to leave for the country. The city, it would seem, is no place for controversial behavior, but the country offers safety, seclusion, and anonymity.

The abject construction or marginalization of transgendered characters is also produced and maintained through narrative strategies such as focalization and point of view. "The Mouse, the Thing and the Wand" and "The Counterfeit Marquise" are idiosyncratic even within the transgender paradigm (given their dates of publication/origin), because they do not limit the voices or agency of their transgendered characters. Narrated in the third person (as conventionally befits the fairy tale and folktale genres), each tale contests the cultural marginalization of transgendered characters by allowing the stories to be focalized through transgendered eyes.

The transgender paradigm, as illustrated by "The Mouse, the Thing and the Wand" and "The Counterfeit Marquise," brings an unusual dimension to the representation of cross-dressing and gender in children's literature through its direct engagement with the adult transgender arena, particularly in relation to sexual identity. At the same time, representations of cross-dressing within the transgender paradigm interrogate conventional gender boundaries and introduce the concept of gender deviance to young readers in an environment that encourages tolerance and compassion for individuals who violate socially dictated gender norms.

Cross-dressing has many different manifestations and effects within children's literature and film, each cross-dressing paradigm generating a range of unique issues relating to how the concept of gender is presented to young audiences. The female-to-male paradigm, which occurs most frequently, is actively dissociated from the adult realm of transgender. Female cross-dressing is desexualized and temporary, used as an effective critical technique for a radical questioning and reevaluation of gender based on the ease with which the cross-dressing heroine performs masculinity. The male-to-female paradigm is remarkably different, distinguishing itself with a humorous, carnivalized construction of cross-dressing that reinscribes, rather than challenges, conventional gender stereotypes. The transgender paradigm is different again, providing a representation of cross-dressing that bridges the children's and adults' cross-dressing worlds. This paradigm acknowledges the relationship between sexual identity and transgendered subjectivity, engaging with the concept of transgender in a contemporary social and political sense, yet also sustains cross-dressing as a critical strategy for gender deconstruction.

Each cross-dressing paradigm communicates a specific message regarding gender to the young reader/viewer, raising a variety of questions relating to the distinction between sex and gender, the social construction of gender norms, and the consequences of deviant gender behavior. The assumption that cross-dressing is not a suitable topic for younger readers is refuted in the context of its widespread appearance in children's literature, most of which would not be considered controversial or provocative in any way. For the most part, cross-dressing is used positively in children's texts, providing the child reader with an opportunity to experiment with the concept of gender in a unique manner that is rarely afforded by other types of children's literature. Representations of cross-dressing that can be construed as less liberal in their thematic scope (most likely belonging to the male-to-female paradigm) are limited by an implicit fear of negotiating the adult cross-dressing realm. Adult sensibilities invade, and the simple act of disguising oneself as another gender is imbued with a heavier (i.e., sexualized, and therefore dangerous) significance. These differences aside, it is difficult to ignore the power of the cross-dresser. Regardless of whether the cross-dressed figure is used to critique or confirm the traditional gender binary, there is no denying that cross-dressing representations reveal a great deal about the ideological function of gender in children's literature and film. Cross-dressers in children's literature disclose how the discourses of femininity and masculinity operate in children's texts, problematizing masculinity and femininity by way of their gender disguise and prompting a critique of existing gender categories. As such, cross-dressers in children's literature redress the way in which transgressive gender behavior is traditionally culturally marginalized, using cross-dressing to destabilize the very foundations that underlie gender and its construction, and providing a unique contribution to the study of gender in children's texts.

3

ICONIC FEMALE CROSS-DRESSING

*The Problem of Gender in Children's
Retellings of the Story of Joan of Arc*

The woman shall not wear that which pertaineth unto a man.

Deuteronomy 22:5

The uncertainty points to a reality at the centre of transvestism for women: that it unsexes and dehumanizes her, but does not confer manhood upon her. She remains ambiguous. But in the process, she rises rather than falls.

Marina Warner
Joan of Arc

INTRODUCTION

The most culturally celebrated case of female cross-dressing belongs to Joan of Arc, a woman who inspired pious devotion in her followers and whose story has taken on mythic proportions in contemporary retellings. Joan of Arc was denounced by the Inquisition in 1431 for "asserting that her cross-dressing was a religious duty" (Feinberg 1996, 35), and subsequently executed. Her refusal to abandon her masculine costume was one of the grounds upon which she was tried and executed (Garber [1992] 1993, 216; Warner [1981] 2000, 5), but retellings of the legend of Joan of Arc for preadult audiences generally offer a sanitized reconstruction of events which minimizes the significance of her cross-dressing. Joan of Arc's gender transgression is either divested of importance or overtly justified, downplayed as a necessary measure of safety for a woman surrounded by male soldiers. The narrative reconstruction of Joan of Arc's life in children's literature is in many ways the antithesis of the female cross-dressing paradigm: cross-dressing rarely functions as a thematic strategy designed to interrogate gendered social practices in retellings of her life. Point of view and focalization strategies limit the reader's access to Joan of Arc, whose life is frequently presented through the eyes of another. Restrictive focalization techniques affect Joan of Arc's construction as an agential subject because, prevented from telling her own story (or framing her experiences within the more intimate narration of another character), she appears to lack emotional complexity as a subject. Joan's status as a revered historical figure and saint is communicated to readers through overtly sympathetic interpretive positions, which applaud her character and behavior while leaving her subjectivity and spiritual convictions largely unexplored or underdeveloped. These strategies diminish the subversive effects of Joan's cross-dressing in children's retellings, which are characterized by their valorization of her spiritual convictions over and above her gender and class transgressions.

CROSS-DRESSING SAINTS: CHRISTIANITY AND GENDER

Joan of Arc was not the first religious woman to cross-dress as a man. Several Catholic saints, whose stories feature in works such as *Butler's Lives of the Saints* (1985) (a text from which children, even in the present, are instructed in matters of faith), are known to have cross-dressed for the purpose of bringing themselves closer to, or emulating, (a masculine) God. Saints such as Athanasia of Antioch, who lived as a man for twelve years, and Pelagia, who cross-dressed in order to escape a proposed marriage and live a monastic life, were commended by their male counterparts, argues Marjorie Garber. She provides a quotation from St. Jerome as evidence that a woman could transcend the limitations of her gender through spiritual devotion: "...a woman who wishes to serve Christ more than the world . . . will cease to be a woman and will be called a man" (Garber 1992, 214). These religious women practiced cross-dressing in order to reach a higher spiritual state (by living the life of a monastic hermit, unfettered by sins of the flesh). Men could legitimately choose a life of religious devotion, but for women, whose socially prescribed roles were wife and mother, the abdication of such responsibilities in favor of a commitment to God was frowned upon. Cross-dressing allowed a small number of women to escape this predicament and embrace an agential subjectivity, their lives later honored as models of spiritual piety. Dekker and van de Pol declare that the explicit prohibition of transvestism in the Bible "was sufficient to make cross-dressing a criminal offense, even if the act was not included in contemporary compilations of criminal law" (1989, 75), but it is clear that the Church was prepared to make exceptions for some cross-dressing female saints. The cross-dressed female body functioned as a symbol of unity with Christ, simultaneously signifying the site of destruction and salvation (Davis 2002).

The cross-dressing female saints of the Christian monastic tradition were models for Joan of Arc, and Garber argues that "Like them she broke with her parents, refused to marry the husband they had chosen for her, and rejected male domination even as she assumed male privilege. Yet, unlike these women she did not choose the costume, or the life, of a monk; instead, crossing class as well as gender lines, she maintained herself as a knight" ([1992] 1993, 215). Garber's characterization of Joan of Arc's cross-dressing as behavior that overtly contravened both class and gender structures succinctly demonstrates why she was perceived as a dangerous figure. As the champion of the French peasantry, her cross-dressing was not only tolerated but exalted by the French populace, and since her death she has been resurrected in popular culture as a heroic martyr. The destabilizing and subversive power of her cross-dressing is widely recognized and actively discussed in contemporary cultural discourse, as is evident from discussions of her legacy by Bullough and Bullough (1993), Feinberg (1996), Garber (1992), and Warner (1981). Given this cultural fascination with Joan's transgressive gender identity, it is surprising that this aspect of her life and subsequent legendary cultural status as a female cross-dresser are largely absent from children's retellings. Rarely examined in detail, Joan's cross-dressing is presented to readers as a measure of feminine security. Moreover, her spectacular performance of masculinity on the battlefield is constructed as a corollary of her spiritual devotion to God, not a successful subversion of the patriarchal gender binary.

This chapter will focus specifically on three versions of Joan's life which reflect a diversity of genres and intended audiences: *Joan of Arc* ([1998] 2000), written by Josephine Poole and illustrated by Angela Barrett, is a picture book that is aimed at young but relatively sophisticated readers (its verbal text is dense and quite complex). Michael Morpurgo's *Joan of Arc* ([1998]) 1999), illustrated by Michael Foreman, is directed at a slightly older audience, indicated by a heavier emphasis on the verbal rather than visual text. Last, *Dove and Sword* ([1995] 1997), a fictionalized account of Joan's life by Nancy Garden, is a historical novel for adolescent readers. Each of these texts portrays Joan of Arc as a young woman who dressed as a man. Nevertheless, her cross-dressing is not awarded the same significance it earned in its own historical context, nor in the cultural discourse that later formed around her legend. Her cross-dressing is not centralized within the narratives but mentioned only once or twice. Its effect on the construction of gender is much less remarkable than in most other examples of female cross-dressing in children's literature.

Narrativity is a significant issue in retellings of the Joan of Arc story, as the chosen mode of focalization usually operates to limit Joan's inner voice. The reader is not invited to witness Joan's subjective development because she is denied interiority as a character. Poole's picture book employs limited and shifting third-person narration; Morpurgo's illustrated retelling uses close third-person narration, but the reader's access to Joan is compromised because it is framed within the more immediate first-person narration of another character; and Garden uses the fictional character of Gabrielle as its naïve first-person narrator, who follows Joan into battle but whose perspective of Joan is limited because they interact with each other only rarely. The retellings in question are all "traditional" texts in the sense that they perform a didactic function: their purpose is to educate young readers about the great deeds of this famous and legendary saint. Literature about the lives of saints is intended to be inspirational, a tool of instruction for the religious faithful. Cross-dressing is accordingly problematic in this context, a controversial aspect of Joan's otherwise heroic and pious existence. Limited focalization allows each retelling to reinforce its theme of spiritual devotion, overtly constructing Joan as extraordinarily devout and gifted. Narration which silences Joan's inner voice, telling or explaining her perceptions, neatly averts the need to explore the issue of her cross-dressing. Without access to Joan's interior thoughts on the subject, apart from those she expresses in her speech (which suggest that she is a reluctant cross-dresser), her transgressive gender identity remains a matter for speculation only.

Joan of Arc's cross-dressing behavior is systematically downplayed in each retelling. It is explained merely as a direction from God or from certain individuals (invariably male) concerned about her safety. Her cross-dressing is not depicted as a voluntary act and therefore cannot be associated with subjective agency, as it is within female cross-dressing narratives such as *Alanna* and *Mulan*. For example, Poole deals with Joan's cross-dressing in a single line, using limited third-person narration to state simplistically that after visiting Robert de Baudricourt and demanding to be taken to the Dauphin, "she cut her hair and dressed like a man." This is then followed by the qualifying phrase "so that she could travel more safely." Garden's novel reveals Joan's cross-dressing in a dialogue between Gabrielle and Joan's brother, Pierre. Gabrielle's lack of proximity to Joan means that information about her is always secondhand, relayed through the perception of another character. For example, when Pierre tells Gabrielle of Joan's cross-dressing, he does so by reporting what he has heard from someone else: "Laxart came to us and said that she has been given men's clothes..." ([1995] 1997, 38). Garden's use of the word "given" denotes Joan's passivity in the cross-dressing process. She is the object of another's direction. Morpurgo's approach is similar, but in his case traditional gender ideologies are more visible because Joan is persuaded to cross-dress by male family members concerned for her welfare: "It was Jean and Bertrand and Uncle Durand. They were all quite adamant" ([1998] 1999, 45). Morpurgo's closely focalized third-person narration discloses Joan's interiority more effectively than either Poole or Garden (whose representation is of course more limited because Joan is not a focalizing character in her novel), but even so, Morpurgo's retelling denies Joan's volition in the decision to cross-dress. Cross-dressing is addressed in a discussion between Joan and the men selected to ride with her on the journey to see the Dauphin, which allows Joan to reply to the suggestion that she should dress as a man in the first person: "It is my voices that have arranged it, as they arrange everything in the end. I had thought to defy them in this, but I see I cannot" (46). Morpurgo is prepared to fictionalize Joan's subjectivity in much greater detail and complexity elsewhere, investigating her personal perceptions of herself and her behavior, but is much more reticent about examining her attitude to cross-dressing. He avoids the issue by inserting the subject within the context of a public dialogue, which allows Joan to articulate her position clearly and directly in the first person. Joan's statement decisively concludes the matter, which is not referred to again until the time of her trial.

Cross-dressing is openly linked with subjective agency in the female cross-dressing paradigm, a symbolic act of resistance against patriarchal ideologies that restrict feminine activity. Retellings of the Joan of Arc story oppose this type of cross-dressing construction. Joan's experiences are framed within a religious discourse, in which she is a woman specifically chosen by God to do His bidding. Her decision to cross-dress is indicative of her willingness to carry out His designated mission for her. Hence Joan's subjective agency is a troublesome issue within children's retellings because it is always presented in terms of her religious subjection: "Joan simply did what God told her to do, and nothing, nobody could prevent her" (Poole). Her unprecedentedly sub-versive behavior, which enabled her to abandon the life of a female peas-ant and successfully lead the French army into battle, is always qualified by her repeated insistence that she did not act independently but under the auspices of God's direction: "...everything I have done, I have done at God's command" (Morpurgo, 111). The most significant theme in these versions of Joan's life is her spiritual devotion, a concept that revolves around contradictory notions of agency, resistance, morality, and obligation. Joan struggles to fulfill her mission in the face of great social and political adversity. At the same time, she tries to reconcile God's will with her responsibilities to her beloved French countrymen. Morpurgo is most successful at thematically examining the nature of religious devotion. He uses Joan's private conversations with Belami (a small sparrow who befriends Joan and accompanies her everywhere) as a device to examine her developing selfhood. Even Poole's picture book text, which is most limited in terms of length, successfully conveys this theme: "The citizens said they would sooner die than surrender. Joan could not bear to leave them to their fate, although the Voices warned her that if she went, she would be taken prisoner." Within this spiritual context, Joan's cross-dressing and refusal to abandon her masculine costume when interrogated are reconstructed as religious obedience rather than gender transgression.

A central concern in female cross-dressing texts such as *Alanna* and *Mulan* is the interrogation of dominant gender ideologies. This idea is explored with regard to the central character's inability (or lack of desire) to fulfill the prescribed requirements of conventional feminin-ity and subsequent performance of masculinity. The contrast between the cross-dressing protagonist's nonconformist gender identity and conventional femininity is further developed in relation to Joan's cross-dressing performance. Her newly formed masculine subjectivity is contrasted with the behavior of biological men. *Alanna* and *Mulan* the-matize the issue of gender by using different strategies, such as structure, focalization, and point of view, to make symbolic contrasts between the conventional discourses of masculinity and femininity. These are then blurred by the female cross-dresser's performance of masculinity. *Alanna* opens with Alanna and her brother Thom taking turns to lament their gendered fate, each violently opposed to the activities and charac-ter traits conventionally attributed to their respective gender identity. This introduction frames Alanna's decision to cross-dress as a response to her dissatisfaction with traditional femininity and desire to escape it by assuming a masculine identity as a royal page. Alanna's subjective development is illustrated by incidents that cause her to assess her own performance of masculine behavior from a feminine perspective. The process inevitably results in conflict. For example, at an early point in the novel Alanna is bullied by another page. She responds by inviting him to fight her, strategically beating him by exploiting his weaknesses. Alanna's tactical skills are marked as feminine in this instance, and she employs them to compensate for her physical disadvantages in what I would argue is a demonstration of her ability to integrate masculine and feminine behaviors and skills. Alanna, however, feels that her victory is a travesty, a demonstration of her inability to assume an authentic masculine subjectivity:

> Myles ruffled her hair. "So now you've proved you're a warrior to the whole palace. Surely you want to celebrate."
>
> Alanna made a face. No matter what Myles said, she had used fancy tricks to beat Ralon, that was all. She was still a girl masquerading as a boy, and sometimes she doubted that she would ever believe herself to be as good as the stupidest, clumsiest male. (78)

Alanna's self-loathing is plainly evident. The novel uses a third-person narrative style which is closely focalized through Alanna, unambiguously revealing her innermost thoughts and subjective experience of the masculine world around her. Alanna's point of view is the only one offered to the reader. The close relationship between narration and focalization draws attention to the issue of gender by repeatedly referring to Alanna's sense of failure. This is ironic, however, as it is undermined by her performative success. Alanna's gender identity segues easily from masculinity to femininity, not fragmented as such, but in a process of constant momentum and evolution. A focalized passage of narration tells readers that "fighting was becoming second nature to her" (142), and is followed by a scene in which Alanna's masculine performance is validated by a coveted invitation to accompany Sir Myles to his estate because of her achievements as a page. Proudly relaying this invitation to her manservant, Coram, Alanna finishes by commenting upon the duke's "brocade dressing gown." The attention that she pays to his clothing is a display of conventionally feminine behavior. It prompts Coram to remark, "It's things like that that remind me who ye are. Sometimes even I forget ye're not a lad" (145). Coram's statement counters Alanna's frequent disappointment at herself for not giving an adequate masculine performance. At the same time it foregrounds her ability to assimilate both masculine and feminine subjectivities, drawing attention to the ways in which behaviors and gestures are heavily gendered.

Mulan also interrogates patriarchal gender relations by depicting symbolic contrasts between the discourses of traditional femininity and masculinity. These are then problematized by Mulan's nonconformist feminine identity and successful masculine performance. In conjunction with her song solos, Mulan's interactions with Mushu are direct reflections of her developing subjectivity. Mushu, the miniature dragon, is significant in terms of focalization because he enables Mulan to communicate her inner feelings to the audience. Their relationship is intimate and personal in nature—as a family guardian it is Mushu's responsibility to protect Mulan—and the film uses their dialogue to allow Mulan to articulate her inner thought processes and emotional responses. Mushu and Mulan's discourse is the literal embodiment of the intersubjective nature of identity formation, as Mushu's pertinent input assists Mulan in reconceiving herself as masculine:

Mushu: Okay, this is it! Time to show them your man-walk. Shoulders back, chest high, feet apart, head up, and strut! Two, three, break that bone, two, three, and work it!

[They pass men trimming their toenails and picking their noses.]

Mushu: Beautiful, isn't it?

Mulan: They're disgusting.

Mushu: No, they're men. And you're gonna have to act just like them, so pay attention.

Mushu's masculine identity complements Mulan's femininity. Their partnership is a visual symbol of the film's juxtaposition of masculine and feminine discourses. This theme is also articulated in the film's structure, where scenes double or mirror each other, but are different in relation to the gender that they emphasize. After learning that he has been conscripted, Mulan's father unsheathes his sword and begins to practice his swordsmanship. Soon after, he falls and is forced to stop, breathing heavily as he leans against the wall for support. As an elderly man whose health is fragile, he no longer embodies patriarchal masculinity. The scene in which Mulan steals her father's sword and armor parallels the earlier image of her father's weakness and failure. In Mulan's case this defeat is replaced with promise and action—the significance of her decision to cross-dress clearly conveyed by the use of dramatic music punctuated by loud, urgent beats. When Mulan holds up her father's sword, an image of her face is reflected in its blade, half feminine and half masculine, in a visual representation of her doubled gender identity. The film's climactic ending continues this mirroring strategy when Mulan rescues Shang from Shan Yu (the leader of the Huns) and prevents Shan Yu's victory for the second time. Shan Yu cries out, "No! You! You took away my victory!" Mulan counters by responding, "No, I did!" She quickly pulls her hair back off her face and Shan Yu instantly recognizes her as the male soldier responsible for his previous defeat. The film relies on this structure of parallel scenes, in combination with recurring motifs (such as cross-dressing, which is inverted when Mulan's fellow soldiers cross-dress as concubines), to thematize the concept of gender and foreground its performative nature. Mulan's unconventional feminine subjectivity and assumed masculine subjectivity are contrasted against stereotypical gender behaviors. The intersection of gendered discourses initiates a reevaluation of conventional gender categories.

Children's retellings of the legend of Joan of Arc approach the subject of her cross-dressing differently. They tend to shy away from the implication that such behavior may have affected her feminine gender identity. In all probability it is Joan's iconic cultural status and the widespread popularity of her story that have caused this conservatism. The metaphoric power of other female cross-dressing narratives, which enables the cross-dressing heroine's behavior to function as a rigorous critique of traditional gender categorizations, may indeed exist because of the general anonymity surrounding the central cross-dressing character.[1] The lack of cultural awareness that generally surrounds female-to-male cross-dressing—in both history and literature—is perhaps beneficial in rendering the female cross-dresser as relatively ordinary prior to her cross-dressing, and extraordinary during and after it. Her cultural invisibility invites a radical interpretation of her behavior, as there is no point of comparison or cultural reference for her gendered identity. The same cannot be said for Joan, for as Warner indicates, "She is one of the few historical personalities who, like Henry VIII, Florence Nightingale, Robin Hood and Davy Crockett, is immediately known to every child" (6). In children's versions of her life, Joan is depicted as a saint and patriot, a woman who achieved cultural and spiritual greatness. She is not portrayed as a cross-dresser who challenged the gender status quo by leading the French army into battle—regardless of the obvious gender transgressions this unprecedented behavior signified. Warner comments at length upon Joan's subversive gender identity, but it is her reference to spirituality which best reflects Joan's construction in children's literature:

> Through her transvestism, she abrogated the destiny of womankind. She could thereby transcend her sex; she could set herself

apart and usurp the privileges of the male and his claims to superiority. At the same time, by never pretending to be other than a
woman and maid, she was usurping a man's function but shak-
ing off the trammels of his sex altogether to occupy a different,
third order, neither male nor female, but unearthly, like the angels
whose company she loved. (145–146)

Warner's remarks about Joan's "unearthly" qualities are apposite to the
retellings of Poole and Barrett, Morpurgo and Foreman, and Garden,
each of which emphasizes Joan's spiritual devotion to the extent that she
becomes a godlike character who resists human categorizations. Confronted with the devastation of war during the battle at Orléans, Joan
is consistently represented as distressed in each text. Yet her unrest is
not constructed as a feminine response to the brutal fighting that has
just occurred (and which she has never experienced until now). Her
grief is caused by her propinquity to premature death. Her sorrow at
seeing the wasted lives of soldiers elicits a Jesus-like, rather than a feminine, response: "And Joan wept for the pity of him, and of all who died
that day" (Poole); "she was closeted with Father Pasquerel, weeping and
confessing" (Garden, 145); and "'Can God really have meant this?' And
when she wept, she wept like a child" (Morpurgo, 82). (Morpurgo's use
of the word "child" here emphasizes Joan's innocence and purity, not
her humanity.) Joan of Arc's cross-dressing is distinctive from other
stories of female cross-dressing because she never pretended to be a
man. However, she did perform masculinity in both a social and political sense. Children's retellings of her legend understate the significance
of her cross-dressing, refusing to engage with the gender implications
of such behavior. This is made possible by the use of limited focalization
which selectively addresses Joan of Arc's inner thoughts, producing a
closed and unengaging representation that diminishes her capacity to
be an agential and emotionally complex character.

Poole's picture book provides an interesting contrast to female cross-
dressing narratives such as *Alanna* and *Mulan* because of obvious shifts
between narration, focalization, and point of view. Intrusive third-person omniscient narration is focalized from the historical perspective
of Joan's subsequent cultural status. It is used in conjunction with her
restricted focalization. Aside from Joan's perspective, other points of
view are interwoven, including that of the French king and the French
population as a whole (who saw Joan of Arc as their savior):

The King knew that only a miracle could save him from his enemies. But—Joan was such an ordinary girl! Besides, suppose her
power didn't come from God? Suppose she was a witch!

He couldn't make up his mind. But Joan knew what would happen. There was no time to waste—she learned to gallop a war-horse and use a lance.

And at last her orders came.

Orléans was buzzing with rumors. God was sending a maiden with miraculous powers! (**Poole**)

The verbal text has a dialogic construction representative of the many responses Joan of Arc provoked in the people whom she encountered (hostility, mockery, loyalty, patriotism, awe). This strategy effectively develops the theme of Poole's story, which examines how an ordinary, lower-class French girl was able to convince a king and a nation that she was on a mission to liberate them from the English. Although written in English, the narration is overtly sympathetic to the French campaign against the British. The example below demonstrates the way in which the narration demonizes the English as aggressive marauders, as well as directly implicating issues of class in the contrast between Joan (farmer's daughter) and her eventual foes (lords and soldiers):

English ships set sail for France. English lords and soldiers captured many cities that belonged to the young French King. It looked as if he would be driven out, and he hadn't even been properly crowned.

Deep in the country, there lived a girl called Joan. She was a farmer's daughter. (**Poole**)

Joan is revealed to be a pious and determined young woman, but because of constant shifts in point of view, her character is underdeveloped and underfocalized. Her perceptions are incorporated into the narration, reported rather than developed or explored. This prevents the reader from gaining anything but a superficial glimpse of her thought processes and emotional reactions. Joan is thus heroic, but never quite real; her motivations for attempting such extraordinary feats are left largely untouched. For example, when establishing the history of Joan's voices, Poole's narration is initially detached, simply stating a sequence of events. It then shifts briefly, as Joan focalizes the emotional impact that her voices produced in her, before finally returning to a statement that again conveys a straight sequence of events. Joan's inner voice is fragmented, couched among narration that explains her behavior and effectively silences her ability to express herself:

Joan was thirteen when this happened. During the next four years, the Voices often spoke to her, but she never told anyone about them. To hear them was more important to her than anything in the world, although sometimes, when they spoke of the fighting in France, they made her cry. As time passed, her heart was filled with a great will and desire that her King should have his kingdom.

Cross-dressing is mentioned specifically on only one occasion. This reference occurs at the beginning of the text, just after Joan has approached Baudricourt (called only "the Captain" here) to arrange for her to journey to Orléans to meet the king. The text informs the reader that "he gave her a horse and four guards. She cut her hair and dressed like a man so that she could travel more safely. Now she was ready to start…." (Poole). Joan's cross-dressing is rationalized in practical terms as a safety precaution rather than as a compunction or spiritual calling. The only other allusion to Joan's gender status, which indirectly addresses the issue of gender performativity, is made before the battle at Orléans. When Joan rides into the city with her army, she is greeted by people "cheering and rejoicing." As they throng about her, a "flaring torch caught the pennant of her standard and set it alight. By spurring her horse, she turned him quickly and gently so that she could put out the fire. Everyone who saw it marvelled at her horsemanship. …" Although not explicit, this remark indicates that Joan's behavior is atypical and unexpected—the assumption being that it is unconventional only because she is a woman. Apart from these two minor instances, the text does not address Joan's cross-dressing and performance of masculinity.

In contrast to the narrow verbal exploration of Joan's cross-dressing, Barrett's pictorial representation of her life tells an altogether different story. Barrett's illustrations challenge the diminished position of cross-dressing in the verbal text, allowing Joan to perform masculinity in a visual sense. The dichotomy between the words and pictures is most evident in relation to the rather insignificant verbal text used to describe Joan's decision to cross-dress. The words "she cut her hair and dressed like a man so that she could travel more safely" are accompanied by a highly symbolic illustration of Joan cutting off her hair as she stands before an open window.[2] Although the verbal reference to cross-dressing is embedded among text that lessens its importance (the focus is the journey to Orléans and the king), the illustration of Joan cutting her hair repositions gender as the most significant issue. Barrett repeatedly uses a distant perspective of Joan in her other illustrations, favoring the depiction of her entire body which situates the reader farther away from her. In this illustration, however, the profiled figure of Joan, seen from the waist up, dominates the picture, creating a more intimate relationship with the reader than any of the other illustrations. Half of Joan's auburn hair has been shorn off, and she holds a pair of scissors that are in the process of removing the rest of her girlish locks. A pronounced vector runs in a diagonal line from the top left-hand corner to the bottom right-hand corner of the illustration, formed by the way in which Joan's head, eyes and hand are directly aligned with the edge of the open window. This vector explicitly includes the large pair of scissors she is holding, emphasizing their significance on both a literal and a figurative level. Cutting her hair is symbolic of political and gender severance—from her life as a peasant and also from the limited feminine roles available to her as a woman. This illustration is also a vivid demonstration of the pictorial strategies Barrett uses throughout, as although the relationship between Joan and the reader is most intimate here, her eyes do not meet the viewer's. They are downcast, and she does not look toward the open window—possibly representative of her reluctance to embrace her future, but also symbolic of the way in

Figure 3.1 From *Joan of Arc* by Josephine Poole, illustrated by Angela Barrett, published by Dragonfly Books (2000). Reprinted by permission of The Random House Group Ltd.

which she is perpetually disconnected from the viewer by an indirect gaze that never fully engages the viewer's attention.

A dramatic change occurs in Barrett's visual depiction of Joan of Arc after she abandons her feminine clothing. The overtly feminine Joan of the first two double-page spreads (shown with long, flowing hair adorned with a ribbon and elegantly draped dresses) is replaced by a cropped-haired, convincing young man. The differences between Joan's formerly feminine features and her facial characteristics when she is cross-dressed are subtle, but noticeable—a certain hardening and thickening of the nose, accompanied by changed features that offer no defining indications of gender and are the epitome of androgyny. For example, the image which depicts Charles's coronation shows both Joan of Arc and Charles in profile. Their facial features and physical attributes are remarkably similar: both have hair and skin in similar shades; each has a straight and well-defined nose. No discernible gender differences are evident in the pictorial techniques used to portray their faces. The only noticeable distinction is that although both are outfitted in robes befitting the regal occasion (reminiscent of dresses), Joan's presentation is arguably more masculine because her armor is plainly visible underneath the robe.

This "masculinization" of the physical features of the female protagonist when cross-dressed is also evident in *Mulan*. However, in *Mulan* this strategy is consistent: when Mulan is in men's clothing her facial characteristics are always masculine; when she reverts to her feminine identity, her visual appearance concurs. In Poole's picture book, however, this is not the case. Joan's visual representation corresponds with her behavior, not her clothing (Joan remains in men's clothing in Barrett's illustrations until her execution). Barrett presents Joan as physically masculine when she exhibits masculine behaviors (during battle or in political situations with the king), but her illustrations of Joan regain a conventionally feminine appearance when Joan displays vulnerability or spiritual devotion.

The pictorial spread that shows Joan arriving in Orléans, before she has had a chance to prove her military capabilities, shows a young and uneasy Joan. Clad in battle armor and sitting astride a powerful horse, her eyes once again do not meet those of the viewer; instead, they are fearfully cast back behind her. Joan's features are soft, youthful, and androgynous. More than anything else, she looks like a lost and frightened child. This image stands in contrast to the next two double-page spreads, which depict Joan confronting the English. The self-doubt and fear—so obvious from her eyes and facial expression on the previous page—have disappeared. Joan holds her standard proudly aloft as the

Figure 3.2 From *Joan of Arc* by Josephine Poole, illustrated by Angela Barrett, published by Dragonfly Books (2000). Reprinted by permission of The Random House Group Ltd.

English soldiers deride her, unconcerned by their presence; on the next spread she sits astride her horse, galloping into battle. Presented in profile, her body leans down low to the horse, ready for action. Her mouth is open, aggressively, as if in the middle of chanting a war cry. On this spread and the next, Joan's face takes on masculine physical attributes, such as hardened features and a longer and more prominent nose. Her body also becomes more active (and therefore conventionally masculine), as in each instance she is presented in profile, leaning toward her enemy, a physical manifestation of her courage and self-assurance. She appears as a soldier, indistinguishable from the other soldiers around her, and the verbal text corresponds by attributing masculine behaviors such as anger and aggression to her: "That made her angry and she stormed back into the city." (Poole). Joan's facial features undergo another gender shift on the next spread, returning to feminine softness in order to complement how she "wept for pity" at the violent deaths of English soldiers.

Although *Mulan* employs a similar visual strategy to Poole's picture book, the results are very different. This is due to the significance that the film places on the issue of performance, and the fact that animation (as a medium) allows for a more comprehensive exploration of behavior than does the static medium of still illustrations. By depicting Mulan as more physically masculine when she is cross-dressed, it allows the viewer to focus less on her outward appearance and more on the types of behavior that she must learn in order to pass successfully as a man. In contrast, the issue of passing is not relevant to the story of Joan of Arc, as she never attempted to disguise her biological sex. Poole's verbal text does not actively engage with the fact that Joan must have modified or changed her behavior in order to command an army, handle a weapon, confront an enemy soldier, or conduct a military campaign. The text simply states that "She learned to gallop a war-horse and use a lance," but fails to express the gender significance of such masculine-oriented skills. This is partially due to the limited narrative mode that Poole uses, which only enables a simple reconstruction of events, but it is interesting that the narration is particularly straightforward and events-focused when it comes to explaining any behavior that relates to cross-dressing or to Joan's performance of masculine activities.

The verbal text's reluctance to engage with the issue of cross-dressing openly, thereby denying an important historical aspect of Joan of Arc's life, is offset by the way in which the illustrations visually reclaim the significance of cross-dressing to the story. The illustrations provide the reader with an "unfixed" image of Joan of Arc: as a young girl, a frightened young man, a courageous warrior, a noble hero venerated by the king, and finally as a pious martyr. This visual attempt to engage with the issue of gender as it related to Joan of Arc as a historical figure is noteworthy for its subversive potential. Its effect is ultimately too subtle to challenge the conservative nature of the verbal text. Furthermore, the visual strategies Barrett uses to portray Joan never ask the reader to enter into a "relation of social affinity" (Kress and van Leeuwen 1996, 123). Joan is almost always depicted in profile, or, if depicted front on, her eyes never meet the viewer's. Barrett's visual portrayal of Joan never "creates a visual form of direct address" or demands "that the viewer enter into some kind of imaginary relationship" with her (Kress and van Leeuwen, 122). Joan's eyes always evade the viewer, creating a sense of detachment that is reinforced by Barrett's depiction of her in profile or from a distant perspective. These pictorial strategies thus collude with the verbal text's marginalization of Joan as a character through shifting points of view and limited focalization, producing a verbal and visual construction of Joan that separates her from other female cross-dressers in children's literature and restricts the significance of her cross-dressing.

FEMALE CROSS-DRESSING AND THE LAW

Poole's picture book is the only retelling among those discussed here to expunge cross-dressing as an issue that was relevant to Joan of Arc's trial. Morpurgo and Foreman's retelling, and also Garden's, link her cross-dressing behavior to her execution, but the exact relationship between cross-dressing and heresy, for which Joan of Arc was tried and executed, is never made explicit.

Joan of Arc's refusal to abandon her masculine attire contributed directly to the harsh legal sentence she received. She stood accused, among other things, of "the unwomanliness and immodesty of her costume" and during her trial her questioners "returned to the subject of her dress with as much persistence as they had used about her voices" (Warner [1981] 2000, 143). The judicial characterization of Joan of Arc's cross-dressing as a heretical crime of the highest degree is notable within the historical context of female cross-dressing in Europe, because data suggest that European judges were at times sympathetic to women who had committed similar cross-dressing crimes.

The act of clothing oneself in the garments characteristic of the opposite sex—"cross-dressing" or "transvestism"—is currently not a crime in contemporary Western society. It may be regarded as perverse or immoral, but cross-dressing is not considered a criminal behavior worthy of punishment at the hands of the law. The legal history of cross-dressing, however, attests to the fact that this was not always the case. Cross-dressing has enjoyed a somewhat complex (and often paradoxical) relationship with Western legal institutions, due to the correlation of transgressive gender behavior with immorality and social deviance. Yet, in spite of the Bible's condemnation of cross-dressing, a "flourishing tradition of female cross-dressing" (Dekker and van de Pol 1989, 99) occurred in the sixteenth, seventeenth, and eighteenth centuries. Vern and Bonnie Bullough's historical and cultural examination of cross-dressing explains that during this period, "Changing social conditions had loosened some of the hierarchical ties and made it much easier for women to escape some of the confines of the female role by dressing like and passing as men. Most of these women were probably never uncovered, but hundreds of them are known" (1993, 94). Our knowledge of these women and the lives they led while cross-dressed as men is generally the product of court transcripts, the result of trials that were held after the seemingly inevitable occurred—a cross-dressed female's biological gender was discovered. In their study of European female cross-dressers (*The Tradition of Female Transvestism in Early Modern Europe*), Dekker and van de Pol cite a number of case histories that provide evidence of the judicial/official leniency extended to women whose cross-dressing was discovered. They argue that a number of "women who had successful careers as sailors and soldiers and who had resumed respectable lives as women met with praise and reward. Successful female soldiers or sailors were sometimes even granted exceptional favors from monarchs ..." (101).

In situations where no crimes other than the act of cross-dressing itself had been committed, women were able to escape with little or no punishment. It may well have been that the attitudes of the judiciary and other authority figures toward these cross-dressing women were based partly on admiration for their courage and resourcefulness in the military arena, as social conventions of the time strictly segregated feminine and masculine activities and rarely allowed for any kind of comparisons between the genders. Female cross-dressers, however, were able to demonstrate that (some) women could perform just as successfully as men—even in traditionally male-dominated fields. Children's literature which contains depictions of female cross-dressing is also primarily concerned with this theme, using the cross-dresser's performance of masculinity to orchestrate the destruction of gender stereotypes and reveal the cultural practices which inscribe and regulate them. Texts such as *Alanna* and *Mulan*, for example, replicate the circumstances of historical female cross-dressers who were treated leniently by European judges and authorities. They enlarge upon the principle of gender equality which was raised by sympathetic members of the judiciary during their trials. The pattern to which these fictional and historical cases of female cross-dressing conform is mostly identical—their cross-dressing is nonsexual and noncriminal. It is motivated by the location of the female cross-dresser in a patriarchal world which seeks to limit her behavior. It ceases once the subject has attained some form of gender liberty.

The major difference between Joan of Arc's cross-dressing and other historical women who disguised themselves as men in order to join the army or navy is that Joan of Arc's behavior not only affronted gender mores, but also threatened to destabilize social and political hierarchies. Her status as a peasant and her agenda to restore Charles VII to the throne had a far more revolutionary implication than her contravention of subordinated feminine gender roles. Nevertheless, the criminal nature of her cross-dressing was a central issue during her trial. Perhaps due to the youth of its intended readers, Poole's picture book exorcises the matter of Joan's cross-dressing from its reconstruction of her trial: "A special court was set up to accuse her of heresy—pretending to hear heavenly voices, pretending to talk with saints and even see them. The punishment for heresy was death." The accompanying illustration shows Joan surrounded by five angels, a visual rebuttal to the accusation that her voices were only imagined. The angels all look down kindly at Joan, one holding her hand, another tenderly caressing her forehead. She is encircled and protected by them. Poole's verbal text is unusual in its complete elimination of cross-dressing from Joan's trial. Morpurgo and Garden engage with the controversial nature of Joan's dress more effectively, but they are also tentative about awarding it too much significance. Their texts do not explore cross-dressing in relation to gender, and it therefore cannot function (as it generally does in other female cross-dressing narratives) as subversive behavior that has potentially liberating or positive effects.

The characterization of cross-dressing as a crime is not alien to children's literature. The paradoxical way in which cross-dressing is creatively eliminated from portrayals of Joan of Arc's trial in children's literature, when history attests to its vast significance, is countered by the presentation of female cross-dressing in the film *Mulan*. *Mulan* directly confronts the relationship between cross-dressing and the law, reconstructing the transgressive nature of cross-dressing into an empowering act of subjective agency. The legal ramifications of Mulan's cross-dressing are addressed at the film's outset, where the seriousness of her cross-dressing behavior is conveyed by her father's revelation that the punishment for such a crime is death:

Granny Fa: Mulan is gone!

Fa Zhou: What? It can't be! Mulan! No!

Fa Li: You must go after her. She could be killed.

Fa Zhou: If I reveal her, she will be.

The scene where Mulan's female sex is revealed, after she has been injured in battle, clarifies the gravity of her crime. Chi Fu demands that Mulan be killed, in accordance with the law. Cross-dressing is not named as her crime, but Mulan is accused of treason, and therefore of betrayal. Her crime is deception, so although cross-dressing is not specifically criminalized, the gender fraud which her cross-dressing enabled is constructed as illegal:

Chi Fu: I knew there was something wrong with you! A woman! Treacherous snake!

Mulan: My name is Mulan. I did it to save my father!

Chi Fu: High treason!

Mulan: I didn't mean for it to go this far!

Chi Fu: Ultimate dishonor!

Mulan: It was the only way! Please, believe me!

Chi Fu: Captain?

Shang: Restrain him. You know the law.

[Shang walks over to Mulan, but then abandons his intention to kill her. He drops his sword in front of her.]

Shang: A life for a life. My debt is repaid. [to the soldiers] Move out!

Chi Fu: But you can't just … .

Shang: I said, "Move out."

Shang's exoneration of Mulan complements the film's thematic exploration of socially constructed gender roles, as it adheres to the structure of earlier scenes in the way that it contrasts conformist and nonconformist gender behavior. After her sex is discovered, Mulan is situated in a position of vulnerability in the lower left-hand corner of the screen as she begs for her life. She is terrified and desperate, her head and eyes downcast as she awaits her punishment from Shang, who in striking contrast stands tall and powerful above her. It is the first time Mulan is presented as conventionally feminine, the scene offering a visual representation of the traditional gender hierarchy (despite Mulan's male costume) in its depiction of Shang's masculine power over Mulan's feminine identity and continued existence. Shang's decision to pardon Mulan problematizes this reading, however, as it immediately repositions Mulan with a masculine discourse. She escapes death because of her heroically masculine behavior, which was responsible for saving Shang's life just minutes before. The soldier's military code of honor overrides her cross-dressing crime of treason, validating her masculine heroism at the expense of her female sex.

Mulan's gender identity is constructed in more fluid terms than Joan of Arc's, even in children's versions of her life, such as Morpurgo's and Garden's, which directly address her cross-dressing behavior. The problem lies within the historical chronology of events in Joan of Arc's life. Her refusal to abandon men's clothing during her trial was a significant act of political and gender defiance. This was immediately followed by her execution, a fate which repositions Joan as the self-sacrificing embodiment of feminine piety. Morpurgo's illustrated retelling of her life, simply titled *Joan of Arc*, is distinct from both Poole's picture book and Garden's novel because it allows Joan to reflect introspectively on her behavior and to achieve interiority as a character. Morpurgo's primary strategy for exploring Joan's subjectivity is his clever use of Belami, a sparrow which befriends Joan and becomes a device through which Joan can articulate her emotional response to the circumstances of her life. Joan's conversations with Belami give voice to her interior character perceptions, revealing her to be an emotionally complex young woman fully cognizant of the politically subversive nature of her behavior:

> She talked to him mostly of her family and of Hauviette, about how odd they thought she had become recently, how quiet and distant. It was her father who worried about her more than anyone else, it seemed. "You know the worst of all this, Belami?" she asked him. "I am deceiving my own father. By not telling him of my voices, of what they say I will one day have to do, I am deceiving him. And he loves me so much, and he trusts me, too. (28)

Joan's conversations with Belami permit readers to view her character from an interior rather than exterior perspective, distinguishing her construction in Morpurgo's text from Poole's picture book, where Joan's thought processes are incorporated into the narration. Joan's reactions and responses are explored through her dialogue with Belami, who performs a similar function to Mushu, in *Mulan*. Like Mushu, the text anthropomorphically constructs Belami as Joan's confidant, using conversations with him as a device through which to explore her thought processes. Belami focalizes minor parts of the narration, but this narration is limited to a description of his perceptions within the narration: "Sometimes, particularly when she was at her prayers, he would keep his distance, knowing how she liked to be alone with her voices" (28). Belami's purpose is more symbolic than Mushu's role in *Mulan* because, unlike Mushu, he is not able to speak or respond to Joan. Mushu's dialogue with Mulan is a literal representation of the way in which individual subjectivity is constructed intersubjectively. However, Joan's conversations with Belami are more figurative than literal revelations of her internal thought processes and emotional reactions, Belami's lack of response highlighting the private and internal nature of her dialogue with him.

The less restricted focalization of Joan of Arc in Morpurgo's text is mediated, however, by the presentation of her experiences within another story. Morpurgo constructs his narrative on two levels: Joan's story is framed by another character, Eloise, who falls asleep on a riverbank one day and dreams of Joan's life. Joan's story is mediated by the contemporary character of Eloise. The initial and concluding parts of the narrative are told by Eloise in the first person, while the middle portion (which is Joan's life, as dreamed by Eloise) reverts to third-person narration. Although the middle section of the story is closely focalized by Joan, the shift in narrative mode from first to third person implicitly creates a level of distance between Joan and the reader. Eloise contextualizes Joan's story within her own, and the immediacy and intimacy of Eloise's narration are replaced by a more restricted perspective when Joan becomes the focalizing character. Eloise speaks directly to the reader—"My name is Eloise Hardy. I was seventeen this May" (11)—and her conversational discourse and emotional honesty are disarmingly attractive in the way that they articulate adolescent fears about the world and their situation as subjects within it:

> Now that Joan was in my room, she became even more my secret familiar, my guardian angel, and my talisman. I would reach up and touch her face every night before I went to sleep, and in times of trouble I would even talk to her, but quietly, in whispers, so no one could ever hear me. It sounds silly, but I began to hope for, even to expect perhaps, replies to my questions, solutions to my troubles. (13)

Joan's private thoughts and motivations often lack the same degree of intimacy and detail: "In the privacy of the dark she would weep her

silent tears and share with Belami her most dread doubts and fears"
(109). Joan's more limited focalization affects the representation of her
cross-dressing in Morpurgo's story, which (like Poole's) is constructed
merely as a measure to protect her vulnerable feminine sexuality. Based
on historical research, however, Warner asserts that Joan never justified
or explained her cross-dressing in practical terms:

> But neither at this point in the trial nor at any other time, until
> the very end, did she specifically give a practical reason. She never
> said she had done it to live with greater safety amongst soldiers, to
> preserve her chastity, or to ride a horse. No pragmatic explanation
> was ever offered by Joan.... ([1981] 2000, 144)

Warner's argument contests the construction of cross-dressing as a
precautionary measure of safety in children's retellings. In these texts,
Joan of Arc's gender ambiguity is purged, replaced by declarations that
her cross-dressing was not rebellious and transgressive, but simply necessary. Joan of Arc's own attitude toward it is never clearly expressed.
Distant focalization ensures that it remains hidden from the reader.

In Morpurgo's retelling, Joan of Arc's limitations as a character are
most evident in the representation of her trial. Rather than eradicating
the specifics of Joan's trial, as Poole does, Morpurgo attempts to re-create a version based on historical evidence. The result is an edited, and
therefore reconstructed, account of Joan's inquisition, which for historical veracity Morpurgo reproduces as a reported series of questions
and answers. Joan is prevented from focalizing at all, her subjective
response and emotional reaction to each question a matter of conjecture
only. Moreover, Morpurgo substantially reduces the length and extent
of the questions and answers as they were historically documented. His
abridgment of the proceedings encompasses the nature of the questions
directed at Joan, but the details surrounding each of the charges against
her are absent. The full implication of her cross-dressing is all but lost,
as its significance to her inquisitors is difficult to ascertain:

"What age were you when your voices came for the first time?"

"Thirteen."

"What teaching do your voices give you?"

"They taught me how to behave."

"Who advised you to take male dress?"

"My voices."

"When you found King Charles at Chinon, how did you recognize him?" (104)

The reality of the situation that Joan faced is conveyed much more clearly in this extract from the historical transcripts of the proceedings:

Asked if God ordered her to wear a man's dress, she answered that the dress is a small, nay, the least thing. Nor did she put on man's dress by the advice of any man whatsoever; she did not put it on, nor did she do aught, but by the command of God and the angels.

Asked whether it seemed to her that this command to assume male attire was lawful, she answered: "Everything I have done is at God's command; and if He had ordered me to assume a different habit, I should have done it, because it would have been His command."

Asked if she did it at the order of Robert de Baudricourt she said no.

Asked if she thought she had done well to take man's dress, she answered that everything she did at God's command she thought well done, and hoped for good warrant and succor in it.

Asked if, in this particular case, by taking man's dress, she thought she had done well, she answered that she had done nothing in the world but by God's commands. (paras. [61]–[62])[3]

Morpurgo's disinclination to engage with Joan of Arc's cross-dressing as anything other than a practical measure does not pose a problem until her imprisonment, whereupon her cross-dressing behavior becomes logically inconsistent with her previous defense of it. Joan's continued refusal to put on women's apparel once she is imprisoned contradicts the text's initial construction of cross-dressing as a device to protect herself from masculine impropriety. Indeed, when she is held in captivity by Jean of Luxembourg, Joan's rebellious noncompliance with the orders to remove her masculine clothing suggests that her attitude toward her cross-dressing was considerably more complex than mere protection from men:

Secure in her tower, Joan was at last among women: Jean of Luxembourg's wife, and his aunt and stepdaughter. Under the circumstances, they could not have been kinder. They did try to persuade Joan to change out of her men's clothes, and even made her a dress, white with embroidered wild roses. It fit perfectly, but still Joan would not put it on. "I thank you, but I may not," she told them. "My voices have forbidden it. I am a soldier, you see." (96)

Joan of Arc's response in this instance capably articulates the plurality of significance attached to her cross-dressing. The discourses of religion and gender intersect in her explanation, which also simultaneously constructs her as both an agential and interpellated subject. Since Joan is surrounded by women, her continued refusal to stop cross-dressing contests its representation as protection from men; her assertion that she is a soldier implies that she has abandoned her femininity in favor of a masculine role, with which her fiercely resistant behavior concurs. At the same time, by stating that her voices have forbidden her to dress as a woman, she presents herself as an individual who is subjected to greater powers, incapable of resistance. A consequence of this ideological conundrum is that Joan of Arc's cross-dressing is presented to the reader at this moment in the same light as it has since been considered by cultural critics and gender theorists alike: transgressive, illusory, and endowed with a wealth of contradictory symbolism and meaning.

The relationship between words and pictures with regard to Joan of Arc's gender identity in Morpurgo's version is both subversive and complementary. As with Poole's retelling, the interplay between text and illustrations operates to detach the reader/viewer from the events and characters represented. Foreman's visual presentation of Joan in Morpurgo's retelling is not as contradictory as that of Barrett, who chooses to portray Joan as a subject with two distinct gender identities that are not seamlessly integrated. Barrett deliberately constructs a visual masculine/feminine dichotomy in Joan's appearance which culminates in the presentation of Joan as a mystical subject capable of maintaining two separate identities: a masculine hero/warrior *and* a pious and gentle saint devoted to God. This dualistic visual depiction of Joan reduces the importance of her cross-dressing. Barrett portrays her as physically masculine when involved in masculine activities (such as war and politics), and as physically feminine when placed in a more vulnerable context (such as in prison or being led to her execution). This leads the reader to view Joan as an individual with a fragmented and contradictory gender identity rather than as one, cohesive, transgendered subject. Foreman's illustrations, however, participate in constructing Joan as a consistent, but ambiguously gendered, character. This consistency is not always maintained in the verbal text, which initially presents Joan as a reluctant cross-dresser loath to relinquish her feminine identity. Morpurgo also emphasizes Joan's femininity leading up to and during her execution, attributing conventionally feminine behaviors to her such as weakness and fainting, which contrast sharply with her previous demonstration of military aggression and resolute willfulness during her trial. The accompanying illustrations undermine the verbal text's emphasis on Joan's behavioral femininity during the final stages of her life, because in the visual text she is shown with a shaven head. She displays no visual indicators of either gender in these illustrations: with her shorn hair, she is attired in a shapeless robe that alludes intertextually to the habits traditionally worn by monks. Her image is completely ungendered.

Foreman's androgynous visual representation of Joan is coordinated with his equally androgynous depiction of Eloise. The book's first major illustration is of Joan (10), but the same style of facial representation is repeated in the first close-up illustration of Eloise, creating a direct relationship between these characters, one historical and one contemporary, because of their similar physical features. The visual relationship between Eloise and Joan encourages readers to associate the two girls with each other, using Eloise to anchor Joan's story in contemporary reality. Eloise's visual representation, however, also operates to lessen the significance of Joan's cross-dressing. Eloise's short hair and jeans mirror Joan's masculine clothes, but her gender identity in the verbal text is unquestionably feminine. Eloise wears the mandatory denim uniform of contemporary adolescents, but by outfitting her in jeans (a piece of clothing universally regarded as unisex), Foreman averts the implication that, like Joan, she also has a transgressive gender identity. The visual relationship between Eloise and Joan normalizes Joan's cross-dressing, explicitly suggesting that trousers are acceptable dress for modern women and, by extension, contextualizes Joan's behavior within modern gender mores. The huge furor caused by her cross-dressing behavior, which was completely unacceptable in its fifteenth-century context, is ideologically erased.

Eloise's physical representation is not the only pictorial strategy which undermines the significance of Joan of Arc's gender ambiguity in Foreman's illustrations. The issues of the represented character's gaze and the perspective from which the character is viewed, strategies which prevent the viewer from establishing a direct relationship with Joan in Barrett's illustrations, are more exaggerated in Foreman's imagery. Foreman never allows Joan's gaze to meet the viewer's, constantly portraying her in profile or in a position where her eyes are averted. Foreman also chooses to depict Joan frequently among groups of other characters, often from a distant perspective, where the low modality of his imagery makes it impossible to distinguish Joan's facial features from the other represented participants (her white standard is the only device used to identify her). These visual strategies are most pronounced in the illustration which depicts Joan being sentenced to death for her crimes by Cauchon. The image is full-page, positioning the viewer behind Joan so that only the back of her body is visible. Cauchon's face is discernible, as are those of the spectators, but their eyes are fixed firmly on Joan, not on the viewer. Cauchon's pointing arm forms a vector between him and Joan, visually connecting them, but because Joan's face is obscured, it is a relationship from which the viewer is excluded.

Foreman's illustrations forcefully demonstrate the issues concerning representation that arise in children's retellings of the legend of Joan of Arc. On the one hand, his imagery engages with the issue of Joan's gender identity by presenting her as genuinely (and consistently) androgynous. At the same time he employs the pictorial strategies of perspective and the gaze to detach viewers from relating to Joan of Arc intimately, as an empathetic character. Foreman's images of Joan constantly evade the establishment of a direct relationship with the viewer, as her profiled or distant representation, combined with a lack of eye contact, never allows the viewer to be positioned within the picture. We are always situated outside the represented event, on the periphery rather than in the center.

CROSS-DRESSING AND PERFORMANCE IN JOAN OF ARC RETELLINGS

In an interesting inversion of the way that gender is linked to performance in the female cross-dressing paradigm, Morpurgo's *Joan of Arc* also associates cross-dressing with performance, but does so by using a narrow theatrical concept of performance which elevates it to art and severs its relationship with gender and daily life. Morpurgo uses Eloise as a framing device for the narrative, and closure occurs when Eloise is able to apply her newfound knowledge of Joan of Arc (acquired through her dream) to her role as Joan in the town's annual reenactment of the triumph at Orléans. Eloise must cross-dress in masculine armor for the role of her heroine, Joan of Arc, but her cross-dressing is obligatory for the part. The theatrical necessity of cross-dressing in this context reconstructs it as a required costume or prop. The analogy between gender and performance, which texts like *Alanna* and *Mulan* draw on and explore comprehensively, is forsaken in this particular retelling. Eloise's participation in the town pageant situates her cross-dressing behavior within the playful and imaginary world of the staged spectacle. The subversive potential of her cross-dressing is reconstructed as permissible on the stage, a space where transgressive behavior becomes temporarily permissible.

The relationship between cross-dressing and gender is not explicitly explored in either the retelling by Poole or Morpurgo, but each text engages with the issue of gender through visual imagery. Nancy Garden's novel, *Dove and Sword*, is therefore unusual because it thematically addresses the associated concepts of gender and performativity. Garden's novel also offers the most overt demonstration of the way that children's retellings of the Joan of Arc legend employ narrative strategies such as focalization and point of view to prevent readers from gaining an interior perspective of Joan of Arc's subjectivity, and thereby constructing Joan as an inscrutable, mythic, and above all, distant, character. *Dove and Sword* uses the same strategy of a fictional, first-person narrator, whose experiences mirror Joan of Arc's, as in Morpurgo's *Joan of Arc*. Instead of a modern character, however, *Dove and Sword* uses as its narrator a young girl named Gabrielle, who is placed within Joan's story and offers an account of Joan's life from her own perspective. The use of Gabrielle as the narrative's focalizing character confirms the tendency (also evident in Poole and Morpurgo's texts) for children's fiction to distance itself from more personal, closely focalized (i.e., first-person) constructions of Joan's subjectivity. Joan becomes a secondary character to Gabrielle's experiences, and Gabrielle's frequent lack of proximity to Joan, coupled with her awe of Joan's achievements, results in a portrayal of Joan as a heroic but nevertheless secondary character. The events of Joan's life are fragmented, constructed out of Gabrielle's minimal interactions with her, but otherwise revealed to the reader in the same way that they are made known to Gabrielle—through information she gleans from others. This produces a disjointed representation of Joan, as Gabrielle is only present during her brilliant but short-lived military successes against the English. The circumstances surrounding Joan's capture and trial are therefore reconstructed by Gabrielle, who is not present but uses the information she has learned from others to narrate the unfolding events to the reader:[4] "When I pieced it all together, it seemed that Jeanne had indeed tried to escape..." (390); "And so I passed the first part of early winter, until one cold December day when I heard that Jeanne had been sold to the English..." (307). Accordingly, Joan's motivations and thoughts are only those that Gabrielle supposes of her, and Joan is thus denied any genuine emotional complexity or depth: "My eyes were on Jeanne, who stood silently and patiently, looking towards the sky, and then at the stake, and then at the crowd. She appeared puzzled, sometimes, as if she did not understand what had brought her here. I could feel my heart hammering in my breast and I wondered if she felt her own" (330).

Gabrielle, who is a childhood friend of Joan's, follows her into battle, facilitating a doubling of Joan's cross-dressing (as occurs with Eloise in Morpurgo's version). Instead of cross-dressing to *be* Joan, as Eloise does, Gabrielle cross-dresses for the same reasons attributed to Joan within this novel and the other retellings so far discussed: so that she can venture in safety into the masculine domain of warfare. But Gabrielle's response to the idea of cross-dressing, in relation to her own and Joan of Arc's, is framed within a discourse of subordinated femininity. Gabrielle immediately recognizes that cross-dressing has far-reaching social implications because it will allow her to participate in behavior denied to her as a feminine subject. When she hears that Joan has been seen wearing masculine clothing, Gabrielle immediately relates to this information on a personal and gendered level. Her reference to the impractical skirt of her red dress is symbolic of the regulatory social forces which restrict femininity: "'Men's clothes!' I said in awe and envy, lifting the skirt of my red dress, on which I had often tripped" (38–39).

Gabrielle's pleasure at the thought of being able to disguise herself as a man, her emotive response conveyed by the use of words such as "awe" and "envy," and the potential for this desire to be interpreted as a comment critical of the gender limitations socially imposed upon feminine subjectivity, are promptly frustrated by the reaction it provokes in Joan's brother, Pierre. Confronting the connection between cross-dressing and perversion, Garden uses a secondary female character (Pierre's fiancée, who is also named Jeanne) to address the biblical prohibition of cross-dressing. She queries Joan's cross-dressing, asking Pierre, "But surely that is a sin, for a woman to wear men's clothes?" (38). Typical of the rationalization for cross-dressing offered in both Poole's and Morpurgo's narratives, *Dove and Sword* frames female cross-dressing within the boundaries of safety and feminine honor:

> "If a woman is to ride among men as a soldier," Pierre said sternly, "she had better wear men's clothes. You do not know what beasts men are, my Jeanne." (38)

Pierre uses his social superiority as a man to chastise his fiancée "sternly," reprimanding her with the pronouncement "you do not know" in reference to her ignorance of masculine behavior. Pierre's equation of men with "beasts" also serves to reinforce the traditional gender hierarchy by frighteningly alluding to the animalistic and predatory qualities of men, a sentiment that correspondingly constructs women as innocent victims. Further, Pierre's conversation regarding Joan's cross-dressing reveals that it is not of her own volition. He tells Gabrielle that "Laxart came to us and said that she had been given men's clothes"

(38), a construction of female cross-dressing that prevents it from being associated with feminine agency because it is behavior compelled by masculine direction. (Both Poole and Morpurgo also participate in constructing Joan's cross-dressing as the product of male coercion.)

Dove and Sword does not focus on Joan's cross-dressing, however, preferring to use Gabrielle's personal experience of gender disguise as an analogy for Joan of Arc's behavior. In many respects Gabrielle's cross-dressing reproduces key elements of the female paradigm. Gabrielle resembles characters such as Alanna and Mulan because she also fails to fulfill the prescriptive requirements of conventional femininity. Her feminine failure is communicated through her successful assimilation of masculine behaviors:

> And yet, though I knew Jeanette [Joan of Arc] was more pious than I, I felt much more suited than she to lead an army into war. It was I, not Jeanette, who hated to spin and cook; it was I who had played with the boys; it was I, alone among the girls of our village, who had fought the boys of Maxey. (39)

This passage of introspective, first-person narration effectively communicates Gabrielle's yearning to escape the passivity of subordinated femininity, a familiar trait of cross-dressing heroines. However, it also discloses that she is a solipsistic and naïve narrator who is overly ambitious. The exaggerated repetition of the pronoun "I," accompanied with the dismissive reference to Joan of Arc, belies Gabrielle's immaturity and self-involvement. Her youthful self-assurance is also evident in the way that she approaches a masculine performance while cross-dressed, which she reflects upon with confidence and superiority:

> I found I was enjoying the masquerade of being a boy. I had taught myself to swagger, and to make my voice squeak so the men would think it was changing, as boys' voices do. Pierre had given out that I had been sickly as a child and so was not strong. But in truth I was stronger than some boys, and lacked few skills country boys possess.... (106)

The novel's construction of gender as performative, a socially regulated routine of learned gestures and behaviors, is supported by Gabrielle's choice of the word "masquerade," a term that conjures up images of elegant playfulness and bourgeois role-playing. Yet this passage is more effective at portraying Gabrielle's inflated self-confidence than providing a meaningful critique of stereotypical gender attributes. Gabrielle's perspective of her cross-dressing diminishes its significance because, although she is perfectly aware of the need to alter and modify her behavior in order to present herself as a convincing male, she simplifies the difficulty associated with such a transformation. Mulan's and Alanna's experiences with cross-dressing are considerably more complicated. Their performance of masculinity is a struggle, as they each try to "unlearn" conditioned behaviors and responses that identify them as feminine within a context where the discovery of their sex is potentially dangerous. Gabrielle, on the other hand, finds cross-dressing "enjoyable." Her assertion that she is physically stronger than other boys and already possesses the requisite masculine skills for her role in the army appears to be far-fetched, if not deluded, and belittles the extensive implications of socially enforced gender codes.

Gabrielle's blithe estimation of her cross-dressing abilities is dramatically confounded by her experience of war. Once she is confronted with the reality of battle, her self-assurance quickly drains away and is replaced by doubt, fear, and self-remonstration. Gabrielle often reflects upon her unsuitability for the masculine role of soldier, becoming increasingly unconvinced of her own abilities: "I wondered what she would do when there was fighting, for she was no war-horse, and what I would do myself. Though I was eager, I knew I was not a soldier..." (109). A similar attitude is evident on page 144, where she states, "...I had seen enough blood that day, and had begun to think that perhaps I was not suited to this adventure," and again on page 164, where Gabrielle's previously successful performance of masculinity is replaced by failure:

> Unthinking, carried by the men's fervor as a twig is carried by a swift stream, I seized an abandoned cross-bow, and put my foot on it, as I had seen bowmen do. I tried to draw its string back with its windlass to prepare it for firing, but I could not get the knack of it.

Although it is typical for female cross-dressers to feel anxious about their masculine abilities, these feelings are much more pronounced in the character of Gabrielle than in, for example, Mulan or Alanna. Gabrielle's self-doubt overshadows her earlier performative successes, implying that her assumed masculinity is not, and never will be, authentic. In the passage above, Gabrielle's acknowledgment that she is aware of the skill required to operate a crossbow, but still cannot master it, reinforces the patriarchal gender binary by suggesting that Gabrielle's femininity is the cause of her failure. Cross-dressing is a frightening experience for Gabrielle. It does not lead to agency, but confirms her gendered inferiority as a feminine subject.

Story closure also plays a contributory role in emphasizing Gabrielle's "natural" feminine subjectivity and constructing her cross-dressing as ill-conceived. *Dove and Sword* commences in 1455, twenty-four years after Joan's execution in 1431. The story is structured around Gabrielle's meeting with Pierre, Joan of Arc's brother, for the first time since they served together in the French army under Joan's leadership. This beginning, which is also the end of the narrative's circular structure, reveals that since Joan of Arc's death, Gabrielle has been living in a convent. She is not a nun herself, but serves as their resident healer. Gabrielle's return to conventional femininity after her cross-dressing experience is a common ploy in female cross-dressing narratives, but Gabrielle's decision to remove herself to a cloistered environment of women suggests that her cross-dressing has negatively affected her perception of the world. Pierre teases Gabrielle about her patients, referring to her medical work in the army when he asks, "But no soldiers anymore, eh, Gabrielle? No sword cuts or caltrop punctures, no cross-bow bolts to probe for....Do you miss it?" (2). Pierre's question subtly invokes a masculine discourse by his use of the word "soldier," but Gabrielle's emphatically negative response ignores the issue of gender. Reflective of the novel's resolution of Gabrielle's cross-dressing, wherein the thematic examination of gender performativity is addressed but later abandoned in favor of the patriarchal gender hierarchy, the novel concludes with a direct address to the reader about the futility of war. The gendered discourse that traditionally surrounds war demands and constructs a tough and aggressive masculinity from its participants, and it is this discourse which directly compels Gabrielle to assume a masculine identity during her military experience. Gabrielle's last words, however, which specifically address the reader, avoid any association between war and masculinity:

> No matter how much I have thought and read and prayed and studied, I have in the end not been able to find it right that people choose to kill and maim one another.... (336)

Gabrielle's substitution of the word "people" for the more historically accurate "men" is emblematic of the way in which this and other retellings strategically abolish gender as a relevant concern within a narrative that nevertheless provides detailed but inexplicable accounts of Joan's continued refusal to abandon her masculine costume. Joan's execution, reconstructed in each retelling as an exercise of political power, orchestrated by a group of men who were determined to victimize and eliminate the subversive woman before them, clearly invites a gendered reading. However, none of these retellings attempts to engage with the patriarchal gender politics of such a situation.

Cross-dressing, which is as much a part of Joan of Arc's life and legend as her military successes and untimely death, is a subject that is reluctantly broached in children's retellings. Joan's cross-dressing is constructed in a coercive context, a directive issued by men rather than an act of her own volition. The relationship between cross-dressing and gender is obscured in these retellings, two of which raise the issue of performativity but revise its contemporary theoretical application to socially constructed gender categories so that it produces the opposite effect. Performativity is taken out of the everyday and elevated to art (Morpurgo), or used to reinscribe the patriarchal gender binary by reason of the performer's failure (Garden). Moreover, the association of female cross-dressing with agency, a central principle of the female paradigm, is problematized by Joan's execution, an event that repositions her within a discourse of patriarchal femininity as a subordinated and self-sacrificing victim of hegemonic masculinity.

Stories about Joan of Arc pose a particular challenge within the broader context of female cross-dressing in children's literature. The relationship between cross-dressing and feminine agency is inconsistent with Joan's violent demise, but each retelling discussed here ameliorates this dilemma by supplying readers with a range of peritextual material that attests to Joan of Arc's enduring cultural legacy. A map of France is included in each, locating the town of Joan's birth and the sites of her battles against the English, adding historical veracity to these fictionalized accounts of her life. Poole's picture book concludes with a historical chronology of events that lists the dates of Joan's official pardon and canonization as a saint. Morpurgo includes a short author's note at the end of his retelling, detailing the historical and literary sources he drew on for his narrative. Garden's novel commences with an acknowledgment of the people and historical institutes which assisted her research, followed closely by a lengthy author's note. Garden's note begins, "This book is, before anything else, a story. It is a story with a good deal of history in it, but it should be viewed as fiction..." (xiii). Garden's caution to readers that her novel should be treated as fiction rather than fact is contradicted by her subsequent testament to the historical "truth" of her novel. She writes, "Most of the military and political people mentioned in the book were real, too," and "...wherever possible, I have tried to base Joan's lines in this book on those that have been recorded" (xiv). Garden also expresses gratitude to a historical scholar, Jules Quicherat, whose research assisted her reconstruction of events, characters, and dialogue. This extensive testament to the historical accuracy of her novel undermines its status as fiction. Garden readily admits that Gabrielle was not a real person, but even this admission is underscored by her assertion that historical evidence suggests that there were "some amazingly feisty women in Joan's time" (xiii). Garden's historical justification of her characters and represented events highlights the conflict between historical discourses and narrativity which arises in Joan of Arc retellings. Garden ends her epistle to the reader with an apology for any historical errors she may have made, a conciliatory gesture that epitomizes the reticence with which children's retellings approach the problem of fictionalizing the story of Joan of Arc, a woman who left an extensive trail of historical evidence and scholarship in her wake.

Morpurgo's retelling is clearly the most ambitious of the texts discussed here, his fictional attempt to re-create Joan's interiority obviously influenced by the work of George Bernard Shaw and Vita Sackville-West, in combination with historical documents. The wealth of historical and cultural research widely available on Joan of Arc compromises her fictional depiction in children's retellings, particularly in relation to the issue of gender, because of a demonstrated reluctance to engage with matter that is not factual, such as her attitude to her cross-dressing, of which there is little or no historical evidence. Transcripts of Joan's trial attest to her refusal to stop cross-dressing, and also record that she characterized it as behavior ordered by God, but her own thoughts about it are unknown. Perhaps in fear of lessening the historical and educational value of their narratives, children's retellings re-create only the uncontentious aspects of her life. A retelling such as Morpurgo's, for example, takes liberties with its fictionalized re-creation of Joan's inner thoughts with respect to her self-doubt about the validity of her mission to restore the French king to the throne, but her transgressive gender behavior is left unexplored. Morpurgo articulates the problem precisely, observing that "Many biographies by learned authors have been written about her. There have been numerous plays and films, too; but in many cases I found the Joan in them too remote or too saintly" (124). In spite of his perceptive analysis regarding the cultural reproduction of Joan's legend in literature and art, Morpurgo's own retelling partly succumbs to the narrative construction of Joan in children's literature as a distant and unknowable character. The narrativity of Joan of Arc retellings is peculiarly homogeneous—the extensive use of limited focalization effectively marginalizing the contentious nature and impact (personal, social, political) of her cross-dressing. This homogeneity can be ascribed to the traditional purpose of literature about saints, wherein the lives of these historical men and women were supposed to serve as inspiration for the common reader. The saints' lives were not meant to be emulated or studied, but were intended to be reflected upon and commemorated—to stimulate "a growth in faith," asserts the Archbishop of Westminster in the foreword to Butler's Lives of the Saints

(1985, v). The construction of Joan as a character whose subjectivity is never fully revealed or explored, and which remains either wholly or partially obscured in both the visual and the verbal narrative, complies with the religious function of legends about saints. In the words of the archbishop, Joan and her saintly brethren have "bequeathed to us an inspiration that transcends ordinary history" (ibid., 5). She is a legend, not a human being, and this is clearly reflected in the use of visual and verbal strategies which limit the reader's access to her inner voice and also, therefore, to her humanity.

Reflecting on the extent to which gender and sexuality have been brought to bear on Joan of Arc's legend, Andrew Matzner argues that "It is difficult adequately to address these personal issues based on the historical evidence that we now possess. It is clear, however, that Joan's cross-dressing was a significant part of her life, and that as a cross-dressed warrior and military leader she was venerated by French royalty, soldiery, and peasantry alike" (2004). Matzner's comments are apposite to children's retellings, because although these versions of Joan of Arc's life tentatively skirt around the issue of cross-dressing, they unambiguously construct her as a woman of heroic passions and devout religious convictions who was beloved by her people. The subversive effect of Joan's cross-dressing is therefore implicit. Unexplored and unremarked upon, her transgressive behavior is reconstructed in retellings as valid, legitimate, and even heroic. The significance of contemporary children's literature that undoubtedly honors the life and legend of this most celebrated female cross-dresser, within an environment where cross-dressing is still popularly perceived as taboo, cannot be overstated.

4

REFRAMING MASCULINITY
The Destabilizing Effect of the Female Cross-Dresser

... I opposed those regimes of truth that stipulated that certain
kinds of gendered expressions were found to be false or derivative,
and others, true and original.

Judith Butler
Gender Trouble

INTRODUCTION

Masculinity is a peculiar commodity in children's cross-dressing narratives. When boys put on women's clothing, they generally do so in a gesture of masculine larrikinism. The results are humorous—often overtly
so—and are rarely perceived as sinister or sexually deviant. Although
contemporary conceptualizations of cross-dressing invariably involve
adult males and sexually deviant motivations, the male cross-dressers in children's literature are distanced from such associations by the
specific form of traditional masculinity they project. The masculinity
of the majority of these characters is never questionable (a testament
to the way in which hegemonic masculinity has traditionally maintained a position of dominance in all aspects of society and culture),
thus producing comic situations when these palpably male characters
dress themselves in women's clothing and are suitably uncomfortable
(and unconvincing) when doing so. Representations of female-to-male
cross-dressing are radically different, because in these cases girls dress

themselves as boys in order to escape societies which seek to repress and limit femininity. Cross-dressing allows them to inhabit the world of men and experience many of the liberties denied them when they are dressed and perceived as feminine. Female-to-male cross-dressing thus facilitates an analysis of gender itself, and of the constructs that constitute and divide masculinity and femininity.

There is, then, a sharp disjunction between representations of the male and female cross-dressing experience in children's literature. While this difference was addressed in Chapter 2 in terms of the paradigmatic structure of male and female cross-dressing narratives, my focus here is more specifically on the construction of masculinity in both female and male cross-dressing narratives. (Femininity will be discussed more implicitly, as male cross-dressers rarely master a convincing feminine performance and female cross-dressers construct their subjectivities against feminine gender norms.) In order to address this issue, some of the material covered here will reiterate arguments presented earlier. I hope, however, to expand these theoretical tenets by widening the scope of analysis to include a discussion of how the female cross-dresser's masculine identity is situated within a more general textual construction of masculinity. This will involve an examination of how the masculinity of other biologically male characters within the text is constructed and contrasted against the type of masculinity performed by the female cross-dresser.

One of the more interesting aspects of female cross-dressing narratives is that the interrogation of normative gender categories which is initiated by the cross-dressing heroine is rarely confined to her alone, but extends to encompass an exploration of other constructions of masculinity and femininity (as represented by other masculine and feminine characters) within the text. Female cross-dressing is constructed in such a way that it tends to problematize the notion of gender itself, the gendered identities of other characters being measured and assessed against the cross-dresser's masculine performance. The result is a critical assessment of gender on all levels. But, of course, not all female cross-dressing narratives are completely successful at deconstructing gender norms. It is to some of these less successful examples of female cross-dressing which I now turn, in order to consider why the masculine performances of these particular cross-dressers are poor or unconvincing. The reasons for their failure provide an equally significant perspective on the ideological construction of gender in children's literature and film.

For young girls, the cross-dressing experience commonly represented in children's literature is liberatory. It exposes the artifice of gender constructions, permitting the female cross-dresser to construct for herself a unique gendered niche that is not grounded within a single gender category, but incorporates elements of both. This phenomenon is evident in a range of female-to-male cross-dressing texts. The most comprehensive collection of stories in which female-to-male cross-dressing appears in this specific fashion is Sharukh Husain's collection, *Women Who Wear the Breeches* (1995). From this collection I will discuss the tale "What Will Be, Will Be" as the most symptomatic example of how such narratives can deconstruct traditional notions of gender by using cross-dressing to interrogate the social construction of gender and to introduce empowering feminist agendas. For male cross-dressers, however, the attempt to perform a feminine role is rarely approached in a similar manner. The masculinity of male cross-dressers is seldom as fragile as the femininity of female cross-dressers, nor is it so easily forsaken. Because their behavior presupposes the superiority of masculine over feminine, their self-assured masculinity permeates every aspect of their cross-dressing experience, rendering comic their inability to comprehend femininity as separate from their own biologically male experience of gender.

Female-to-male cross-dressing narratives are invariably concerned with the rejection of traditional gender stereotypes, even though many long precede modern feminism or the social acceptance of transgender identities and behavior. They seek to destabilize the polarized conceptions of masculinity and femininity and to create a gendered realm outside conventional expectations and stereotypes. Not every female cross-dressing text, however, achieves this with absolute conviction. With some, their ability to challenge gender stereotypes is hindered by the prevalence of conventional gender constructions. Clear examples are afforded by Terry Pratchett's *Monstrous Regiment* (2003) and Robin McKinley's *Rose Daughter* (1997), McKinley's second novel-length retelling of the Beauty and the Beast myth. Pratchett's fantasy novel conforms almost exactly to the paradigmatic structure of the female-to-male cross-dressing model in its portrayal of a cross-dressed girl, Polly, who joins the army in order to find her lost brother. Her cross-dressing success is perhaps more successful than most other examples of female cross-dressing, due to the acute consciousness with which the novel engages with the notion of gender as a performance. The heroine's cross-dressing success is compromised, however, by the novel's use of generic conventions. A tale of battle and warfare, *Monstrous Regiment* fails to destabilize the historical construction of war as a masculine domain. Its cross-dressing protagonists (there are multiple ones within this novel) are successful at bringing an end to the war that has devas-

tated the fantasy country of Borogravia, but do so within a traditionally militaristic framework that reinscribes patriarchal masculinity
rather than interrogating it. McKinley's fairy tale suffers a similar fate.
The cross-dressing depicted within this novel is secondary to the main
events of the tale and is less successful in reassessing conventional gender codes than the atypical, gender-bending tales in Husain's *Women
Who Wear the Breeches*. In some ways, *Rose Daughter* confirms traditional gender stereotypes in its portrayal of a Beast who personifies
conventional masculinity in many respects and a female character who
cross-dresses yet is never totally able to escape her essential femininity. Despite the depiction of relatively unsuccessful female cross-dressing, however, the treatment of gender in both *Monstrous Regiment* and
Rose Daughter is nevertheless more accommodating of individuality in
gender identity than the majority of portrayals of male cross-dressing
available in children's literature.

TO BE A SUBJECT IS TO BE A MAN

The representation of masculinity within female-to-male cross-dressing narratives offers a unique conceptualization of masculinity and
the machinations of gender constructions, and will be the focus of the
rest of this chapter. These narratives provide an arena in which gender constructions (as they appear in each individual text) are laid bare
and essentially (re)constructed in the cross-dresser's performance. The
breadth of gender construction in female cross-dressing narratives
contrasts with the more limited type of masculinity evident in male
cross-dressing narratives. These encompass canonical literature such
as Kenneth Grahame's *The Wind in the Willows* (1908), where Toad disguises himself as a washerwoman, and also Anne Fine's novel *Bill's New
Frock* (1989), in which Bill wakes one morning to find himself attired in
a pink dress and is then subjected to the gender discrimination which
often characterizes feminine experience in school classrooms. Within
this model the authenticity of the masculinity of the cross-dressing male
subject is never in doubt. The characters are first and foremost "male,"
and their inherent masculinity permeates the cross-dressing context,
even though they may appear outwardly female. The form of masculinity which these characters embody, in spite of their brief transvestite
transgressions, is characterized in terms of traditional gender values.
It is defined against femininity and encompasses the range of specific
behaviors that have become symbolic, through controlling social practices and popular representations, of hegemonic masculinity.

One of the most significant features of this masculine construction is that it is never presented as vulnerable, precarious, or subject to any form of fragmentation. The gender of the male subject, regardless of playful forays into the seemingly dubious gender area of transvestism, is always upheld and never attains the same ambiguity that is created in relation to female cross-dressers. Psychoanalyst Robert Stoller even claims that actual adult male transvestism is grounded in such a presupposition:

> The whole complex psychological system that we call transves-tism is a rather efficient method of handling very strong feminine identifications without the patient having to succumb to the feel-ing that his sense of masculinity is being submerged by feminine wishes. The transvestite fights this battle against being destroyed by his feminine desires, first by alternating his masculinity with the feminine behavior, and thus reassuring himself that it isn't permanent; and second, by being always aware even at the height of feminine behavior—when he is fully dressed in women's clothes—that he has the absolute insignia of maleness, a penis.

(cited in Garber [1992] 1993, 95)

Although the situation in male cross-dressing literature is quite different, devoid as it is of sexual connotations, a similar assertion of phallocentrism is inherent within the cross-dressing performances of male protagonists. As Garber remarks apropos of Stoller, "The concept of 'male subjectivity' to many custodians of Western culture—whether literary critics, psychoanalysts, or rock musicians, should they ever have recourse to the term—is in a sense redundant. To be a subject is to *be* a man—to be male literally or empowered 'as' male in culture and society" (1993, 94).

Female cross-dressing narratives, on the other hand, generally involve a total transformation of feminine subjectivity—indicative of the more variable status of femininity within cultural constructions of gender. The cross-dressing heroine initially embarks upon a process of learning how to "perform" as a male in texts such as "What Will Be, Will Be," a fairy tale from Charles Swynnerton's *Romantic Tales from the Panjab with Indian Nights' Entertainment* (adapted in Husain 1995, 195–229); Terry Pratchett's *Monstrous Regiment* (2003); and the afore-mentioned *Alanna* and *Mulan*. Despite some preliminary stumbling, each female protagonist quickly assumes a "genuine" masculine per-sona that is acceptable to the outside world, and is so successful in her role-playing that she is able to outperform the same males which she originally set out to emulate. Her masculinity is therefore more authentic than the masculinity of her biologically male compatriots—a very anomalous phenomenon in the context of the all-pervasive patriarchal social structures which have long dominated, and continue to dominate, societies the world over.

THE MASCULINE TRANSFORMATION
OF THE FEMININE SUBJECT

The female cross-dressing subject typically embarks on a quest to achieve and sustain masculinity, yet in doing so, she outperforms all other biologically "authentic" renditions of this gender. The masculinity that she originally sets out to emulate, as embodied in the other male characters of the text, is surpassed and outdone. The cross-dressing heroine is ultimately more "manlike" than her biological counterparts within the narrative. This "outportrayal" can be attributed to a number of factors, such as the feminist concerns of the text and the requisite promotion of feminine autonomy and self-determination, or the reassessment of the socially constructed notion of gender as the most essential definer of individual identity; but one of the most compelling is that the versions of masculinity with which the cross-dressing heroine is confronted are inadequate and unconventional in themselves. For example, the father of Mulan is too old and frail to go to war, and it is this which motivates Mulan to dress as a young man and go in his stead. The cross-dressing protagonist of *Monstrous Regiment*, Polly, enlists for war because she is anxious to find her brother Paul, whom she fears will fare badly when faced with the reality of battle. Similarly, Alanna's male twin abhors the traditional masculine pursuits of swordsmanship and horse riding, and is only too happy to exchange destinies with his sister. The male characters within these narratives rarely fulfill the conventional expectations of masculinity, and it is in the context of these failed personifications of traditional masculinity that the cross-dressing protagonist is able to carve her/his own gender niche, which falls outside the socially condoned categorizations of "masculinity" and "femininity." Sizing up the behavioral requirements of masculinity, cross-dressing heroines give a gender performance that highlights the artifice of supposedly "natural" masculine traits. Cross-dressing heroines draw attention to the limitations inherent within the social construction of masculinity, often illuminating the stereotypical components of socially constructed masculinity in a humorous fashion:

> Forget you were ever Polly. *Think* young male, that was the thing. Fart loudly and with self-satisfaction at a job well done, move like

a puppet that'd had a couple of random strings cut, never hug any-one and, if you meet a friend, punch them. A few years working in the bar had provided plenty of observational material.

(*Monstrous Regiment*, 11)

The female cross-dresser's masculine performance is commonly noticed and appreciated by other males, who admire their new acquain-tance without any trace of suspicion as to her/his biological origin, indicative of the manner in which these children's texts seek to decon-struct and re-create the idea of gender itself. As argued by Pettitt (1999, 3) about drag performances, and also resonates within a children's liter-ary cross-dressing context, "in drag the performance of . . . masculinity by a female body demonstrates the mutability of gender. Moreover, it testifies to the arbitrary relation between sex and gender; sex can there-fore no longer be simply understood as that raw material upon which gender is later inscribed."

"What Will Be, Will Be" is a cross-dressing folktale that conforms to the female-to-male cross-dressing paradigm. It tells the story of a young princess, abandoned by her husband and his parents, a king and queen, whose resilience and courage enable her to tackle her fate head-on—by dressing as a man, winning favor with the king of the land and an influ-ential position within the palace, which she ultimately uses to uncover her family's whereabouts and thus initiate a reunion. "What Will Be, Will Be" is significantly contextualized by its retelling within Sharukh Husain's *Women Who Wear the Breeches*, a collection of female-to-male cross-dressing stories sourced from a range of cultures and literary tra-ditions as diverse as Angela Carter's contemporary retellings of fairy tales, Giovanni Boccaccio's *Decameron*, Jewish folklore, and even tra-ditional Tibetan allegory. Although each text differs markedly in nar-rative style and genre, all tell the story of a female cross-dresser. These heroines cross-dress for varying reasons, and the outcome of their cross-dressing forays is never exactly the same, yet they share a com-mon bond in the instance of their cross-dressing. In choosing to cross-dress, these women put themselves at risk. They demonstrate courage and audacity in their decision to transform themselves into a different gender, responding to a need—that originates from within themselves or is generated by outside forces or circumstances beyond their con-trol—which cannot be ignored, and which they embrace wholeheart-edly with resourcefulness and zest.

The representation of masculinity within the female-to-male cross-dressing texts included in Husain's anthology is complex and multi-faceted, because masculinity and femininity become intertwined and almost interchangeable within the portrayal of the cross-dressing subject. In her introduction to *Women Who Wear the Breeches*, Husain evocatively writes about her first exposure to cross-dressing children's stories. When she was ten years old, she heard the tale of a blacksmith's daughter who married a young and feisty prince, then dressed herself as a man in order to rescue her lover from the hands of a wicked fairy princess. Everything about this story impressed the young Husain, who was enchanted by the reckless behavior of the female protagonist: "The blacksmith's daughter did the things that I as a child had already been told were wrong, but which continued to tantalize my child's heart. She answered back, she was wilful and disobedient, she lied and cheated. She was the bad-girl incarnate, the type grown-ups would have told me not to mix with. And what fun she had living dangerously!" (ix). But the most interesting aspect of this editorial anecdote is that the story was told to Husain by "a fierce-looking frontiersman, who was temporarily replacing the nightwatchman in our family home in Karachi, and he was unreservedly delighted by the heroine's romps..." (ix). In dressing herself as a man, the blacksmith's daughter became one in the mind of the male storyteller, and he identified strongly with her headstrong behavior. Husain eloquently articulates the duality and complexity of gender representations within children's tales of female cross-dressing:

> In retrospect, I realize that the frontiersman told the story with such gusto and vibrancy because he identified with the heroine. He and she became interchangeable as he referred to her now in the masculine, now in the feminine, simultaneously sustaining both female and male personae. She was the perfect androgyne, representing the protective and the assertive in male and female. (x)

The ability of female cross-dressing heroines to traverse the boundaries of gender is one of their most remarkable achievements, and the key to their success as an "omni-gendered" subject—with whom readers of either sex can empathize on a multitude of gendered levels. This cross-dressing protagonist reworks and reconstitutes the very idea of gender, appropriating it for her own purposes. The female character assumes a masculine identity through her cross-dressing, and achieves success because her disguise is effective. Her true biological status is not discovered, for at least a portion of the text, and, perhaps most significantly, she is considered to be a "genuine" male by the other characters with whom she/he interacts. A necessary process of the cross-dressing heroine's narrative is the constant comparison that occurs between her own masculine behavior and the behavior of the other biological males that surround her. This comparison occurs to the heroine herself, who in some cases overtly modifies and internally measures her performance against her new male peers, as in the case of *Mulan*, but is also intrinsically evoked throughout the text during each encounter with a biological male. This is equally true in *Alanna*, where the female cross-dressing protagonist must perform her own version of masculinity within the most challenging of contexts—an Arthurian-style school for knights-in-training. Her behavioral battle is made all the more difficult because of the physical, militarist emphasis of her location. Alanna must therefore prove her masculinity in terms of strength and prowess, and is invariably placed in a position where although she is smaller in stature than her male peers, she is still valiantly capable of demonstrating her fighting skills and is often victorious over other "genuine" males.

Jody Norton succinctly addresses the benefits of this form of nonconformist gender representation in children's literature, arguing that they encourage reading practices which acknowledge and are resistant to regulatory gender regimes. According to Norton, children's texts which portray subjects whose "experience and sense of their gender does not allow them to fit their sexed bodies into seamless accord with a congruent, conventional gender identity" play a liberatory role in "creating interpretive strategies, curricular revisions, and pedagogical interventions that will contribute substantially to the amelioration of the condition of cultural, institutional, and political neglect through which transchildren have been denied their reality, and their worth" (1999, 415–16). Norton's focus, however, lies with those particular children's texts which portray transgender potential in a form that is complicit with the general social incomprehension of sex outside the traditional binaries of masculinity and femininity. Thus the situation depicted in Mark Twain's "Hellfire Hotchkiss," where the nonconformist gender behavior of its female narrator, Hellfire, is vastly inconsistent with the representation and experiences of female heroines in *Mulan, Alanna,* and "What Will Be, Will Be." Hellfire is socially ostracized because of her masculine gender identity, her subjectivity constructed as alienated and abject:

> Thug Carpenter is out of his sphere. I am out of mine. Neither of us can arrive at any success in life, we shall always be hampered and fretted and kept back by our misplaced sexes, and in the end defeated by them, whereas if we could change we should stand as good a chance as any of the young people in the town.

> **(Cited in Norton 1999, 423)**

The futility and despair that permeate the words of Twain's trans-gendered character are absent from the texts within the female-to-male cross-dressing paradigm. Social intolerance and rejection play no such role in these texts, as the widespread acceptance of the cross-dresser's masculine performance constitutes an integral component of the nar-rative—it is the very essence of these children's cross-dressing tales. The cross-dressing heroine's role is one which explicitly involves the successful assumption of a masculine subjectivity to the extent that the biologically female subject is considered to be a male by secondary characters in the context of the narrative. She does not fall victim to the socially contrived categorization of gender into the two, oppositional frameworks of masculinity and femininity. In *Vested Interests: Cross-Dressing and Cultural Anxiety* (1992), Marjorie Garber calls attention to examples of female-to-male cross-dressing in adult literature in which the cross-dressing exploits of the female heroine are never quite as revolutionary as they first appear to be, with insistence always placed on, and attention drawn to, the character's biological origin:

> All the more striking were the transvestite heroines, whether dressed as pages, country boys, or clerks. Theirs was a recupera-tive pattern: however outspoken they were, however much they challenged authority in the form of wicked dukes or moneylend-ers, they took pains to let their femaleness show. Rosalind and Julia swoon at moments of stress, Viola, facing the prospect of a duel, laments "a little thing would make me tell them how much I lack of a man" (TN 3.3.307–9), and Portia remarks to Nerissa that in their male disguise "they shall think we are accomplished/ With that we lack." ([1992] 1993, 72)

This "obligation" to remind the reader or audience of the cross-dress-ing character's biology and supposedly "natural" gender does not fea-ture prominently in the portrayal of female cross-dressing in children's literature. Rather than reminding the reader of the protagonist's biol-ogy, these texts strive to elevate the notion of gender to a level where the fact of biology becomes less significant, or temporarily irrelevant, in relation to the cross-dresser's ability to subvert gender stereotypes. The extent to which this is accomplished is demonstrated by the choice of pronoun which is used to identify the cross-dressing character. Although not always the case in female-to-male cross-dressing nar-ratives, texts such as "Secure at Last" (in Husain 1995, 33–75), which conforms to the more radical elements of the female-to-male paradigm, proceed to change the pronoun from "she" to "he" once the protagonist adopts a cross-dressed masculine persona. The cross-dressing heroine of this text also assumes a man's name, thus erasing the relationship between her/his new masculinity and former femininity. In fact, when Sicurano (the name of the male character in "Secure at Last") dwells upon the incidents that once occurred in the life of Zinevra (the original female character) and prompted his "birth," it is as if Sicurano and Zinevra are two distinct persons. This not only cements the cross-dressing character's gender transformation, but also negates any occurrence of the phenomenon described by Garber.

The main character of the tale "What Will Be, Will Be," a young woman named Wahda, is a spectacular demonstration of this phenomenon. "What Will Be, Will Be" contains all of the elements requisite to a fairy tale: gloomy prophecies; an ill-fated king; vampires; ogres; and an ending in which good triumphs over evil. The only difference between "What Will Be, Will Be" and other stories of the same genre is that Wahda fulfills the roles of both hero and heroine in this tale, toying with the traditional notions of masculine and feminine literary roles as her narrative progresses, and (re)creating a position of gendered subjectivity outside and beyond the constructed artificialities of conventional masculinity and femininity. "What Will Be, Will Be" opens with a king who, when riding through a forest, suddenly encounters an evil witch. The witch announces that the king is destined to meet ill fortune at some stage in his life, and gives him the choice of having the ill fortune bestowed upon him now or at a later date. The king decides, after consulting his wife, that it would be better for him to meet his fate now, while still in his prime and able to cope with it. Upon making this choice, the king loses his status and kingdom to a warring neighbor, and is forced to take his family and flee. After wandering for days, with little food and nowhere to go, the king decides that it would be more beneficial if he, the queen, and their two sons abandoned the sons' wives, who, as young and naive women, are nothing but a burden to the party. The two princesses thus awake one morning to find their husbands and family gone. So begins the story of Wahda and her sister.

Finding themselves alone, Wahda quickly assumes control of the situation. She journeys with her sister to the next town, selling jewelry so that both can buy clothes, food, and a place in which to live. Demonstrating her resourcefulness, Wahda decides to dress herself "as a man, because cities are full of people of both good character and bad and two beautiful, inexperienced women on their own would not have been safe…" (199). What follows is a magical tale of courage and fortitude, in which a young woman considered to be worthless by her husband and family achieves wondrous feats of bravery and wit in her quest to be reunited with the man she still loves, despite his abandoning her.[1]

The construction of masculinity in "What Will Be, Will Be" is perplexing because of its contradictory nature. The text weaves the usual gender conventions of fairy tales with its own brand of oppositional gender frameworks, resulting in a construction of gender that is unique in its refusal to be categorized. The narrative begins with a king, and the story initially positions him as its primary character. This king displays, however, a form of masculinity that juxtaposes conventionality with a more challenging and atypical gender construction. When told by the witch that he must make a fundamental choice regarding his destiny, the king falters:

> The King hesitated. It was a difficult question and how could he answer it without asking his Queen? After all, her life would be affected and so would that of their two young sons and the two sisters, their wives. Though of course, the young princesses would go where their husbands went and do as they were told. (196)

The king's behavior in this instance would not be considered "masculine" in the traditional sense of the word. Rather than being headstrong and decisive, attributes conventionally considered to be masculine, he declines to make his choice before consulting his wife. He also displays the virtue of empathy in his acknowledgment that the decision will ultimately affect his wife as much as himself, as well as their family, and that therefore she should play an equal part in its making. The king's capacity to consider the implications of this decision for his loved ones is also an ability not generally associated with masculinity, but rather with the feminine values of sensitivity and emotion. These interesting beginnings, however, are overshadowed by the patriarchal comment that follows them which restores the traditional gender equilibrium: "Though of course, the young princesses would go where their husbands went and do as they were told." In spite of this return to gender conventionality, the potential for interrogating gender binaries has been sown, waiting only for Wahda to awaken it. Until this incident, "What Will Be, Will Be" unfolds as any familiar fairy tale should. Yet instead of continuing to narrate the king's ordeal, the story departs, in dramatic fashion, to document the fortunes of the two abandoned women. The king's narrative is never revisited. In contrast to the foreshadowed gloom that has permeated the text thus far, an entirely different tone is created once the tale's protagonist has changed. Defying the conventional behavior appropriate to her sex, Wahda (who has previously been referred to only as the "older sister") masterfully assumes control of what appears to be an ill-fated and hopeless situation and is finally given a name:

"We must find them," declared the older sister immediately.

"But they have left us here to fend for ourselves."

"Ah," replied the older one dismissively, "we would have done the same in a few days. Besides, we can do better because without them no one will recognize us."

"But where will we find them?" asked the younger, feeling hurt and frightened.

"Leave it to me," responded the older. (199)

Wahda's masculinity is accepted and admired by all whom she/he meets in her/his adventures. The king is so impressed by Wahda that he makes her/him his personal bodyguard, a position of great honor, bestowing on her/him "a mansion befitting a personal aids of the King" (201). Wahda's masculine persona also impresses the women whose village she cleverly rescues from the clutches of an ogre who eats human flesh. Not only are these women in awe of Wahda the young man, but they also find him sexually attractive. Although this presupposes a heterosexual paradigm of desire, the fact that Wahda is biologically female and arouses feelings of sexual attraction in other females offers readers a more subversive queer paradigm from which to interpret the situation:

> Then Wahda returned to the old woman, who was now a different person, all cuddles and kisses and blessings and her daughter all smiles and guiles and flirtation—because, don't forget, she thought Wahda was a young man. What a well-favoured young man and how brave and big-hearted! (206)

The narrator unambiguously reminds the reader that Wahda is not male, as she appears to the old woman and her daughter, but this assertion is closely followed (in a subtle change of narrative focalizers) by the ecstatic pronouncement of the two women on the virtue of Wahda's masculine subjectivity. The juxtaposition of these two conflicting statements concerning Wahda's gender identity furthers the text's construction of gender as indefinite and subject to variation. This incident also explicitly demonstrates that not only has Wahda succeeded in her cross-dressing goal, but she has also accomplished a masculine performance so spectacularly good that both men and women are attracted to the persona she creates. On the night of her wedding to the ogre and ogress's foster daughter, "the young woman was waiting for Wahda decked in gorgeous clothes and jewels from top to toe…. When she saw her future husband enter, she rose slowly from her bed, walked over and threw her arms around his neck" (219). To this woman, Wahda is the perfect incarnation of masculinity. When Wahda does not return her initial embrace, she is discouraged only because she thinks that it may be through a fault of her own. Wahda proceeds to tell her that she is a female, not a male, but the young woman refuses to be disheartened: "… I feel what I feel," she declared, "whether you are a man or a woman…" (221).

The strength of feeling which Wahda generates in the hearts of those she encounters throughout "What Will Be, Will Be" is so great that even upon the revelation of her true biological status she is still revered. In the context of this narrative, gender is never quite what meets the eye. The feminine becomes the masculine; heterosexual attraction becomes homosexual; and the traditional indicators of gender become obsolete in relation to the perceived sex of the protagonist and the varied responses that her cross-dressing performance engenders. The gendered relationships portrayed in "What Will Be, Will Be" never conform to established social conventions, seeking instead to disrupt preconceived notions relating to masculine and feminine gendered persons by demonstrating the artificiality of such constructs through the behavior and actions of a cross-dressing subject—a subject who essentially belongs to neither category, yet also belongs to both in his/her amalgamation and reconstruction of masculine and feminine gendered behaviors.

The extent of Wahda's cross-dressing success can be measured, somewhat ironically, at the point in the text in which her "true" biological identity is revealed and her masculine persona is exposed as a cross-dressing "performance." This revelation is made to the king himself, whose apparent homoerotic feelings at least in part informed his motivation for promoting Wahda to positions which required constant contact with him, and it is this intimacy which confirms the authenticity of Wahda's masculine performance. When she informs him that she is actually a woman, he is astounded:

> Well, the King was beside himself with a flurry of different emotions and thoughts and questions. What was happening? How had she concealed her true self for so long? Who was she? Why was she disguised? (229)

Wahda's cross-dressing accomplishments are absolute, and her success is almost unparalleled within the realm of female cross-dressing narratives. The revelation of Wahda's biology is voluntary, rather than being discovered by other characters in the text, though the voluntary disrobing and self-chosen moment of biological honesty do seem to be facilitated by the relative brevity of the fairy tale form. Female cross-dressing constructions in novel-length stories are often less capable of providing such comprehensive cross-dressing success, for a number of reasons that will now be discussed.

SUCCESS AND FAILURE: COMPROMISED MASCULINE PERFORMANCES

Novel-length texts which include the female-to-male cross-dressing theme, such as *Alanna*, Terry Pratchett's *Monstrous Regiment,* and Robin McKinley's *Rose Daughter,* necessarily involve a more detailed portrayal of the female cross-dresser and her exploits due to the longer duration of the narrative. Her cross-dressing identity must be sustained over a greater period of time, therefore providing more opportunities for her gendered deceit to be discovered. These texts provide an interesting counterpoint to the totality of cross-dressing success in "What Will Be, Will Be." *Rose Daughter* and *Monstrous Regiment,* in particular, are texts that fulfill several criteria of the female-to-male cross-dressing paradigm, but produce a significantly different result in their representation of masculinity and level of cross-dressing triumph. In spite of each novel's shortcomings—which relate to the construction of masculinity and the use of conventions particular to a specific genre that are already gendered in traditional ways, hence restricting the cross-dresser's ability to interrogate and redefine conventional assumptions about masculinity and femininity—both Pratchett and McKinley bring the socially constructed nature of gender to the reader's attention. And while these novels may be less pioneering in their approach to gender than other examples of female cross-dressing, such as "What Will Be, Will Be," their ideological construction of gender advocates the transgression and subversion of conventional gender categories that limit individual agency.

Monstrous Regiment conforms almost absolutely to the female cross-dressing paradigm: the story opens with Polly, its heroine, disguising herself as a boy and then stealing away from home at dawn in order to join the army. Like Alanna and Mulan, Polly lives in a society that rigorously restricts feminine behavior. Pratchett's novel (*Monstrous Regiment* is part of the Discworld series) is set in the fantasy country of Borogravia, a preindustrialized society with comically archaic rules and cultural practices that parody historical Britain. Polly is the daughter of an innkeeper who has raised her to assist him in running the inn, despite prohibitions on women being involved in such activities.

Borogravia is subject to the rule of an autocratic duchess (who may or may not be alive), who governs with the authority of the god Nuggan, according to whom most things are an "abomination," including the color blue (22). As such, "Polly's mother had taught her to read, which was acceptable to Nuggan, and her father made sure that she learned how to write, which was not. A woman who could write was an Abomination unto Nuggan, according to Father Jupe; anything she wrote would by definition be a lie" (37).

The novel implies that Polly occupies a position of ostracized femininity at the commencement of the narrative because of her physical appearance (her body lacks the appropriate feminine curves [9, 11]) and she has rejected the feminine behavioral codes in relation to education, but the text also suggests that Polly's failure to adhere to the prescriptive requirements of conventional femininity is minimized through parental support and also takes place within a social context where compliance with all of the "abominations" of Nuggan is almost impossible. The opening paragraph uses cross-dressing to problematize Polly's perceptions of her gender identity, adroitly displaying Polly's conflicted attitude to stereotypical femininity as she cuts off her beautiful hair:

> Polly cut off her hair in front of the mirror, feeling slightly guilty about not feeling very guilty about doing so. It was supposed to be her crowning glory, and everyone said it was beautiful, but she generally wore it in a net when she was working. She'd always told herself it was wasted on her. But she was careful to see that the long golden coils all landed on the small sheet spread out for the purpose. (9)

Polly does not feel remorse at the loss of her "crowning glory," but realizes that she should, because it is considered to epitomize the conventional standards of feminine beauty. This realization produces guilt, because she becomes aware that her behavior is "unfeminine." The construction of the last three sentences reproduced above is a series of assertions about femininity, quickly countered by qualifying statements (indicated by the repetitive "but") which undermine the previous assertion. The first shows Polly's rejection of societal attitudes to femininity; the second demonstrates her reluctant adherence. Polly's careful preservation of her one truly feminine physical attribute demonstrates her attachment to it, notwithstanding her acknowledgment that it is impractical (much like other traditionally feminine clothing). Alanna's and Mulan's initial reactions to their cross-dressed appearance are quite different, characterized by eagerness and anticipation rather than the same confliction that Polly experiences: when Alanna first sees herself in a mirror, she grins (9); Mulan's excitement is conveyed by a dramatic change in the musical soundtrack, the increased volume and pulsating beat representative of her exhilaration.

Polly's performance of masculinity once she enlists in the army is almost faultless because she at once recognizes that gender is constituted through a series of learned behaviors and gestures. Working at her father's inn has made her a keen observer of men, and Polly is much more conscious of the behavioral requirements for a successful masculine performance than other female cross-dressers such as Alanna and Mulan: Polly is quick to modify her walking style and tone of voice, as well as adopting a general attitude of exaggerated bravado: "'You have to try to occupy a lot of space, she thought. It makes you look bigger, like a tomcat fluffing his tail. She'd seen it a lot in the inn. The boys tried to walk big in self-defense against all those other big boys out there. I'm bad, I'm fierce, I'm cool...'" (11). The shifting narration used in this passage, from second to third to first person, foregrounds the novel's thematic exploration of gender as performance. First, the reader is directly addressed, positioned (with Polly) in the role of female cross-dresser. Next, this direct form of address is replaced by a more distant third-person narration—a transitional sentence—which tells where Polly's knowledge of masculinity comes from. Finally, the reader is placed in a masculine subject position that emulates the coercive power of regulatory gender stereotypes. Pratchett's skill as a writer is demonstrated with great aptitude here, as he linguistically represents the cross-dressing process—using shifts in narrative point of view to demonstrate the transformation of Polly's subjectivity from femininity to masculinity.

Polly's cross-dressing success is more difficult to measure than other examples of female cross-dressing because as the narrative progresses, it becomes clear that each member of Polly's military unit is actually a cross-dressed girl. The one exception is Lieutenant Blouse, a "tired, skinny man" (66) whose military inexperience and fearful response to the realities of war strike an amusing contrast with his regiment of cross-dressed girls, all of whom perform masculinity much more effectively than he is able to. The character of Blouse acutely focuses the novel's thematic exploration of gender performativity in two distinct ways. First, the name "Blouse," which is bestowed upon a male character who is the antithesis of hegemonic masculinity, establishes a relationship between language and gender, revealing that gender can be linguistically (as well as behaviorally) constituted. The article of feminine clothing from which Blouse gets his name positions him as feminine from the outset, and his one truly valuable characteristic within a military context, his ability to think laterally, coincides with the marking of this skill as feminine in both *Alanna* and *Mulan*. Blouse's attitude to his identifiably feminine name is highly satirical, because his greatest desire is, in his own words, "to win the highest accolade that a gallant officer may obtain... .Having either a foodstuff or an item of clothing named after one" (265). The irony of Blouse's ambition is that his role model is General Froc, who got both: "The frock coat and Beef Froc. Of course I could never aspire *that* high" (265). Blouse's failure to identify "frock" as a signifier of feminine clothing is amusing, the irony of his omission reflective of his similar failure to notice that he is surrounded by a regiment of cross-dressed women. Blouse's hero, General Froc, later turns out to be a cross-dressing woman also, a revelation that makes Blouse's aspiration all the more humorous in its inversion of the patriarchal gender binary. The girls' performance of masculinity accentuates the relationship between language and gender, as Polly is quick to notice that not only behavior, but also speech is regulated according to gender. Because their masculine behavior is generally appropriate, it is the girls' unconscious use of gendered language which reveals the truth of their sex:

> "Now, I say a man who knows how to cook is no less of a man for that. But a man who says "sugar" when he swears? Have you *ever* heard a man say that? (80)

Second, it is Blouse who is responsible for drawing a direct correlation between cross-dressing and performance. After some not-so-subtle prodding from Polly, Blouse devises the plan to infiltrate the enemy Zlobenian castle by cross-dressing himself as a washerwoman. (The plan parodies a similar incident in Kenneth Grahame's *The Wind in the Willows* (1908), where Toad disguises himself as a washerwoman to escape from gaol.) Jackrum, when he hears of Blouse's plan, protests, "... dressing up as washerwomen is for gettin' *out* of places! Milit'ry rules!" (217). Blouse's naiveté in electing himself as the only member of the squad capable of giving a convincing feminine performance is highly comic, but it simultaneously draws an effective analogy between gender and performance for a number of different reasons:

> "Well, I'm clearly the only one who's had any practice," said Blouse, rubbing his hands together. "At my old school, we were in and out of skirts all the time." He looked around at the circle of absolutely expressionless faces. "Theatricals, you see?" he said brightly. "No gels at our boarding school, of course. But we didn't let *that* stop us." (219)

Blouse's remarks are pertinent because they are a forewarning of what happens to the girls shortly afterward: having performed masculinity for such a long period, they have forgotten how to be feminine and are immediately identified as males when they enter the castle. Blouse, however, remains unnoticed. His regular performance of femininity in his school "theatricals" has given him practice at behaving like a woman, which is also perhaps why his own masculine identity is so inadequate.

Monstrous Regiment ingeniously exposes how gender ideologies are inscribed and reproduced through language usage and behavior, focusing primarily on masculinity —as it is performed by the female cross-dressers, and not performed by a biologically male character like Blouse. The novel's title is indicative of its gender-oriented theme, as Pratchett's use of the phrase "Monstrous Regiment" is a reference to John Knox's famous essay of 1558, "The First Blast of the Trumpet Against the Monstrous Regiment of Women," which decried the rule of women over men. Knox's work was directed at the female monarchs of his time, Mary Queen of Scots and Mary Tudor, and his use of the word "regiment" was a reference to government rather than the military (Montrose 2002, 908). Pratchett has borrowed and reinterpreted Knox's conservative denunciation of female rule, employing the word "regiment" in its now more commonly used military sense, in order to parody Knox's reactionary gender treatise. The central characters of *Monstrous Regiment* are all cross-dressed women, an aspect that distinguishes Pratchett's novel from other examples of female cross-dressing literature, but this ultimately proves to be troublesome because it turns cross-dressing into a repetitive joke, lessening its impact as a strategy for meaningful gender criticism. The level of cross-dressing success that Polly's squad achieves is consequently marred by the fact that their masculine disguise rarely has to be effective in the eyes of biological men. Furthermore, the risks involved with detection within the unit are minimized when each member is the perpetrator of a similar misdemeanor.

Despite its adherence to the structure of the female cross-dressing paradigm, *Monstrous Regiment* fails to accomplish a similar level of sophistication in the gender criticism it tenders. The reasons for this failure include its reliance on dialogue as the primary narrative mode, which limits each character's ability to be introspective about her cross-dressing; its satiric tone, which is dependent on an observational style of comedy that is outward- rather than inward-looking (and similarly limits character interiority); and generic conventions that reinscribe conventional constructions of masculinity and femininity. Like a film or play with an ensemble cast, *Monstrous Regiment* draws on the conventions of these two genres by using dialogue as its central means for plot and character development. The novel's use of dialogue is effective at expressing the intersubjective nature of individual subjectivity, particularly in relation to the processes that inform Polly's self-awareness and character progression, but at the same time Polly's ability for self-reflection is hampered by this conversational discourse. Roberta Seelinger Trites suggests that a character's subjectivity can be measured by investigating how "the dialogics of the text have enabled a character to perceive herself in more than one subject position" (1997, 31). Polly demonstrates that she is capable of such differentiation at the beginning of the story, as she tentatively adopts new behaviors and transforms her identity from masculinity to femininity, but her interior voice is often stifled. For example, a crucial moment in Polly's cross-dressing-influenced consciousness of gendered behavior and gendered appearances occurs just after she has enlisted in the army, where Jackrum, a sergeant, helpfully points out that her masculine disguise is flawed in one aspect—she lacks male genitals:

"A pair of socks?" she said.

"Right. Wear 'em," said the mystery voice hoarsely.

"Thank you, but I've brought several pairs…" Polly began.

"There was a faint sigh. "No. Not on your feet. Shove 'em down the front of your trousers."

"What do you mean?"

"Look," said the whisperer patiently, "you don't bulge where you shouldn't bulge. That's good. But you don't bulge where you should bulge, either. You know? Lower down?

"Oh! Er…I…but…I didn't think people noticed…," said Polly, glowing with embarrassment. (38–39)

Polly's whispered conversation with Jackrum highlights her naiveté with regard to her physical shortcomings, as well as playfully suggesting that "bulging" in the right place is just as important as looking and behaving like a male (a comic, literal reference to the primary role of the phallus within patriarchal constructions of masculinity). However, her reaction to this revelation is restricted to the response she gives Jackrum. Polly's embarrassment is incorporated into the novel's narration, shown to readers rather than explored. Her self-reflexive narration at the commencement of the novel, which articulately uses the cross-dressing process to comment on cultural gender practices, dwindles as the plot develops. Polly's previously perceptible interiority is curtailed either by scenes constructed entirely out of dialogue; scenes where Polly is not present; or scenes in which Polly's perceptions are directed at observing and reflecting upon the behavior of others, rather than herself (for a large part of the novel she participates in a game of trying to "out" the other members of the squad as females).

Much like children's retellings of the Joan of Arc legend, *Monstrous Regiment* limits the interiority of its cross-dressing characters. Cross-dressing accordingly functions on a public rather than a personal level, contextualized within the specific setting of the story and perceived from an exterior perspective. The lack of character interiority in Joan of Arc retellings produces a construction of Joan as a remote and somehow "unhuman" character, but *Monstrous Regiment* partly avoids this through its use of a satiric narrative mode. The novel constantly pokes fun at individual characters and their behavior, and Polly's self-deprecating attitude is immediately endearing. Pratchett playfully ridicules his characters' behavior, using the fantasy context of the war between the Borogravians and Zlobenians to comment upon a wide variety of social and political phenomena, such as military codes of honor, figurehead monarchies, fundamentalist religions, and, of course, gender stereotypes. As with most parody that is intended to function as social commentary, Pratchett's comedy is typically observational, characterized by its propensity to look outward, rather than inward. As the central focalizing character, Polly's thoughts therefore tend to focus on her perceptions of others, instead of herself, deflecting the reader away from her own subjective development throughout the cross-dressing process.

Genre also contributes to *Monstrous Regiment's* less successful construction of female cross-dressing as a strategy for gender criticism. Although Pratchett's novel aspires to provide a progressive deconstruction of normative gender categories, it is restricted by generic conventions that implicitly reinforce stereotypical gender constructions. Located in a fantasy world that replicates the cultural and political institutions and ideologies which existed in a preindustrialized Britain, the novel imitates the patriarchal gender system of this historical era. The heightened awareness with which *Monstrous Regiment* treats the idea of a gender performance indicates an obvious interest in reassessing social constructions of gender, but this concern is undermined by the conventional representations of masculinity and femininity favored by the text. Set within the militaristic framework of warfare, *Monstrous Regiment* draws on a narrowly constructed definition of masculinity wherein attributes such as aggression, authoritarianism, and self-preservation are marked as key indicators. This type of masculinity is clearly a parody of masculine behavior in times of battle, but Pratchett's satiric construction of masculinity undermines any attempt to evaluate its social construction in a more serious or critical fashion. For instance, as indicated in the passage quoted above, the eventual key to Polly's cross-dressing success is nothing but a pair of socks.

The socks scene also reveals the vulnerability of the masculine disguises adopted by Polly and other members of her squad. Polly's biological sex is discovered on the first night after she enlists (which could set a record for swift detection in female cross-dressing narratives), and the sex of each of her comrades is gradually revealed as the story progresses; it is also replicated at the close of the novel, when they are "revealed" again. By the time the narrative climax occurs, when Polly and her cross-dressed squad secretly invade the enemy Zlobenian castle, the reader is acutely aware that the entire military unit is made up of young women. Acting in accordance with Blouse's plan, the girls dress themselves as washerwomen in the Shakespearean style of double disguise: they are women disguised as men disguised as women. Once they are inside the castle, they are detected by Zlobenian soldiers, who identify the girls as men because they "walk wrong and…stand wrong" (254). This doubling of the girls' cross-dressing disguise has the potential to problematize conventional gender categories but does not, instead turning the situation into a comical farce. Admittedly, the cross-dressed girls react rather ingeniously to this mistaken gender identification—deciding to give an overt performance of femininity to the skeptical guards—but their performance is arranged for comic, rather than critical, effect and is based on a caricature of femininity: Shufti, one of the cross-dressers, reacts to the Zlobenian guards' mistake by "raising her skirt," while Tonker bursts into tears, "accompanied by a long, mournful wail as she threw herself on to the floor" (254). The artfulness of this performance is exposed by Tonker's next comment, which is whispered into Polly's ear "between howls": "If you can take him down I can garrotte the other one with my apron string" (255).

Tonker's remark exemplifies the predicament that plagues the representation of cross-dressing in *Monstrous Regiment*. Situated in a fantasy world that relies on a stereotypical construction of the patriarchal gender binary for much of its humor, it is not possible for a narrative that employs such polarized definitions of masculinity and femininity (particularly in relation to its cross-dressed heroines themselves) to provide a meaningful critique of gender. Unlike Alanna and Mulan, who are better "men" than their biological peers because they perform masculinity successfully but at the same time incorporate elements of femininity into their behavior as they see fit, the female soldiers of *Monstrous Regi-*

ment simply echo the conventional form of masculinity favored within the culture of their army. This point is best illustrated in the climactic scene where Polly and the other members of her squad come before a tribunal constituted by the commanders of their own army, which has been called for the purpose of disciplining the squad in relation to their cross-dressing misdemeanors. The girls are about to be imprisoned for defying the tribunal's orders (which involve making the girls lie about their achievements and paying them off with a dowry), when Sergeant Jackrum arrives and startlingly reveals that half the commanding officers and generals of the Borogravian army are actually women in disguise. Although the scene takes place within a room filled entirely with cross-dressed women, the only gendered behavior on display is stereotypically masculine. The cross-dressed officers and generals show no mercy to the cross-dressed women standing before them, conversely treating them in a misogynist and dismissive fashion. Sergeant Jackrum (who is also revealed to be a biological female at the narrative's end[2]) responds in similarly stereotypical masculine fashion by blackmailing the cross-dressed military personnel with the threat of exposure if they do not treat his squad with more respect—a strategic maneuver flavored with Machiavellian (i.e., masculine) political cunning.

When Polly declares that the key to success in her world is "trousers" (244), she is actually making a pronouncement about the rigid gender structures of her society that appear to be invulnerable to change or subversion. Alanna and Mulan make a much more profound discovery as a result of their cross-dressing. For them, cross-dressing has allowed them to become aware of the socially constructed nature of gender rather than reinforcing the inferiority of women within a patriarchal society. Alanna and Mulan are both happy to return to their former feminine status after their cross-dressing disguise has been revealed, yet each does so with an altered appreciation of the ways in which the world is gendered. Most important, they return to their feminine gender position as triumphant and publicly lauded heroines, having also convinced others that the restrictions placed on feminine behavior are unnecessary and worthy of transgression. Polly's achievements are considerably less spectacular (which she self-consciously acknowledges at the close of the narrative as she sets out, cross-dressed, to enlist for a second time in the army). Notwithstanding the binary representation of masculinity and femininity in *Monstrous Regiment,* which circumvents the cross-dressers' ability to destabilize or subvert either category of gender particularly effectively, Pratchett's novel provides a shrewd counterpoint to the more widespread depiction of female cross-dressing. His novel sharply draws reader attention to the concept of gender as a performance, but his heavy reliance on dialogue, limited character focalization, and the generic conventions of both fantasy and comedy effectively derail *Monstrous Regiment* from achieving greater critical success in relation to the deconstruction of conventional gender categories. If anything, the novel successfully reveals that the gendered conventions of certain literary genres and styles of writing are difficult to escape, regardless of theme or authorial intention. *Monstrous Regiment* does, however, effectively highlight the socially constructed nature of gender because even though its female cross-dressing characters mimic rather than subvert the conventional signifiers of masculinity, the act of gender mimicry which they perform is in itself a powerful reminder that gender is a socially contrived, instead of "natural," phenomenon.

REVISIONS OF TRADITIONAL FAIRY TALES: CROSS-DRESSING, GENDER, AND GENRE

The cross-dressing which occurs in McKinley's Beauty-and-the-Beast novel, *Rose Daughter*, is difficult to compare to *Monstrous Regiment* because it happens on a much more insignificant scale. It is not Beauty, the main female protagonist, who cross-dresses. Instead it is her sister Lionheart, a peripheral character, who cross-dresses only for a brief period. As Beauty is the novel's focalizing character and her experiences with the Beast are central, Lionheart's cross-dressing is relegated to a minor story line. In conjunction with *Monstrous Regiment*, *Rose Daughter* illustrates how the scale of female cross-dressing behavior can affect its narrative construction. The two novels represent different cross-dressing extremes—*Monstrous Regiment* tackles female cross-dressing in a grand and sweeping manner, applying the concept of gender performance to all of its characters, most of whom are women in disguise; *Rose Daughter's* treatment of cross-dressing is of considerably less consequence, practiced by a minor and nonfocalizing character whose own perceptions of her cross-dressing behavior are never directly addressed. These differences produce unexpectedly similar results, because in each novel the exaggerated scale of the cross-dressing contributes to a limited narrative construction of subjectivity. Unless the cross-dresser can scrutinize her behavior both before, during, and after cross-dressing —reflecting on her feminine subjectivity, articulating her conformity or nonconformity to conventional stereotypes of femininity, identifying how she must modify her behavior in order to give a convincing masculine performance, and always conscious of the reactions her gendered behavior produces in others—its significance as a strategy for gender criticism cannot be fully realized. The female cross-dressers of *Monstrous Regiment* and *Rose Daughter* are unable to participate in this kind of introspective evaluation of their cross-dressing, as their limited ability to focalize encumbers their construction as emotionally complex characters.

McKinley's text follows the conventional path—with Beauty leaving her family, joining the Beast, and eventually learning to love him, at which point the magical spell cast on him is lifted. So intrinsic are Beauty's family to the tale that they provide an interesting twist to the conventional fairy tale ending: when the spell is finally lifted, Beauty chooses to shun the life of a queen or princess (depending on which version of the story you are accustomed to) and to bring her new husband home to live in the family's cottage, where he retains his beastly shape. The decision is the result of Beauty's great affection for her father and sisters and the prominence they have played throughout the tale. Beauty's relationship with her sisters is paramount to the text, and the reason why McKinley breathes life into the characters of the two sisters, Lionheart and Jeweltongue. Lionheart's cross-dressing is motivated by the misfortune that falls upon her father at the beginning of the story, forcing the family to sell their belongings and move to a far-off town. Compelled to rely on their own resources for the first time, they rebuild their dilapidated cottage, and one of the sisters, the brash and outspoken Lionheart, dresses herself as a man in order to gain employment. Although Lionheart's cross-dressing does not attain the same level of success achieved by other cross-dressing heroines such as Wahda, Alanna, or Mulan, it is a unique and engaging inclusion in *Rose Daughter* and also in terms of the female-to-male cross-dressing paradigm.

In contrast to *Monstrous Regiment*, which closely replicates the female cross-dressing paradigm, Lionheart's cross-dressing differs greatly from the representation of cross-dressing in texts such as *Alanna, Mulan,* or "What Will Be, Will Be." Unlike the female characters typical of the paradigm, Lionheart's action does not originate from a position of ostracized femininity that is constrained by patriarchal social structures. In *Alanna* the female protagonist is disillusioned by the expectations of femininity, unable to comprehend why she should be locked up inside, learning to sew and dance like a lady, when she would much rather be outside riding horses and practicing to wield her sword. In *Mulan*, the protagonist fails to be feminine. She is unable to master feminine skills, culminating in her disastrous performance at the matchmaker's ceremony. Mulan is not particularly masculine—in fact, she is presented on screen as a typically pretty young woman—she simply falls short of the standards of femininity which the film depicts as a comically absurd stifling of individuality. Lionheart, in contrast, is not portrayed as failing or lacking in any respect. Unlike Mulan or Alanna, she finds herself in the unique position of being permitted to act as she pleases—without criticism or aspersions being cast upon her femininity. Allowed to behave as she chooses, she willfully embodies many of the attributes that are stereotypically considered to be masculine. She storms in and out of the text, raising her voice, gesturing aggressively, and generally creating a certain degree of havoc. The language McKinley uses to describe her is always heavily endowed with militarist metaphors, emphasizing Lionheart's warlike aggression and manner:

> "I didn't know flowers could look like this!" roared Lionheart, and threw up her arms as if challenging an enemy to look at her, and laughed. ([1997] 2002, 9)

Lionheart is audacious and free-spirited, exhibiting behavior that would generally be considered conventionally masculine. Discussing her lack of feminine social graces, she tells Beauty: "I'll try to be polite, but when some buffoon is yammering away at me, my mind goes blank of anything but wanting to knock 'em down and sit on 'em" (25). Lionheart's comment reverses the subordinated feminine subject position typical of "good" fairy tale characters in this particular instance because of its combative attitude, but her character is never completely alienated from conventional feminine discourses. Although her behavior is unusual for a woman, her pride in her appearance is not:

> Lionheart's careless tone did not disguise her bitterness, nor did her sisters miss the glance she gave to her hands. In the old days they had all had lady's hands; even the callouses Lionheart had from riding were smooth, cushioned by the finest kid riding gloves, pumiced and lotioned by her maid. (34)

Lionheart's behavior is often at odds with the stereotypical standards of femininity, but this does not cause her feminine subjectivity to be compromised. In *Mulan*, the protagonist's greatest feminine failure occurs during the matchmaker's ceremony. The prospect of Mulan never being able to marry is the greatest of disgraces in the eyes of her parents and the village community. In *Rose Daughter*, however, Lionheart's impending marriage to an incredibly eligible young man forms part of the book's opening scenes. The marriage is canceled, because of her father's financial disaster, but Lionheart's romantic prospects are not diminished and she quickly finds love again. Lionheart is also perfectly capable of performing feminine tasks, such as cooking, although she does so in true aggressive form. Her decision to dress as a man in order to obtain employment and much-needed money for the family is not greeted with horror or dismay by her tolerant family. Lionheart confides in her sisters almost from the beginning, and they cheerfully assist with her disguise: "Beauty trimmed her sister's hair and then swept the silky tufts into a tiny pile..." (32).

The most significant disparity between Lionheart's cross-dressing and the female-to-male cross-dressing depicted in texts such as *Mulan*, *Alanna*, "What Will Be, Will Be," and *Monstrous Regiment* is that it occurs outside the text. The novel chiefly takes place in two settings, Rose Cottage, where Beauty's family lives, and the Beast's palace, which becomes Beauty's new home. Lionheart begins cross-dressing before Beauty has left for the palace, but the story only recounts her presence when she is at home:

> Neither Jeweltongue nor Beauty saw Lionheart leave, but both saw her return. They had not immediately recognised her. A very handsome young man had burst into the house at early twilight, with the light behind him, and they had stared up in alarm at the intrusion. Lionheart looked at their frightened faces, and laughed, and pulled her hat off so they could see her face clearly.... Her sisters were speechless. (41–42)

Lionheart's disguise is relevant only to her employment, and thus is never in effect in her interactions with her family, where the narrative takes place. The story is focalized by Beauty, so Lionheart's representation is confined to her direct interactions with Beauty or else presented through Beauty's dreams of her family, visions that occur after she has left for the Beast's palace and which give the fragmented scenes she "sees" of her father and sisters a surreal, ghostly quality. Beauty's role as invisible observer is not omniscient; her perception of what she sees reveals her status as a spectator, not a participant: "Lionheart, at the kitchen table, beating something in a bowl..." (161). The visions also have a disjointed effect, because Beauty is forcefully plunged into and out of them, having little control over what she sees: "Beauty felt herself driven out of her own dream, pushed away..." (164). Beauty is unable to contextualize what she learns of her family's life during these night visions, and the reader's interpretation of her sisters' behavior is similarly disempowered. Lionheart and Jeweltongue have little interiority as characters, their subjectivities often disclosed by limited representations of their behavior and speech. Lionheart's interior voice is concealed, as is her performance of masculinity.

Lionheart is never presented within the text as a convincing male, despite enjoying freedoms that may have accommodated a genuine masculine performance. Readers are told that she cross-dresses for the purpose of her job, but her behavior is never shown or explored. Her sisters are aware of her cross-dressing from the outset and continue to treat her as a woman whenever she returns home, which is the only place that the reader can observe her. This said, Lionheart's portrayal in *Rose Daughter* does not occupy enough textual representation to be overly complex and radical, in terms of its feminist possibilities. In many respects, Lionheart is a two-dimensional character. She is wayward and destructive, and capable of defying certain feminine stereotypes, but is also essentially "womanly," as is evident in her failure to present as an authentic male—a failure so complete that it results in the creation of a romantic bond between herself and a heterosexual male. In similar situations which take place between a cross-dressed woman and male in more radical texts such as "What Will Be, Will Be" and "Secure at Last," the resulting relationships are much more elaborate, prompting more serious questions about the (homo)sexual nature of the bond between the cross-dresser and her male admirer.

Lionheart's failure as a cross-dresser is intrinsically related to the general conceptualization of masculinity in *Rose Daughter*—precisely the dilemma which compromises the construction of female cross-dressing in *Monstrous Regiment*. Although a small number of males feature in McKinley's text, masculinity is represented almost entirely in terms of the character of the Beast. The masculinity of the Beast permeates every page, and is constructed not only in terms of his description throughout but also through the reader's prior knowledge of the fairy tale on which *Rose Daughter* is based. His presence is anticipated from the outset, and thus gains potency from the expectation and legend that surround it. The Beast essentially represents masculinity in its most powerful form, and the reader's expectation of this portrayal is linked with various "masculine" expectations that have arisen from various retellings of this story over several hundred years. The Beast is both man and animal: enormous, hairy, and terrifying. He personifies physical power through his animalistic strength and stature, yet is also representative of masculine sexual power. He has demanded Beauty, a young woman, as compensation for her father's theft, and installs her in his deserted palace, over which he has complete control. Beauty's family is terrified that the Beast will kill or injure her, and their fear and her own assist in the construction of the Beast as a predator, both in terms of his strength and his domineering masculine sexuality. Even though Beauty soon learns that the Beast wishes her no harm, and treats her tenderly and with the utmost respect, her own fear of him is palpable. His outward appearance and potential for violence always pose a mask that it is difficult for Beauty—or the reader—to look behind. In terms of this representation, Lionheart's attempts at creating any form of realistic masculinity are destined to fail, overshadowed as they are by this basic construction of animalistic "maleness." And indeed, Lionheart does fail to convince others that she is genuinely masculine.

Similar patriarchal conventions are evident in *Monstrous Regiment*, but it strategically uses cross-dressing to bring the usually invisible cultural gender practices to the attention of Polly and the reader alike. Polly's cross-dressing exploits are not particularly successful at challenging normative constructions of gender (since they merely convince her that to have any impact in her world, she is required to wear trousers) but they do enable her to see the constructedness of masculinity. Polly acknowledges her own cross-dressing failure ("it had been a *joke*" [349]), but her cross-dressing facilitates the realization that she can elect to reject the life of passivity traditionally deemed appropriate for women. Her development as a character is indicated by her resolve to begin again, armed with the discovery of her new knowledge. At the close of the novel, Polly inquisitively reasons, "How many ways can you fight a war?" (349), a question brimming with the possibility of hope for a different and more successful cross-dressing adventure in the future.

Rose Daughter's thematic achievements are more subtle, as it does not use Lionheart's cross-dressing to reevaluate conventional gender norms. Yet, it is successful at destabilizing assumptions about individual identity based on visual appearance. *Rose Daughter* revolves around the premise that things are not always what they initially appear to be. It warns that outward appearances can be deceiving and are often misguided, a concept that becomes literal in the representation of the Beast's palace, where corridors, doorways, and furniture constantly shift and change, much to the consternation of Beauty. This theme is embodied most obviously in the character of the Beast, who inhabits a horrific body within which lives a gentle and intelligent man who is undeserving of the fear that his outward appearance generates. Beauty must learn to look beyond outward signifiers and see the Beast for the man he truly is. Traditional versions of "Beauty and the Beast" also conform to this basic theme, yet their purpose is always to reinforce gender divisions rather than oppose them.[3] McKinley's skill in retelling and reworking this fairy tale is that she attempts to deconstruct its original gender ideology (and mythology) to the point that only the most fundamental principle remains—that outward appearances can often create an illusion far removed from actual reality.

McKinley's approach in *Rose Daughter* is understated rather than radical. Her story ends traditionally, with Beauty's marriage to the

Beast, but the most significant difference between *Rose Daughter* and the original fairy tale is that the Beast does not revert to his former human shape in McKinley's text. Neither do he and Beauty become king and queen after they marry, nor do they take up residence in his palace. The conclusion of *Rose Daughter* is reworked into one of feminine victory, as it is Beauty who chooses her own and the Beast's decidedly unconventional fate. These changes to the traditional text are foreshadowed by McKinley's treatment of gender throughout, a treatment that specifically focuses on each character's lack of traditional gender conformity. Beauty herself is an alienated outsider—a young girl who shuns the bourgeois frivolities of her sisters' lives. Her father is introduced as a man who has similarly failed to live up to the conventional expectations of masculine success, as he has lost his fortune and is responsible for his family's financial ruin. In keeping with this, Lionheart is a woman who refuses to be limited by traditional feminine expectations and lives up to the metaphor of her name through her willfulness and disregard of feminine propriety. These characters each present challenges to gender stereotypes, and their eventual encounter with the Beast provides the ultimate challenge to preconceived notions regarding physical appearance and biological makeup. The character of the Beast demonstrates figuratively that a person can essentially be very different from their outward, physical projection—and it is around this exact theme that female cross-dressing narratives revolve.

Texts such as *Alanna*, *Mulan*, "What Will Be, Will Be," and *Monstrous Regiment* address this notion directly through the actions and behavior of the cross-dressing heroine, who must convince both the reader and other characters that she is capable of a genuine masculine performance despite the impediment of her feminine biology. Her triumph necessarily invokes a rethinking of what it is that the cross-dresser herself, the other participants within the text, and ultimately the readers, consider to be the determining factors that constitute masculinity and femininity. Even a text such as *Monstrous Regiment*, which ultimately fails to provide a particularly insightful deconstruction of gender owing to its limited definitions of masculinity and femininity, encourages the implied reader to think about gender as socially constructed and performative.

Gender is not the most important factor in *Rose Daughter* (as the most significant review of initial impressions, based on what is signified visually, takes place in relation to the Beast), but its implication in the process of interpretation is validated. Female cross-dressing texts emphasize the fallibility of visual cues, particularly as they relate to the assessment of gender. They achieve this through the endless portrayal of characters that are not conventionally masculine or feminine, and by ultimately suggesting that it is not all-important to be considered as such. "What Will Be, Will Be" tells the story of a successful female cross-dresser, but at the same time is also a tale of a husband and father-in-law who initially epitomize masculinity in the traditional sense yet are ultimately reduced, in the text's conclusion, to men riddled with regret, poverty, and a complete lack of self-worth. This text also portrays an emperor unable to make or fulfill political strategies without assistance, which is then rendered by the cross-dressing protagonist. *Rose Daughter* contains characters that are also positioned outside of conventional categorizations.

The inescapable dilemma of female cross-dressing representations is that their potential for insightful gender criticism is contingent upon the use of narrative strategies which encourage readers to reflect on the responses and reactions it provokes—from both the perspective of the cross-dresser herself as well as from others who interact with her while she is disguised. Husain's tale "Secure at Last" provides an interesting remedy to the problems of limited focalization which plague *Monstrous Regiment* and *Rose Daughter*. This fairy tale relates the revelation of Sicurano's female sex from the perspective of the sultan, an unusual strategy that is highly effective in conveying the victorious nature of her masculine performance:

"I am a woman," she repeated.

The Sultan watched the transformation in amazement. He had never once doubted that Sicurano was who he appeared to be: a man—a very talented man.

He waited a moment, expecting the wisps of confusion to disperse and clarity to come. This was perhaps a dream from the early hours of morning. Any moment now, he would wake up and find that he had experienced a strange and detailed dream—a vision, almost....But when a few moments later the scene did not change or vanish and he found himself still on his throne and not in his bed, he knew he was firmly in reality...as he forced his mind to ingest and process the transformation of a man—and a pretty constant companion of his, at that—into a woman, he realized quite what a magnificent man Sicurano really was. And that this exceptional man had really been a woman meant that the woman was truly twice the paragon of virtue that anyone had ever claimed she was, for to be a woman and yet to be twice as good as a man...oh, stop! (73–74)

The profound nature of this man's reaction to the revelation that Sicurano is biologically female belies the depth of his affection for this young man/woman. His feelings are presented to the reader almost as if he were Sicurano's lover—a lover presented with a dilemma about his beloved, but whose adoration is so great that the discovery not only fails to jeopardize his love, but actually increases its depth. Unlike "What Will Be, Will Be," the homoerotic undertones of "Secure at Last" are implicit rather than explicit. The sultan's reaction illustrates the text's deconstructive approach to gender and its revision of gender myths as they apply to the construction of individual identity. In this context, the sultan's response is an affirmation of the fallibility of socially constructed gender stereotypes. The "uncovering" of Sicurano's/Zinevra's true identity makes no difference to his estimation of Sicurano's/Zinevra's worth as a human being, but serves only to make him admire the character even more. The exclamation "oh, stop!" which recalls the Sultan's reverie from an absurd aporia, is precisely illustrative of the response which stories of female cross-dressing wish to engender in relation to the application of conventional gender classifications and signifiers to their cross-dressing protagonists and, to a lesser extent, the secondary characters of the narratives. Although texts such as *Monstrous Regiment* and *Rose Daughter* are unable to fulfill this criterion in as specific a fashion, the issue of gender is nevertheless raised in relation to the way that we read, interpret, and evaluate the behavior of others.

In the words of Sigmund Freud, "When you meet a human being, the first distinction you make is 'male or female'?" and you are accustomed to make the distinction with unhesitating certainty" (cited in Garber [1992] 1993, 1). Female-to-male cross-dressing texts, however, are actively involved in challenging and destabilizing this notion. They strive to prove that the distinction between masculinity and femininity is never as clear, or as "readable," as it may initially seem. Within these texts gender is removed from the traditional and limiting categories of "masculinity" and "femininity," divisions created out of artifice and unworkable expectations, and reconstructed into a notion that is unfettered and autonomous. The "unhesitating certainty" of which Freud speaks is replaced by ambiguity and nuance, as each character within this paradigm asks only that they be considered on their own individual, ungendered terms. "Oh, stop!" is exactly what these cross-dressing texts ask of their readers in relation to interpreting the story of the cross-dresser in accordance with prevailing gender assumptions and categorizations. They demand instead that masculinity and femininity, and the supposedly "essential" behaviors, skills, and attributes associated with these two genders, be reassessed and reconstructed into something new and meaningful—a notion of gender based not on differences and divisions, but on intrinsically interwoven shades of gray, where lines can, and will, be crossed by autonomous individuals who exist above and beyond the limitations of "male" and "female."

5

FUNNY BOYS

Masculinity, Misogyny, and the Carnivalesque in Children's Male Cross-Dressing Literature

INTRODUCTION

Masculinity is a concept that is frequently addressed in children's cross-dressing narratives, through cross-dressing heroines who seek to replicate a masculine subjectivity while disguised as men. However, male characters that dress in women's clothing are rare. Presumably this is because adult cross-dressing is generally perceived as a male activity, and a sexual one at that, so it is unsurprising that literature for young audiences would wish to avoid any association with the complexities of the adult transgender world. Notwithstanding this disinclination, the tradition of female cross-dressing heroines in children's literature and film demonstrates that it is possible to use cross-dressing in a manner that is dissociated from adult transvestism, and that enables cross-dressing to function as an effective strategy for a critical examination of socially constructed gender categories. There has been much more hesitation to apply a similarly progressive gender ideology to the construction of male cross-dressing. Male cross-dressing is presented as comic, trivial, and humiliating for the masculine subject. In contrast to the feminine version, it reinforces socially prescribed gender categories rather than interrogating or challenging them.

When males dress up as girls, it is generally not for the purposes of a disguise designed to help them escape their previous masculine experience, as is the case with female characters. Instead, it is part of a brief theatrical "act" or performance, often presented to the reader or viewer as part of a comedy routine—the humor of which is based upon the male subject's inherent inability to give a convincing feminine performance. The incapacity of male cross-dressers to discard, albeit only temporarily, the behaviors and attributes they have internalized as socially appropriate indicators of masculinity stands in stark contrast to the manner in which female characters take on a similar task with relish and aplomb. Their lack of success makes a pointed statement about the powerful status of hegemonic masculinity, revealing the obvious unwillingness of masculine subjects to relinquish their traditional gender dominance by exploring any aspect of (obviously inferior) femininity. Children's literature containing male cross-dressing thus stands in disheartening contrast to its enlightened feminine formation. Instead of critically questioning the notion of gender to make a progressive statement about its application to individuals, male-to-female cross-dressing narratives seem unable to construct cross-dressing as anything other than a short-lived, often silly, comic gesture, preferring to use it as a means through which to reinforce oppositional gender relations.

The construction of female cross-dressing in children's texts as non-sexual and temporary behavior, and therefore unrelated to its existence in an adult context, is an approach that male cross-dressing representations also adopt. Nevertheless, male cross-dressing representations face a much harder task in dissociating themselves from the adult concepts of transvestism and transsexualism because of a popular perception that transvestites and transsexuals are male, rather than female. Children's literature typically handles the cultural association of male cross-dressing with (homo)sexuality in an extreme fashion, taking excessive care to ensure that the male protagonist's masculinity is not compromised by his cross-dressing behavior. The male character's cross-dressing transgression is generally presented as brief and humorous, followed by an exaggerated reassertion of his masculinity. This conscious attempt to reinstate the invulnerability of hegemonic masculinity, momentarily challenged by a cross-dressing interlude, often appears overly contrived, successful only in confirming the fragility of hegemonic masculinity as a socially constructed concept.

The behavioral achievements and public celebration of the cross-dressing heroine are prizes denied to the male cross-dresser. His transvestic exploits render him a more humble status because of the accompanying personal humiliation or public denigration. While a feminine subject appears to achieve a higher social status through her cross-dressed masculine performance, gaining the social privileges traditionally associated with masculinity, which she then astutely redeploys, the reverse occurs to masculine subjects who cross-dress as women. Instead, by relinquishing their primary phallic identification they also "lose" their social standing, a situation presented as humorous in most male-to-female cross-dressing texts. The loss of social status and agency that results from the male subject's cross-dressing induced exploration of femininity, regardless of its failure to reproduce any genuine feminine attributes or behavior, later becomes a condition in need of desperate remedy—prompting the reassertion of the male character's hegemonic masculinity. The heavy-handed nature of this reassertion ironically constructs patriarchal masculinity as easily susceptible to threat, a category of identity just as artificial as the feminine subjectivity forced upon the male cross-dresser.

Like its feminine version, although much more limited in number, male-to-female cross-dressing representations occur in a variety of genres of children's literature—from the celebrated children's stories *The Wind in the Willows* (Grahame 1908) and *The Adventures of Huckleberry Finn* (Twain 1884), picture books such as *Princess Max* (Stiller 2001) and *Min Syster är en Ängel* (Stark 1996), and junior fiction such as *Bill's New Frock* (Fine 1989), and *Alias Madame Doubtfire* (Fine 1988). In most of these examples, male cross-dressing is used for comedic purposes. The male cross-dresser, adorned in feminine apparel worn in such an inexpert manner that his true sex remains no secret, is a familiar and well-established comedic strategy in an adult cultural context. It is evident in numerous mainstream films such as *Some Like It Hot* [1959] and *Tootsie* [1982], and also popular musicals such as *South Pacific* [1949]. An obvious element of the comedy in these adult male cross-dressing texts is that the protagonists must defend themselves from the common assumption that transvestite behavior signifies homosexuality, a supposition that the male cross-dressers rigorously resist. Male cross-dressing representations in children's literature are hence problematic because they do not directly address the popular association of cross-dressing with sexuality. However, the adult discourse of transvestism is often implicitly present in male cross-dressing texts for children. These texts engage with the adult concept of transvestism on two different levels. The first of these is the misogynistic representation of feminine subjectivity that occurs when a male character is made to surrender his masculine identity for a feminine one. The second is the assumption that male subjects are emasculated by feminine impersonation, a notion which refers to the conceptualization of drag as a homosexual behavior. These allusions to the adult world of transvestism and its concomitant associations with sexuality are evident, to varying degrees, in most depictions of male-to-female cross-dressing. While engaging with the adult model of transvestism might initially seem to be a progressive step for children's literature, the reverse is true. Although references to the adult model are typically subtle and implicit, the manner in which male cross-dressing is deployed engages with a regressive adult discourse that is inherently patriarchal, heterosexual, and condemnatory of transgender behavior. The common representative feature of the male-to-female cross-dressing characters that appear in children's literature (aside from their sex, unconvincing feminine performance, and humorous presentation) is an essentially conservative attitude toward cross-dressing. These texts do not accept cross-dressing as a valid sexual practice or lifestyle choice for adults. It is instead something shameful and dangerous. Nor are they willing to embrace cross-dressing as a viable and highly effective textual strategy through which to interrogate the socially constructed nature of gender. This potentiality is denied, substituted with a conservative affirmation of traditional gender values.

THE ROLE OF THE CARNIVALESQUE IN MALE CROSS-DRESSING NARRATIVES

Mikhail Bakhtin's ([1968] 1984) analysis of the practices associated with Renaissance carnival provides a useful critical framework for examining the construction of male cross-dressing in children's literature. Like the carnival, male cross-dressing representations constitute a theoretical space in which the normal cultural codes and ideologies of society are twisted and inverted. Bakhtin argues that "Carnival celebrated temporary liberation from the prevailing truth and from the established order; it marked the suspension of all hierarchical rank, privileges, norms, and prohibitions" (10). Male cross-dressing stories symbolize a disruption of this nature, as the traditional gender binary is destabilized by the male character assuming (or being forced to assume) a feminine gender position. The conventional notion of masculine social superiority is mocked through the relatively simple strategy of dressing a masculine subject in feminine clothing—an occurrence which divests him of his social and cultural status. John Stephens suggests that "Carnival in children's literature is grounded in a playfulness which situates itself in positions of non-conformity" (1992, 121), which is illustrated in male cross-dressing texts by the comic situation of a boy dressed in girls' clothing, desperately trying to come to terms with his new (and inferior) feminine gender status.

Humor is central to Bakhtin's concept of the carnivalesque and plays a primary role in the construction of male cross-dressing. (The term "carnivalesque" refers to the "general application of a certain 'carnival' spirit to the world of literature" [Danow 1995, 4].) The inversion that occurs when the masculine subject "becomes" feminine and loses his dominant gender status is almost always portrayed as comic within children's literature and film. His parodic and incompetent performance of femininity, as well as the public humiliation he suffers as a result of being placed in an inferior gender position, constitute a playful and comic spectacle for the reader/viewer.

According to Stephens, the carnivalesque mode is used in children's literature to offer "characters 'time out' from the habitual constraints of society," at the same time providing "a safe return to social normality" (121). Stephens's comments encapsulate the phenomenon of male cross-dressing in children's texts. While male cross-dressing is carnivalized to the extent that it notionally inverts society's normative gender codes, each narrative concludes by abandoning its subversive and interrogative potential and instantiating a return to more traditional gender constructions. Male cross-dressing representations purport to give their cross-dressing characters a chance to experience and understand femininity, but what they discover only reinforces their view that masculinity is the more attractive subject position. In this regard, representations of male cross-dressing found in children's literature are not truly carnivalized because their purpose is to socialize child readers with regard to socially prescribed gendered behaviors. They are carnivalesque in the sense that their cross-dressing involves an inversion of the world as we know it, which occurs through the use of exaggerated juxtapositions and parody with regard to the male cross-dresser's inexpert performance of femininity. However, Bakhtin's concept of carnival also has a more serious agenda—which is to interrogate socially received ideas and ideologies through the "free" space that the spirit of carnival offers. This agenda is not fully embraced by male cross-dressing narratives. Despite employing a carnivalesque discourse, male cross-dressing is used to maintain, rather than subvert, the gender status quo. Male cross-dressing representations thus contest the liberal gender criticism that occurs in female cross-dressing texts. They abandon the interrogative possibilities offered by the carnivalesque, choosing instead to reinforce the hegemony of normative gender categories.

A CULTURAL HISTORY OF MALE CROSS-DRESSING

The origins of the presentation of male-to-female transvestism as humorous is a perception of cross-dressing that has played an informative role in the widespread denigration of cross-dressing behavior in Western Societies and dismissal of it as a valid practice. It can be traced back to the eighteenth and nineteenth centuries, a period during which the medicalization of sexuality occurred, and people "whose public [sexual] activities departed from societal norms were likely to be adjudged criminals instead of sinners" (Bullough and Bullough 1993, 203). Bullough and Bullough go on to suggest that:

> One of the more fascinating aspects about the medicalization of cross-dressing … is what was ignored in setting definitions and presenting examples. It was not only in everyday life that an increase in cross-dressing, particularly among men, occurred, but on the stage as well. As the gender divisions became more formalized over the course of the nineteenth century, gender impersonation became a staple of the stage. During the first part of the nineteenth century, more women than men played cross-dressing roles, but increasingly toward the end of the nineteenth century, female impersonation dominated the scene. (226)

What was notable about this increase in theatrical male-to-female cross-dressing was the kind of cross-dressed female performance which gained popularity with audiences. Although female impersonation had decreased since women gained the legitimate right to perform on stage, it was resurrected in Britain during the nineteenth century and became an entrenched feature of British pantomime (232). Bullough and Bullough suggest that "Major actors often took a woman's role, but it was always clear that the person playing the *dame* (the pantomime term for female roles played by men) was a man: he dressed as an absurd and ugly woman, and much of the comedy was derived from the fact that he was burlesquing himself as a male actor" (232). Robert Toll, to whose work Bullough and Bullough also refer, explains that "Women, like Negroes, provided one of the few stable 'inferiors' that assured white men of their status" (1974, 163).

The use of cross-dressing to confirm the status of hegemonic masculinity is regularly evident in male cross-dressing literature for children. In texts such as *Another Perfect Day* (MacDonald 2002), *The Gizmo* (Jennings 1994), and *Bill's New Frock*, cross-dressing is a form of punishment for the male protagonists. For these male characters, being forced to wear women's clothing in public is the ultimate humiliation—a situation construed as comic in each text. The reader's pleasure in such stories arises out of seeing the "hero" struggle desperately with being perceived as less "manly" because of his shameful feminine attire. Children's texts also engage, however, with the adult discourse of male cross-dressing in relation to its connection with homosexuality. In particular, this is a reference to the emasculating potential of female impersonation when performed by a homosexual male subject, or "drag," as it is commonly known.

CROSS-DRESSING AND DRAG—THE EMASCULATING THREAT OF HOMOSEXUALITY

The conflation of cross-dressing and homosexuality occurs often in contemporary Western culture. This is partly because of the phenomenon of drag, which has gained tremendously in popularity since the 1990s and crossed over into mainstream culture, as is evident from the increasing number of films which feature drag queens but are ostensibly aimed at straight audiences (and also contain straight actors performing homosexual roles). As a result, cross-dressing and homosexuality have become inextricably linked, despite the reality, as observed by the pioneering sex researcher Magnus Hirschfeld, "that transvestism was not in itself a sign of underlying homosexuality and in fact occurred most frequently in heterosexuals" (Garber [1992] 1993, 133). Yet, in spite of the crossover status of drag, the perceived link between cross-dressing and homosexuality remains contentious. The simple act of a man wearing feminine clothing holds a powerful signification within our culture precisely because of the equation of such behavior with homosexuality.

Cross-dressing and homosexuality will not be discussed in detail here, as Chapter 7 deals specifically with the relationship between cross-dressing and sexuality. Suffice to say, the texts which feature within the male cross-dressing paradigm rarely delve into the more complex area of cross-dressing and sexuality. However, the cultural connection between homosexuality and cross-dressing is still present in a number of male cross-dressing narratives, even if only indirectly evoked. The allusion to homosexuality occurs in the construction of cross-dressing as an emasculating and shameful experience for male characters. Cross-dressing is portrayed as something to be feared, an experience both unsettling and humiliating for boys and men who define themselves in accordance with the values of hegemonic masculinity. The menace of homosexuality hovers ominously, threatening to deprive these cross-dressers of their masculinity and self-worth. Indeed, a text such as *Princess Max* makes the association between cross-dressing and deviant (i.e., homosexual) behavior clear, using the term "weirdo" in connection with Max's cross-dressing. The picture book *Another Perfect Day* is more overt in connecting cross-dressing with homosexuality. Derogatory words such as "poof" and "funny" are used in conjunction with a male character wearing a dress, constituting a depiction of male cross-dressing that is rare because of its unrestrained homophobia.

To avoid connotations of homosexuality, children's literature containing male cross-dressing uses a common strategy: after the crossdressing of the male character has ceased, his masculinity is heavily reinforced in a framework of traditional masculine values. The necessity of this gesture becomes heavily codified within the text(s), pointing to the emasculating potential of cross-dressing. Discussing the history of female impersonation on the stage, Bullough and Bullough comment that it was problematic precisely because the act of cross-dressing "was increasingly linked with homosexuality, and instead of the curiosity that had greeted an earlier generation, impersonation was often denounced as a perversion; to be successful, the impersonators had to emphasize their maleness offstage" (237). This statement articulates the dilemma of male cross-dressing in our contemporary cultural context: it is perceived as a perversion, but is acceptable on occasion under the condition that the inherent masculinity of the heterosexual crossdresser is not compromised. Children's literature powerfully subscribes to this formula, featuring male cross-dressers whose "success" lies in their inability to be considered as anything but a unified masculine subject. Cross-dressing success is consequently heavily gendered. For females who cross-dress, their achievement lies in their ability to replicate masculinity authentically. For males, their cross-dressing accomplishment is just the opposite, measured in terms of their failure to give a convincing feminine performance due to their inescapably potent (and heterosexual) masculinity.

The social stigma attached to transvestism, and its association with homosexuality and deviance, make cross-dressing an unlikely subject for children's texts, particularly in light of the assumption that a moralistic educational agenda should govern literature produced for children. The abundance of female cross-dressing representations, however, demonstrates that this does not have to be the case. Such narratives have reclaimed cross-dressing for themselves, turning the simple act of putting on the clothes socially designated as belonging to the subject's "opposite" gender into an effective and empowering strategy of gender critique and deconstruction. In this context, children's literature has been much more reticent to perform a similar act of transformation on the male-to-female version of cross-dressing.

THE CONSTRUCTION OF THE MALE CROSS-DRESSING SUBJECT IN CHILDREN'S LITERATURE

Just as female cross-dressing has a long-established history in children's literature, examples of male cross-dressing are not limited to contemporary texts. In fact, male cross-dressing makes an appearance within two classic books considered part of the children's literary canon: Mark Twain's *The Adventures of Huckleberry Finn* (1884) and Kenneth Grahame's *The Wind in the Willows* (1908). Cross-dressing plays only a very minor role within these novels, and in each case the cross-dressing of the male protagonist is brief—mostly because his masculinity is never very effectively disguised by his female clothing. However, despite the brevity of the cross-dressing episodes, both texts cumulatively illustrate the primary features of the male cross-dressing paradigm: an unconvincing rendition of femininity; a carnivalized spectacle that inverts the normative gender binary; and a misogynistic attitude toward femininity.

In *The Adventures of Huckleberry Finn*, Huck's cross-dressing is particularly short-lived. It occurs when Huck and Jim are anxious to discover if any news of their exploits is circulating in the town. To ensure that he remains unnoticed and safe, Jim suggests to Huck that he should disguise himself as a girl. Huck thinks the idea a "good notion," and proceeds (with Jim's help) to put on a calico gown and a sunbonnet ([1884] 1966, 108). Huck is clever enough to realize that in order for him to pass as a woman, the appropriate clothing is only half of what is actually required. Recognizing that gender is performative, Huck decides to rehearse:

> I practiced around all day to get the hang of things, and by-and-by I could do pretty well in them, only Jim said I didn't walk like a girl; and he said I must quit pulling up my gown to get at my britches pocket. I took notice and done better. (109)

Although he realizes that to pass successfully as a girl he must act appropriately, as well as wear the requisite clothing, a convincing performance eludes Huck. Due to his ignorance of the necessary feminine behavioral traits, Huck's first encounter while cross-dressed ensures that his masculinity quickly reveals itself:

> "What's your real name? Is it Bill, or Tom, or Bob?—or what is it?"

> I reckon I shook like a leaf, and I didn't know hardly what to do. But I says:

> "Please don't poke fun at a poor girl like me, mum. If I'm in the way, here, I'll—"

> "No you won't. Set down and stay where you are. I ain't going to hurt you, and I ain't going to tell on you, nuther. You just tell me your secret, and trust me, I'll keep it; and what's more, I'll help you . . . .Bless you child, I wouldn't tell on you. Tell me all about it, now—that's a good boy." (114–115)

The significance of this cross-dressing episode is relatively simple—Huck can't quite pull off being a girl. This element is an integral feature of the male cross-dressing paradigm. Huck is more able than most male characters, as he at least recognizes the need to change his behavior in order to give a successful rendition of femininity. However, his attempts are comprehensively poor. The failure of male characters to give a convincing feminine performance means that femininity itself can never be examined in a consequential way. It remains an elusive concept, subject to ridicule and parody, that is never fully defined or articulated.

The minor cross-dressing episode which occurs in *The Wind in the Willows* is effective at illustrating the two remaining features of the male cross-dressing paradigm: the carnivalized construction of cross-dressing as a comic spectacle and a misogynistic attitude to women. The incorporation of comedy reinforces a familiar adult narrative motif, as there is a traditional association of male cross-dressing with humor in an adult cultural context. The cross-dressing character in *The Wind in the Willows* is Toad, who dons women's clothing to escape from gaol. He does so at the insistence of the gaoler's daughter, who is kind and anxious to help him. She says to him:

> "...I have an aunt who is a washerwoman; she does the washing for all the prisoners in this castle . . . .Now, I think if she were properly approached—squared, I believe, is the word you animals use—you could come to some arrangement by which she would let you have her dress and bonnet and so on, and you could escape from the castle as the official washerwoman. You're very alike in many respects—particularly about the figure."
>
> "We're not," said the Toad in a huff. "I have a very elegant figure—for what I am."
>
> "So has my aunt," replied the girl, "for what she is...." ([1908] 1973, 101–102)

The humorous banter in this scene is characteristic of the carnivalesque mode in children's literature, which often involves a form of linguistic playfulness designed to mock official social structures (J. Stephens 1992, 122). In this case, the dialogue between Toad (who is an anthropomorphic representation of a British aristocrat) and the gaoler's daughter is subtly subversive on both a class and gender level, as well as semantically drawing attention to the fact that Toad is not a human being at all, but rather an animal. The carnivalized nature of this exchange establishes the humorous tone used to construct Toad's cross-dressing, particularly since Toad's protestation that he has an "elegant figure" reverses the usual application of such physical appraisals to feminine bodies rather than masculine ones.

Toad's feminine disguise enables him to escape the gaol successfully, but when he arrives at the station, hoping to board a train that will take him back to his home, he discovers that he has forgotten his money. Although this would appear to be a disaster in itself, Toad has one more supposed injustice to suffer:

> An old gentleman who had been prodding him in the back for some moments here thrust him away, and what was worse, addressed him as his good woman, which angered Toad more than anything that had occurred that evening. (105)

Toad's outrage at being addressed in a feminine manner is symptomatic of the hostile manner in which male cross-dressers in children's literature generally respond to the idea of disguising themselves as women. His cross-dressing is carnivalized through the text's playful construction of his humiliation at being addressed as a woman, with the implied reader invited to take pleasure in the spectacle of his exaggerated indignation. However, the aspiration of carnival is to interrogate and challenge dominant social ideologies, which does not occur here. Toad's behavior simply reinforces the normative gender binary rather than engaging with the subversive function of the carnivalesque. Although it might be possible to interpret the extremity of his anger as parodic, thus confirming the ridiculousness of his sentiments, the next sentence situates the reader in a position of sympathy for Toad, as opposed to perceiving him as foolish or contemptible: "Baffled and full of despair, he wandered blindly down the platform where the train was standing, and tears trickled down each side of his nose" (125). The misogyny inherent in Toad's comments is left unquestioned, replaced by sympathy for his dejected state.

MALE CROSS-DRESSING AS MISOGYNIST AND CARNIVALESQUE CHARADE

Historically, male-to-female cross-dressing—where the subject is typically a heterosexual male and which is performed for the benefit of a heterosexual audience—has had a misogynistic focus, providing what Garber characterizes as a "cruel travesty of the feminine" (239) founded on the patriarchal assumption that femininity is by nature inferior to masculinity. Garber describes its effect in this manner:

> To cross-dress on the stage, in an all-male context like the army or the navy is a way of asserting the common privilege of male-

ness. Borderlines like officers/"men" or gay/straight are both put in question and redrawn or reaffirmed: "woman"—the artifact made of wig, makeup, coconut breasts, and grass skirt or sailor's "frock"—offers a space for fantasies that are at once erotic and misogynistic. (60)

The eroticism commonly associated with adult male-to-female cross-dressing is absent from children's narratives, but a misogynistic view of women is often visible. *The Gizmo* (1994), by Paul Jennings, and two books written by Anne Fine, *Bill's New Frock* (1989) and *Alias Madame Doubtfire* (1988), are all examples of junior fiction in which a young male protagonist is compelled to wear girls' clothing against his will or better judgment, and finds his cross-dressing experience to be essentially humiliating and loathsome. Within these narratives dresses metonymically signify feminine subjectivity, and as the male cross-dressers so clearly indicate, this construction of subjectivity is something they are desperate to escape. The male protagonists' return to their former masculine gender position is accordingly greeted with joy and tremendous relief.

The representation of cross-dressing in *The Gizmo* further enunciates the carnivalesque possibilities suggested in *The Wind in the Willows*, and at the same time engages with the misogynistic construction of women inherent in Toad's humiliation at being taken for a female. *The Gizmo* is told in the first person by its young male protagonist, thus ensuring that the reader's perspective is closely aligned with that of the narrator (as is the case with Toad). It is the story of a small gadget which the narrator steals from a market, and which then wreaks havoc on his life. The gizmo's strange power is that when "it starts to hum it means trouble. It hums for about twenty seconds. Then it beeps. Then I get a bit of the nearest person's clothes. And they get a bit of mine" (32). A series of comic situations ensues, with the narrator finding himself wearing the socks of a passing jogger, the shoes of a man walking past him on the street, and then the outfit of a tramp. The gizmo's power (and the narrator's fear) escalates in each episode, and when the narrator accidentally stumbles across a wedding, his fear is palpable. Despite his screams, he is soon wearing the bride's wedding dress.

Until this point, the narrator has only encountered men, so the clothing he has mysteriously acquired has been masculine. His accumulation of other characters' masculine garments is presented as frightening and strange, but not horrific—which is the tone that permeates the wedding dress incident, and its even more terrifying aftermath, where the narrator is attired in a pink bikini. The story is constructed around the pivotal moment when the narrator discovers that the gizmo is able to force him to wear women's clothing. At this moment the representation of the gizmo takes on a more sinister form. Previously, the gizmo has been responsible for causing friction between the narrator and the nearest individual whose clothing he soon happens to be wearing, but the effect has been limited until this point to a private, two-person exchange. When the narrator encounters the wedding, however, and finds himself in the bride's outfit, the gizmo's power is elevated from the private to the public domain—as he is set upon by an angry mob. The chasing of the protagonist by a mob of people embodies the spirit of the carnival. The polite niceties of civilized behavior are forgotten as the enraged crowd charges after the narrator, hurling insults at him in exaggerated fashion. Normal social rules and practices are inverted: the traditional formality of a wedding is disrupted; the feminine beauty associated with a bridal outfit is challenged by the fact that it is worn by a young boy, atop a horse, who is being chased. The wearing of women's clothing by a male is constructed in *The Gizmo* as capable of inspiring public outrage, a phenomenon that also occurs in *Another Perfect Day*. Male cross-dressing is constructed not only as socially subversive, but also as behavior which provokes social and institutional outrage.

The potent symbolism of feminine clothing is used in male cross-dressing texts as a means through which to present an unsettling challenge, and threat, to the protagonist's masculinity. The case in female cross-dressing narratives is very different, as masculine clothing is less loaded in terms of its signifying power (in that it has been acceptable for women to wear masculine clothing for a considerable period of time). The notion of specifically gendered behavior, or the type of gender performance socially recognized as masculine or feminine, is surprisingly irrelevant in male cross-dressing narratives. Within these texts the simple act of wearing feminine clothing is enough to provoke a gender crisis of some magnitude. The crisis is designed to be a humorous one for the reader—a tactic made explicit through the illustrations of *The Gizmo*, which depict the hero in carnivalized positions of exaggerated terror—yet the humor comes at the expense of feminine subjectivity. The wearing of women's clothing by a male constitutes a diminution of subjective agency, evident in the narrator's loss of control while wearing the wedding dress and being pursued. The implicit message is that feminine subjectivity is passive, undesirable, and humiliating when viewed from a patriarchal perspective. The repetition of the word "shame" in the two examples below equates femininity with ignominy and social embarrassment:

> The bride's outfit is too baggy. It gets in the way. I can't get up. My bra is twisted. My pantyhose are coming off and my knickers are slipping.
>
> Oh, the shame of it. A boy in a bride's outfit. (43)

And again on page 52:

> I look around for the boys' showers. Where are they? Where, oh where? People are staring at me. A boy in a bikini. Shame.

"Shame" operates differently in each instance. It is first used to refer to the narrator's own sense of personal humiliation, but later implies the reaction of other people to the narrator's unconventional gender appearance. Cross-dressing is constructed as shameful on both a personal and a public level. The ideological conservatism of this text is couched within the broader construction of the gizmo as a magical plaything gone awry, intent on wreaking havoc because it has been wrongfully possessed by the narrator. The two cross-dressing incidents are the pinnacle of its revenge, events which are described by the narrator as a "nightmare" (52). Both *Another Perfect Day* and *Bill's New Frock* use similar "nightmare" imagery to describe the horror of males forced to wear dresses. The suggestion is that being dressed in feminine clothes is a young male's worst fantasy. This construction of feminine clothing as repugnant leads to the assumption that femininity itself (as the natural "wearer" of the feminine clothing) is subordinate to masculinity.

The construction of masculinity as superior to femininity is confirmed in *The Gizmo*'s conclusion. At the commencement of the story, the narrator is depicted as deviating from the standards of conventional masculinity. He is coerced by his aptly named friend, Floggit, into stealing the gizmo from a stall at the market. Perturbed at the thought of stealing, he is so anxious that he thinks he will vomit (1), and acknowledges his own lack when measured against the standards of hegemonic masculinity: "I did promise, too. But I was just showing off. Pretending to be tough. What an idiot" (4). The narrator evinces a more considerate and sensitive element of his character with his desire to return Floggit's stolen spanner and the gizmo to their rightful owners. This figuring of the narrator as a "sensitive new man" is therefore initially reinforced, but then disrupted, by the gizmo. The gizmo's strange powers frighten him at first, until he realizes the nature of its magical abilities and embarks on a course of action to free himself. This course of action reinforces the narrator's masculinity in accordance with traditional gender values, as it pits him competitively against Floggit: *The Gizmo* concludes with the narrator finally freeing himself from the gizmo by tricking Floggit into stealing it. Floggit is then publicly humiliated (the gizmo ensures that Floggit's clothes end up on the narrator, while Floggit is left in the nude).

The narrator's final gesture situates him fully within the realm of traditional hegemonic masculinity, perpetuating a masculine model of rivalry and contest. This is verified by his parting comment to Floggit, the childish exhortation, "Suffer" (64). The gizmo is responsible for instantiating the narrator within a conventional schema of masculinity, leading him to demonstrate a range of behaviors appropriate to a stereotypical construction of masculine identity—and seemingly contradictory to his introduction as a character whose identity diverges from this well-established gender pattern. Cross-dressing plays a significant role in this representation of masculinity. The narrator's masculinity is momentarily depicted as fragmentary precisely because of his cross-dressing, but cross-dressing is ultimately used as a strategy to reinforce traditional gender constructions. This effect is counteracted, however, by an overt reinforcement of the protagonist's masculinity in accordance with traditional masculine values. The transgressive potential suggested by the carnivalized construction of the chaos wrought by the gizmo is thwarted by this conformist narrative closure; the possibility for any genuine interrogation of social rules and practices is lost in the face of maintaining the gender status quo. Cross-dressing is thus deployed in *The Gizmo* (and many other male cross-dressing narratives) as a strategy for confirming, rather than subverting or questioning, the superior status of hegemonic masculinity.

The pattern of male cross-dressing established in *The Gizmo* is illustrated more comprehensively in two examples of junior fiction written by Anne Fine. Since male-to-female cross-dressing is a relatively rare phenomenon in children's literature, it is unusual that Fine has produced two texts that deal with this taboo-like subject. Perhaps less curious is that both *Bill's New Frock* (1989) and *Alias Madame Doubtfire* (1988) construct male-to-female cross-dressing in a misogynistic and negative fashion. In each, cross-dressing constitutes a major part of the storyline—unlike *The Gizmo*, which utilizes cross-dressing as only one component of its narrative. However, *Bill's New Frock* and *Alias Madame Doubtfire* are similar to *The Gizmo* in that their male protagonists are also unwilling participants in cross-dressing. Forced into a feminine subject position, they make no attempt to change their patriarchal behavioral patterns. Nor do they gain any genuine insight into femininity from the responses which their outward appearances garner. Instead, each is simply relieved when the cross-dressing finally ceases and they are allowed to resume their former masculine subject positions—conclusions which actively reinforce the superiority of patriarchal masculinity. *Bill's New Frock* and *Alias Madame Doubtfire* also differ from *The Gizmo* because the cross-dressing of their male protagonists is not carnivalized. Laughter is not evoked by either of these texts, despite the comic potential suggested by the plots. The male characters' outrage and self-loathing at being forced to inhabit a feminine subjectivity thwarts the possibility of a carnivalesque reading. *Bill's New Frock* and *Alias Madame Doubtfire* are anything but playful in their construction of femininity as an undesirable and subordinated subject position.

Alias Madame Doubtfire, the novel on which the popular children's film *Mrs. Doubtfire* [1993] was based, offers a conservative depiction of male-to-female cross-dressing that is almost vitriolic in its negative construction of women and femininity. (A comprehensive discussion of *Mrs. Doubtfire*, the film, can be found in Chapter 6) *Alias Madame Doubtfire* can be distinguished from the other texts within this paradigm in that it portrays an adult male as a cross-dresser, thus invoking a connection with the adult world of drag and sexualized transvestism. Bullough and Bullough write that contemporary drag has evolved, in many respects, into what can be termed "gender-bending." This "emphasizes not so much traditional kinds of cross-dressing but a confusion of costume whereby the illusion of assuming the opposite sex is not intended to convince the viewer of authenticity but to suggest ambiguity" (246). *Alias Madame Doubtfire* strenuously resists this implication, its representation of cross-dressing situated poles apart from any notion of gender ambiguity, and hence removing any connection to contemporary drag. It is the story of Daniel Hilliard, a father whose divorce settlement allows him only limited access to his children. To circumvent this, he cross-dresses as a woman in order to be hired as the children's nanny. Despite being attired in very odd women's clothing, there is never any ambiguity about the authenticity of Daniel's masculine identity. The novel offers an overtly negative portrayal of cross-dressing (and feminine subjectivity) to its readers. As indicated by the use of the word "alias" in the title, Madame Doubtfire is never constituted as a genuine or "real" subject—she is always a false and phony component of Daniel's own masculine (and uncompromising) subjective identity. Daniel is depicted as inwardly loathing his cross-dressing exploits, which are portrayed as the desperate actions of a man who can think of no other way in which to deceive his wife into letting him be with their children.

Alias Madame Doubtfire is a serious examination of how divorce can affect both children and parents, and it therefore lacks the exaggerated comic (and carnivalized) spirit which characterizes the cross-dressing in books such as *The Wind in the Willows* or *The Gizmo*. Fine attempts to weave a comic strand throughout the book, but Daniel's bitterness at his predicament subsumes any suggestion of lightheartedness. An example is when Daniel takes a job as a nude artists' model prior to hatching his Madame Doubtfire scheme. His children discover what he is doing for a living, a situation ripe with comic potential. Instead it becomes symptomatic of the impotence Daniel feels at his lack of "proper" employment and his continuing alienation, enforced by his wife, from his children. While his children laugh and tease him, Daniel lifts "a few coils of imaginary rope from an imaginary heap on the floor, and idly started to tie a hangman's knot" ([1988] 1993, 26). The children proceed to tell him of their mother's disgusted reaction to the news of his job, and while they do, Daniel ties his imaginary knot tighter (obviously destined for his wife's imaginary neck) and then "began to lash his imaginary rope to an overhead fitting" (27). The giggles of the children are forgotten in the face of Daniel's violent role-playing. Its sinister and misogynistic undertone represent the hostility of Daniel toward his wife (and the unknowing atrocity she commits in forcing him to cross-dress so that he can spend time with his children) throughout the rest of the novel.

In terms of cross-dressing success, Daniel is a failure in the eyes of everyone except his wife. His children can see through his (poor) disguise almost immediately, becoming aware that the huge and strangely attired woman who arrives at their house for an interview for the position of nanny is in fact their father (71). Miranda's blindness to the disguise is typical of her characterization in the novel. She is the unsympathetic villain, responsible for creating Daniel and the children's misery by forcibly keeping them apart. It is therefore not surprising that Miranda is portrayed as the most idiotic member of the family, the only one unable to perceive that the awkward woman wearing a turban, of all things, is in actuality her ex-husband. The children's recognition of Daniel means that he does not have to conceal his gender while spending time with them each afternoon. His concessions to being feminine are minor:

> He learned to drink his lunchtime beer from a porcelain teacup. He formed the habit of smoking his occasional cheroot upstairs on the landing, where he could blow the smoke out of the window.... .And, toward teatime each day, when he shaved closely for the second time, he made a point of shutting the bathroom door between himself and his small daughter. (83)

Daniel's cross-dressing is a miserable experience for him, a humiliating and degrading sign of the impotence forced upon him by his wife.

Although his children are at first supportive of his Madame Doubtfire disguise, they soon become disillusioned with it. Lydia, Daniel's eldest daughter, appeals to him to stop cross-dressing, saying, "Oh, I know that you did it for us. We've not forgotten that. But it's not *right*" (134). Her comment demonstrates an awareness of the immorality and social disapproval generally associated with cross-dressing, with which the novel engages through Daniel's self-disgust. This is patently evident when Daniel's cross-dressing is discovered by Miranda and he is finally able to rid himself of the disguise. He is hugely relieved to do so:

> The first thing Daniel did when he reached home was rip off his turban and frock, and stuff everything that belonged to Madame Doubtfire into a huge black plastic sack and carry it down to the garbage cans. "Good riddance!" he shouted, stuffing the bag down among the chicken bones and tea leaves and carrot peelings. "Goodbye, turbans! Farewell, lavender water! Adieu, Apricot Crème Foundation! Good riddance to you, Madame Doubtfire! Thank God we'll never meet again!"
>
> Then he kicked the garbage can hard, once, for good measure. (182)

Daniel's eagerness to discard his disguise is indicative of the conservative position taken by the book toward the issues of both transgender and femininity. Daniel's fierce response conflates cross-dressing and femininity, eliciting a deep-seated opposition to both. The bag full of women's clothes is compared to household debris, but whether Daniel's hatred is directed at what he considers to be immoral behavior, or more simply at femininity in general, is never made clear. Irrespective of this distinction, his reaction directly confirms his patriarchal masculine subjectivity. By using the pronoun "we" to refer to himself and Madame Doubtfire, he implies that he never considered them to be one and the same person. Madame Doubtfire did not allow him to explore a feminine side of himself; she was always something exterior, other, different. His aggressive masculine action in kicking the garbage bin after depositing the feminine costume in it emphatically reasserts his hegemonic masculine status—violently demonstrating his contempt for Madame Doubtfire and all that she signified. The implicit gender ideologies of *Alias Madame Doubtfire* are accordingly highly problematic, precisely because Daniel's contempt for his feminine disguise is never accurately defined as either an opposition to transgressive gender behavior or a misogynistic reaction to femininity. The two issues remain confused, their coexistence in the text maintained by Daniel's stridently patriarchal masculinity—an identity clearly resistant to any form of transgressive gender behavior. As the novel is closely focalized by Daniel, the reader is not exposed to any alternative gender perspectives. The text's inevitable conclusion is therefore that masculinity is the superior and more desirable gender status.

Bill's New Frock continues Fine's interest in male cross-dressing characters, but is perhaps the more curious of her two novels, specifically because it outwardly purports to be of feminist intent. It features a young male protagonist, Bill, who wakes up one morning to find that he is a girl. Attired in a frilly pink frock, Bill goes to school and unwillingly discovers that being a girl means that he is treated differently by his peers and teachers alike. Bill's horrified reaction upon first discovering himself dressed in a frock, and being treated as if he were a girl, is preempted by the title of chapter 1—which is not so subtly called, "A Really Awful Start." Bill continues to express his dismay and terror at his cross-dressing situation, saying to himself, "This can't be true…this cannot be true!" ([1989] 1999, 9). As in *The Gizmo*, wearing feminine clothing is presented as the worst possible masculine fantasy, described in nightmarish terminology:

> He left the house at the usual time, too. He didn't seem to have any choice. Things, though odd, were just going on in their own way, as in a dream.
>
> Or it could be a nightmare! (10)

The construction of male cross-dressing in children's narratives as a freakish kind of bad dream which male cross-dressers must endure contrasts remarkably with the presentation of female cross-dressing. Female cross-dressers in children's literature embrace with fervor the chance to adopt masculine clothing, reveling in the opportunity to play a different gender role. This phenomenon is illustrated by the following extracts from *Alanna* and *Dove and Sword*, both of which demonstrate the willingness of feminine subjects to adopt masculine clothing:

> Alanna stared back at herself in the mirror. Her twin stared back, violet eyes wide in his pale face. Grinning, she wrapped herself in her cloak. With a last peek at the boy in the mirror, she followed Maude out to the courtyard.
>
> (*Alanna: The First Adventure*, 8)

> "Men's clothes!" I said in awe and envy, lifting the skirt of my red dress, on which I had often tripped.
>
> (*Dove and Sword*, 38)

Notwithstanding issues of practicality (in relation to the quotation from *Dove and Sword*), these examples highlight the difference between the male and female cross-dressing experiences in children's literature. For females, cross-dressing is exciting and thrilling, while for males it is disastrous and terrifying. In *Bill's New Frock*, the anxiety that Bill feels as a result of wearing a frock is not just because of his changed physical appearance, but also because of the behavioral conventions and expectations that the dress imposes on him. The frock is constructed as symbolic of feminine subjectivity, and Bill's experience of this is anything but pleasant. He soon learns that there are certain behaviors expected of girls that are not required for boys, and vice versa. Ignorant of the behavioral conventions appropriate to femininity, Bill finds himself in trouble at school. He is expected to have a higher standard of written work and to perform menial tasks for the teachers, and is banished to the outskirts of the playground while the boys play football. Bill's response to this situation is to become angry, a typically masculine reaction, resulting in a climax when he beats up the male bully who has whistled at him on his way home from school—a stereotypically masculine gesture of feminine objectification.

In spite of his experiences as a feminine subject, however, Bill is unable (or unwilling) to identify himself as feminine. The narrative supports Bill in his refusal to do so, reiterating time and again that feminine subjectivity is a despicable site from which to experience the world. This is evident, for example, when Bill is forced to read the part of Rapunzel in class. He finds Rapunzel, who is traditionally perceived as a fairy tale heroine, repugnant:

> The lovely Rapunzel didn't seem to do very much. She just got stolen out of spite by the Witch, and hidden away at the very top of a high stone tower which had no door. There she just sat quietly for about fifteen years, being no trouble and growing her hair.
>
> She didn't try to escape. She didn't complain. She didn't even have any fights with the Witch. (19–20)

Bill objects to Rapunzel's passivity and lack of subjective agency, but fails to recognize that these virtues (particularly within the patriarchal world of fairy tales) were traditionally prized as feminine attributes. He then attempts to impose his own masculine model of aggressive action on Rapunzel ("She didn't even have any fights with the Witch"), unable to perceive that there may be other, more viable, behavioral alternatives to his own combative (and therefore traditionally masculine) attitude. Fine's choice of language when describing the various situations in

which Bill finds himself while wearing the frock (most of them personally humiliating to his former masculine identity) contributes to the
construction of femininity as an undesirable gender position. This is
reinforced by its recurring representation as a nightmare: "Bill ignored
everyone. He just sat there, waiting for time to go by. Even a bad dream
couldn't last forever. His torment had to end some time, surely" (42).
The illustrations, by Philippe Dupasquier, are complicit in this process,
depicting Bill in an alienated (in terms of his gender position) light. He
does not appear authentically masculine, because of the frock, but neither does he look convincingly feminine, due to his inability to disguise
the visual, physical indicators of his masculinity. This is most apparent
on the book's front cover, which shows Bill in his frock, but apart from
the pink dress itself, everything else about the picture is distinctly identifiable as masculine—from Bill's unkempt, short hair, sturdy brown
shoes, and defiant stance (hands on his hips, legs wide apart) to his
surroundings, a messy and cluttered bedroom littered with rockets, toy
planes, tennis rackets, and posters of sports heroes. Bill's discomfort
at the situation is clearly conveyed by the hostility of his posture and
the set line of his mouth, signaling to the reader/viewer that his is an
unenviable position. Most of the illustrations portray a miserable or
confused-looking Bill attempting to come to terms with the new gender
identity rudely forced upon him. For Bill, the imposition of a feminine
subjectivity results in a loss of identity and agential power. This induces
an existential crisis in Bill, who perceives feminine subjectivity as a loss
of identity:

Kirsty shook her head, sighing.

"It's just that somehow you seem different today. I can't think what
it is about you that's odd. But you're not you."

She turned to go.

Bill reached out to try to stop her.

"But who am I?" he asked her desperately.

"Who *am I*?" (88)

Rather than learning anything about the positive attributes of femininity, or being able to view masculinity from a different (i.e., feminine)
perspective and thus recognizing that patriarchal masculine behavior
is responsible for the myriad injustices dealt out to women on a daily
basis, Bill is simply eager to return to his former gender position. He is
sickened by the treatment he receives as a girl, but this does not extend

to repulsion for the type of conventional masculinity to which his peers subscribe. After spending the day as a girl, all Bill gains is confirmation that this is an undesirable subject position to inhabit:

> Bill needed no prompting. He ran up to his bedroom and pulled on a pair of jeans and a shirt.
>
> Then he took the tiniest sideways peep in his mirror... .
>
> He was a boy!...
>
> Never in his whole life had Bill felt such relief. (94–96)

Beverley Pennell comments upon the masculine reading position constructed in *Bill's New Frock* in *Ways of Being Male* (J. Stephens 2002), suggesting that:

> ...the obvious achievement of *Bill's New Frock* is that the unitary masculine subject position is made visible by the oppositional representation of the space of the feminine. But there is no representation of empathetic gendered social relations between the characters and no dialogue about gender issues across the gender boundary. The girl reader is expected to identify against herself because the implied reader is clearly masculine. (63)

The negative construction of femininity in *Bill's New Frock* begs the obvious question—if women are supposed to live like this, who would want to be one? Bill clearly does not: "Bill was *amazed*. How was a person in a frock like this supposed to *survive*?" (49). Bill's amazement is ostensibly related to the impracticality of his frilly pink dress, but it metonymically articulates the gender dilemma presented within the text. Femininity is exposed as unattractive, but readers are not offered any strategies of resistance or subversion.

ASSUMING A FEMININE GENDER IDENTITY

A text which provides a less pessimistic answer to Bill's cross-dressing dilemma is *Marvin Redpost: Is He a Girl?* (Sachar 1993). Sachar's junior novel parallels the situation that occurs within *Bill's New Frock*. However, it does so in a carnivalesque mode which ultimately results in Marvin experiencing a more intersubjective appreciation of gender as it operates in the world around him. Marvin is told by a girl in his class one day that if he kisses his elbow, he will turn into a girl. Marvin is intrigued, practicing several times to see if it will really happen. That night while asleep, Marvin gets jumbled up in his blankets and falls out of bed, whereupon he accidentally kisses his elbow. The next morning, Marvin notices a change in the way he perceives the world. Where his behavior was once the epitome of hegemonic masculinity, he suddenly becomes more aware of how a girl would think and act. Of course Marvin believes he is turning (or has turned) into a girl, and like Bill, he is terrified. Marvin's plight is differentiated from Bill's, however, in that he does not actually turn into a girl, or have to wear feminine clothing. (Indeed, the novel suggests that the crisis is all in Marvin's head, as everyone else can see that he is still male and treats him accordingly.) Technically, *Marvin Redpost: Is He a Girl?* is not a representation of cross-dressing as such, but it does involve a masculine subject assuming a feminine identity. Marvin's first "feminized" thoughts also happen to fixate upon feminine clothing and hair, providing a link with the concept of cross-dressing: "But girls were lucky. They could wear anything! Pants or skirts or dresses. And they could wear sparkles on their clothes. Boys didn't get to wear sparkles" (33).

Marvin's concept of femininity is predicated on patriarchal assumptions. To him, femininity is associated with physical beauty. He is interested in this distinction between masculinity and femininity, but at the same time horrified at the thought of actually occupying a feminine subject position. Like Bill, Marvin first experiences femininity with fear. This begins with a clichéd dream, where Marvin is playing baseball. The dream soon turns into a nightmare when he discovers that he is wearing a dress. Unlike Bill, however, Marvin's reaction to finding himself in a dress (although only in a dream) is carnivalesque in its exaggeration. He wakes up screaming (17), a response which confirms his previous thoughts about girls being "stupid and weird" (10).

The panic that grips Marvin when he begins to think that he is becoming feminine is different from the unbelieving dismay of Bill. Marvin's panic is constructed as exaggeratedly comic: "*Girls are lucky,* he thought. They could wear their hair in lots of fun ways. Pigtails. Ponytails. Bangs. He liked bangs. *No, I don't!* he told himself. *I don't like bangs. I don't want bangs. I don't want to wear my hair like a girl*" (31). Marvin's behavior is carnivalized throughout the text, grounded in subversive playfulness and constructed as a kind of elaborate role-playing game. From the incident in his bed which causes him to assume a seemingly impossible physical position and kiss his elbow, to the desperate measures he takes to remedy the situation (such as bending his elbow around the legs of a chair and then attempting to meet it from the other side with his mouth), and the ensuing events at school which show him fantasizing about different girls' hairstyles, Marvin's exploits are presented to the reader as playfully comic. The reader is positioned in the role of spectator, enjoyably watching Marvin's antics as he struggles with the idea of becoming a girl, the humor of the situation arising out of Marvin's oscillation between enjoying and detesting his new subjectivity.

The function of carnival, according to Bakhtin, is "to liberate from the prevailing point of view of the world, from conventions and established truths, from clichés, from all that is humdrum and universally accepted" (34). Marvin's belief that he has assumed a feminine identity fulfills this agenda, exposing him to a new world that he finds both horrifying and also a little exciting. Of the texts thus far discussed, *Marvin Redpost: Is He a Girl?* constructs gender-switching in the most authentically carnivalesque manner. Marvin's masculine subjectivity is comically portrayed as in a state of crisis, oscillating between panic induced by the threat of his loss of identity and the secret pleasure of being able to experience "othered" feminine subjectivity. Like carnival, what occurs to Marvin is not just playfulness for the sake of playfulness. His experience of femininity fulfills a much more serious purpose, which is to enable him to appreciate, in intersubjective terms, what it means to have a feminine identity. Marvin's assumption of femininity poses a threat to the traditional gender binary, which seeks to render hegemonic masculinity as "unified..., fixed, complete and forever" (Clark and Holquist 1984, 301).

The problem with Marvin's feminine awakening, however, is that it is constructed upon a limited and stereotypical idea of feminine subjectivity. Femininity is primarily represented in terms of physical appearance, passivity, attention to detail (i.e., in relation to written work, as is the case in *Bill's New Frock*), and the ability to manipulate males. Marvin's sense of masculine identity is tortured by his newfound fascination with feminine beauty, demonstrated by his attraction to sparkles and bangs. He finds himself repulsed by his own pet, a lizard named General Jackson, whose "ugliness" inexplicably frightens him while in his feminized state. Marvin also discovers an aptitude for cursive writing: "But now, instead of rushing, he wrote each letter slowly and carefully.... Marvin smiled. It wasn't so hard to write neatly, he realized. If you just took your time" (37). The most startling discovery Marvin makes about femininity is in relation to the way that power structures operate within the school playground. Unlike Bill, who quickly realizes that the girls at his school passively occupy only those spaces that are not already occupied by boys, Marvin arrives at a completely different understanding of gendered power relations. Upon watching the boys and girls interact on the playground, Marvin suddenly has a revelation:

Marvin remembered he used to like to chase the girls too. He always thought the boys were in charge. Now he knew. The girls liked to be chased. It was a game. And the girls made all the rules. The boys could never win.

Boys are so stupid, he thought. He couldn't believe he used to be that stupid, too. It was embarrassing. (59)

Marvin's perception that the girls occupy a powerful place on the playground, determining the rules of play, provides an interesting contrast to the abject construction of femininity in *Bill's New Frock*. Marvin's high opinion of femininity is devalued, however, by his recognition that the girls wield their power in a covert and disingenuous manner, which involves deceiving the boys into thinking that they are powerless. The representation of femininity as inversely active is supported by the incident that precedes Marvin's revelation. As in *Bill's New Frock*, this occurs when Marvin confronts the bully of the school. He bravely berates Clarence for teasing a vulnerable female student, but his courage is falsely motivated. Marvin is not afraid of Clarence because he is convinced that "Clarence wouldn't hit a girl" (55), as he believes himself to be. While asserting themselves against boys who are an embodiment of tyrannical masculinity, in what is outwardly supposed to be a positive gesture of feminist solidarity, both Marvin and Bill do little else than assert the oppositional gender values of hegemonic masculinity: Bill uses physical aggression to defeat Mean Marty; Marvin has the freedom to confront Clarence because he can rely on the social mores which dictate that a man should never hit a member of the opposite, weaker sex.

Pennell's critique of *Bill's New Frock* makes a distinction between the conflicting story closure (where a hugely relieved Bill symbolically takes his frock off) and thematic closure, which purports to be pro-feminist by enlightening the reader about the gender inequalities faced by girls in the school system. This disjunction is more suitably resolved in *Marvin Redpost: Is He a Girl?*, although elements of conflicting gender ideologies remain within both the story and the thematic significance. The narrative closure in *Marvin Redpost: Is He a Girl?* reflects what occurs to Bill, enabling Marvin to return to his masculine subjectivity. While playing on the "spiderweb" at school (made out of rope and designed for climbing), Marvin ponders the difference between girls and boys. The difference suddenly becomes clear to him, but before he can articulate it (to the reader), he becomes entangled in the rope of the spiderweb. His elbow jerks to his mouth and he is able to kiss it again—the one act crucial for resuming his masculine subjectivity. Naturally, Marvin is unable to remember the secret difference between boys and girls afterward. Like Bill, he is simply relieved that his ordeal is over. Marvin confidently tells himself that his fear of turning into a girl was simply "silly" (66), defiantly asserting: "Girls are just stupid and weird. That's the secret difference between boys and girls!" (67).

A final scene, however, redresses Marvin's happy return to masculinity and rejection of femininity. Returning to school the next day, Marvin behaves compassionately toward Patsy, a girl ostracized by other members of his class. Marvin befriended Patsy when he thought he was feminine, seeking solace in her company because he felt alienated too—from his masculine identity and, hence, his male friends. The story closes with Marvin recognizing that Patsy is in need of friendship, whereupon he invites her to join him and his friends. The gesture is highly metonymic, signaling that Marvin's view of the world has changed and developed as a result of being given an opportunity to see things from a different (i.e., feminine) perspective. Having experienced femininity for himself, Marvin is able to relate empathetically to Patsy. He no longer views her as inherently different from himself because of her sex and gender, which prompts him to behave more considerately. *Marvin Redpost: Is He a Girl?* provides an instructive contrast to *Bill's New Frock*. Using a similar strategy of unwitting gender reversal, Sachar's text offers a significantly more empathetic representation of masculine and feminine gender relations. Marvin develops and matures because of his feminine experience, to the extent that he consciously changes his behavior to reflect his newly acquired understanding of feminine subjectivity. The hostile construction of femininity as an undesirable subject position, as reinforced by Bill's cross-dressing exploits, is not a feature of Marvin's experience. Yet despite this ideological distinction between the two books, there is a similar tension between the passive and the overt (or surface) ideologies in each.

Both *Marvin Redpost: Is He a Girl?* and *Bill's New Frock* profess a desire to promote harmonious gender relations. *Marvin Redpost: Is He a Girl?* is arguably the more successful text. Its male protagonist consciously changes his behavior after temporarily experiencing femininity, in a gesture which signifies his desire to create cooperatively a more intersubjective gender environment. *Bill's New Frock*, on the other hand, is more effective in highlighting the way in which female students are the daily recipients of discriminatory and sexist treatment. This more astute representation of gender differences, however, results in the presentation of femininity as a marginalized and objectionable subject position, which is reinscribed by Bill's palpable joy at escaping it. *Marvin Redpost: Is He a Girl?* suffers from an analogous dilemma in its construction of gender. The overt ideological message of Marvin's adventures is that femininity is not altogether unappealing when looked at from a masculine perspective, a thematic significance that is designed to promote empathetic gender relations. However, Marvin's experience of femininity is grounded in stereotypical assumptions that reinforce conventional feminine attributes. Marvin enjoys being a girl—but this is mostly because he is attracted to the idea of wearing sparkles and skirts, or of styling his hair in pigtails or bangs. Marvin experiences femininity as a "liberating" opportunity to focus on physical appearance, but his viewpoint only confirms the patriarchal construction of femininity as dependent upon physical beauty.

The significance of the final episode in *Marvin Redpost: Is He a Girl?* is also ambiguous. Marvin reaches out to Patsy in an intersubjective gesture of friendship, but his motivation for doing so is unclear and subject to a number of interpretive possibilities. His changed attitude toward Patsy is obviously prompted by what he has learned while inhabiting a feminine subject position, but the dilemma lies in what it is that Marvin has actually learned. His behavior can be read as a mature appreciation of feminine subjectivity, indicating that he can now recognize what it is like to view the world from what he previously thought was an alien and oppositional perspective. Marvin's behavior also suggests that he has gained some insight into the fact that girls are not inherently different from boys, and is able to see the gender binary which exists on his school playground (which is metonymic of the gender binarism in society at large) as placing an unnecessary limitation on social relationships. Alternatively, Marvin's gesture of friendship to Patsy can be read as a demonstration of compassion and empathy, "feminine" values that he acquired in his feminized state. The association of such attributes with femininity reinforces traditional gender values, as well as promoting conventional gender binarism through the inference that these character traits are not naturally masculine, and that for a boy to experience them, he must have a fantastical adventure akin to Marvin's.

Marvin Redpost: Is He a Girl? and *Bill's New Frock* both present the idea of a young male character temporarily forced to experience a feminine subject position, yet the results of this occurrence are widely different in each. The objective of each narrative is clearly to encourage readers to think critically about gender, but the successful communication of this theme is compromised by a construction of femininity that is marginalized and therefore objectionable, or grounded in conventional stereotypes. *Marvin Redpost: Is He a Girl?* is more successful in its promotion of harmonious gender relations due to Marvin's changed attitude at the end of the story, but the significance of Marvin's development is diminished by the text's reliance on an outdated and traditional mode of femininity. The ideological tension evident in both *Bill's New Frock* and *Marvin Redpost: Is He a Girl?* is redressed, however, by two picture books which present male cross-dressing in a context which emphasizes a more fluid approach to gender relations, as well as promoting (or attempting to promote) gender experimentation.

Princess Max, written by Laurie Stiller and illustrated by Gregory Rogers, and *Min Syster är en Ängel,* written by Ulf Stark and illustrated by Anna Höglund, are two picture books which offer a constructive contrast to the male cross-dressing model established in texts such as *The Adventures of Huckleberry Finn, The Wind in the Willows, The Gizmo, Bill's New Frock,* and *Alias Madame Doubtfire.* They feature young boys who voluntarily decide to wear girls' clothing, a feature which distinguishes them quite significantly from the above-mentioned texts because of the element of complicity each boy has in his cross-dressing. (While characters such as Huck and Toad are not forced to wear feminine clothing per se, they do so only out of necessity.) The male characters of *Princess Max* and *Min Syster är en Ängel,* however, are eager to experience life from a feminine subject position.

The protagonist of *Princess Max* is a young boy of four or five, who decides to try on a dress belonging to his mother early one morning as he waits for his parents to wake. The introductory stages of Max's cross-dressing are constructed in a manner that is similar to the representation of cross-dressing in the female-to-male paradigm. Max's wearing of his mother's dress is a form of playful gender experimentation, enabling him to perceive the world, for the first time, from a perspective other than the masculine subject position to which he is accustomed. After crawling into the dress, Max decides that he would like to see his appearance: "Astonishingly, when he looked in the mirror someone else was looking back." Recognizing that this "new" person should behave differently from the old Max, he decides to dance—the accompanying illustration reveals him twirling around and around, or "swaltzing," as he calls it. Max's arms are joyously raised; the dress, a profusion of curving lines which evoke the smoothness of his dancing movements. His eyes do not meet the reader's; they are closed. Together with the gentle smile on his lips, they express his reverie at behaving in this new way.

Max's mother responds to his performance by telling him that he looks "beautiful," an adjective distinctly marked as feminine. Max's behavior is also condoned and encouraged by his father, who upon seeing him exclaims: "Hey Maxie! You look just like a princess." His father chooses to address him with a diminutive of his name, "Maxie,"

He danced and twirled and
swizzled and swirled.

Figure 5.1 From *Princess Max*, by Laurie Stiller, illustrated by Gregory Rogers (2001). Reprinted by permission of Random House Australia.

which could easily be construed as a feminine version of "Max," and thus appropriate to the twirling vision in a dress that appears before him. (Interestingly, the illustration of Max's father that accompanies this text shows him seated at the breakfast table in what looks suspiciously like a woman's dressing gown—as it is covered in bright pink polka dots—perhaps indicating that this is a household which does not subscribe to gendered clothing conventions.)

Max's cross-dressing differs from the general construction of cross-dressing within the male paradigm in that it is both encouraged and condoned by adults. It is also distinct because of the performative element which accompanies Max's transition to a feminine subject position. Despite his youth, Max is conscious that his appearance is not the only thing he must change in order to give a convincing rendition of femininity. Like other female cross-dressers, Max realizes that it is necessary for him to alter and modify his behavior. When his father asks him if he would like to make breakfast, his insightful response is to decline: "Max liked making breakfast, particularly if he could spill cornflakes onto the floor and crunch them with his bare feet. But princesses wouldn't do that. So Max kept swaltzing." Max's recognition of the fact that girls (in accordance with conventional gender constructions) do not like making a mess is followed by an acknowledgment that they are also unlikely to play mischievous games (that could be interpreted as cruel), or to be as blasé about hygiene as young boys: "Max didn't spread Vegemite on the cat and use the same knife to butter his toast. Princesses wouldn't do that either."

Max's adoption of feminized behavior is grounded upon a stereotypical construction of what it means to be feminine, and as such it is open to the same criticism that can be leveled at *Marvin Redpost: Is He a Girl?* Max's observational knowledge of feminine behavior is, however, much more comprehensive than the version of femininity which Marvin experiences. For Marvin, being feminine essentially revolves around physical appearance, while for Max (even though he is much younger), a feminine performance encompasses a range of different behaviors that he must emulate. True, these behaviors embody traditional feminine attributes—such as an awareness of domestic cleanliness and attention to personal grooming—but Max's perceptive realization that adopting these behaviors will enable him to become feminine temporarily signals an interrogative approach to conventional gender categories. Max's behavior critiques the notion of gender as somehow immutable or natural, communicating to the reader that, instead, gender can be practiced and acquired. Max's assumption of a feminine identity is unique in the context of the texts previously discussed because it involves behavioral modification.

The emphasis that the verbal text of *Princess Max* places on the behavioral requirements of femininity corresponds closely to the female-to-male cross-dressing paradigm, which similarly emphasizes the performative nature of gender. The illustrations cooperate in conveying this message, but they do so in a curious fashion—by revealing that Max is anything but convincingly disguised. Visually, Max is clearly identifiable as male: he has short hair, and his green and blue boyish pajamas are very visible under the much-too-large dress. The dress itself looks more like a large sack when worn by Max, rather than anything distinctly feminine. Its value is purely symbolic for Max—representative of femininity in general, which up until now he has never experienced.

At this point in *Princess Max* the reader/viewer is subtly introduced to the idea that Max's wearing of his mother's dress might not always be met with positive encouragement. This is conveyed via the character of Arnold, one of Max's friends. Arnold comes over to Max's house in order to play with him, whereupon he spies Max wearing the dress and dancing around his kitchen:

"You look like a girl."

"I'm not a girl. I'm a princess and I'm swaltzing."

"Want to come outside and squash snails?"

Max liked squashing snails as much as he liked crunching corn-flakes, but he hadn't finished swaltzing yet.

So Arnold went home.

From this exchange it is apparent that Max is aware that looking like a girl is not considered desirable by his male peers. Hence his assertion to Arnold that he is "not a girl," but a "princess." Arnold, however, does not want to participate in Max's gender role-playing, to the extent that he would rather go home than join in. The illustration on this double-page spread further complements the text, revealing Arnold standing at the doorway of Max's house as he looks in at his dancing friend. Arnold is pictured with a broad grin on his face, which perhaps implies that Max's behavior is funny or silly—and is thus in keeping with the established cultural tradition of using male cross-dressing for the purpose of generating situational humor. He is also depicted within a doorway, a representational strategy often used in picture books to signify that the character is standing on a symbolic threshold, about to progress toward either understanding or confusion (Moebius 1986, 45). In this case, Arnold is standing on the brink of Max's kitchen, and therefore on the brink of Max's gender game. Despite the benign smile on Arnold's face, only one of his arms and one leg are visible inside the door frame; the others are obscured, planted firmly outside the door. Arnold's reluctance to enter the kitchen completely is representative of the confusion he feels upon discovering that Max does not want to play any of their familiar games, but would rather "swaltz," as befits the feminine role into which he has temporarily entered.

The reaction that Max's behavior inspires in Arnold serves as a warning for the crisis that next occurs. Max's aunt, uncle, and cousin Marty arrive for a visit, and when the adolescent Marty spies Max, he laughs cruelly and says: "Whoa, Maxie! Don't you look like a little weirdo?" The visual image of Marty is Max's perspective of him. Marty is depicted as ominously tall. His entire body is shown, but his size is distorted to reflect the way a much smaller person would perceive him. Although Max is not visible, the verbal text indicates that Marty is specifically addressing Max. Max's inferiority is clear—a concept made literal by the erasure of his presence from the picture.

Figure 5.2 From *Princess Max*, by Laurie Stiller, illustrated by Gregory Rogers (2001). Reprinted by permission of Random House Australia.

Marty's choice of the word "weirdo" in this context is significant. It conjures up associations with sexual perversion and other forms of socially inappropriate and deviant behavior, initiating a comparison between Max's cross-dressing behavior and the sexually oriented, adult concept of transvestism. After this criticism, Max runs to his room, crying. The joy he had formerly derived from the dress is tainted by Marty's criticism: "His mum came in and gave him a cuddle. 'Maxie, it's all right, you're still a princess.' 'No I'm not,' he sobbed. 'I just look stupid.'"

The negativity with which Marty responds to Max's cross-dressing is harsh and unjustified, but perhaps realistic within a modern social environment which openly discourages young boys from experimenting with gender. Although girls seem able to do so relatively freely (particularly in relation to clothing and appearance), similar experimentation is much less acceptable for boys. It is therefore regrettable that *Princess Max* does not articulate this inequality, or attempt to encourage boys to engage in gender role-playing. On the contrary, it demonstrates how masculine behavior is policed and regulated, revealing that even minor gender transgressions can be remedied and further prevented through forms of social control such as public ridicule. Max's cross-dressing triggers Marty's condemnation, and the severity of Marty's response clearly constructs Max's behavior as inappropriate and abnormal.

The issue of Max's cross-dressing is resolved in a much less profound fashion than the possibilities hinted at in the introductory stages of the picture book. When Max has fled to his bedroom after Marty's criticism, his mother comforts him by asking him to close his eyes: "Max did and when he opened them…his mum was wearing his dad's underpants on her head." In reciprocating Max's cross-dressing with the goofy gesture of placing underpants on her head, Max's mother reconstructs his cross-dressing as an unsophisticated act of buffoonery rather than a deliberate attempt to explore a different gender position. His cross-dressing becomes a game devoid of significance, and as such invokes Bakhtin's notion of the carnival in the limited way commonly associated with male cross-dressing in children's books. Max's cross-dressing is carnivalized during this exchange with his mother, its complex gender significations and implications trivialized to the extent that they become meaningless in their refashioning as a comedy routine. As in *The Wind in the Willows* and *The Gizmo*, the carnivalesque mode is used in *Princess Max* to assist in the representation of male cross-dressing as exaggerated and inconsequential fun. Yet, the true spirit of carnival, which seeks to interrogate conventional social ideas and structures, is absent.

From the representations of male cross-dressing discussed thus far it would appear that male cross-dressing in children's literature is something that, at best, is funny but, at worst, a horrible humiliation for boys/men to suffer. *Marvin Redpost: Is He a Girl?* signals a more progressive departure from this model, but its success in promoting harmonious gender relations is limited by its stereotypical construction of femininity. A text that substantively challenges this depiction is *Min Syster är en Ängel (My Sister Is an Angel)*, a Swedish picture book[1] that offers a thoroughly different, and positive, construction of cross-dressing.

The protagonist of *Min Syster är en Ängel* is a young boy named Ulf, who willingly cross-dresses. Ulf's motivation for cross-dressing is refreshingly poignant and original. He wishes to show his sister, who died before she could be born, the world. For Ulf, "showing his sister the world" is as simple as putting on a wig, a dress, and some high-heeled shoes. The pictorial strategies used to represent the moment when Ulf first cross-dresses foreground the way that the text unusually uses cross-dressing to thematize the concept of intersubjectivity, rather than merely gender. This scene takes place in a bathroom, where Ulf (positioned on the far right-hand side of the page) perches atop the toilet seat in order to see his new feminine reflection in the mirror. On the opposite (left-hand) page, an interior clothesline is hung with several items of Ulf's identifiably masculine clothing: trousers; a shirt; boys' underwear. The double-page spread represents just one room, but the gutter between the left- and right- hand pages invisibly bisects the space into masculine and feminine halves. The room is representative of one entity divided into two coexistent halves—a concept that is also evident in the doubled image of Ulf, who stands on the toilet seat but also appears reflected in the bathroom mirror. Ulf gazes intently at his reflection, which of course reciprocates by staring back—but the verbal text clearly indicates that Ulf sees his sister in the mirror, not himself. Their intense eye contact signifies their intersubjective acknowledgment of one another. Their bond is visually strengthened by a barely visible golden glow that surrounds and connects their images.

The verbal text articulates Ulf's joy at being able to provide his sister with the experience of life. He willingly and easily surrenders himself to her:

I stood on the bath and put on the wig.

And then I smiled at the picture in the mirror.

Figure 5.3 Min Syster är en Ängel, by Ulf Stark, illustrated by Anna Höglund (1996). Reprinted by permission of Alfabeta.

I only wanted to see what my sister would have looked like if she hadn't died before she was born.

I thought she looked divine.

Butler's concept of gender performativity is not at issue in *Min Syster är en Ängel*. Instead, this charming picture book offers an essentially degendered view of cross-dressing and the world. Ulf's masculine subjectivity is easily and immediately swapped for the feminine subjectivity of his sister, a gesture of empathy that Ulf is eager to make. His success in achieving this is depicted simultaneously in both the visual and verbal texts. In the illustrations, Ulf's sister has been portrayed previously in ghostly outline, with long blonde hair and a flowing white dress. Outfitted in his wig and his mother's dress, Ulf simply becomes his sister—the only visible difference in the illustrations being the change of dress from white to red. The verbal text reiterates this blending of masculine and feminine subjectivities, specifically using a combination of pronouns—I, her, my, we—in its construction of Ulf's cross-dressing adventures:

> After that we climbed the highest pine tree so she could experience the feeling of dizziness that comes from sitting on a branch under the sky. There I opened the bag and let her know the taste of toffee on my tongue. Likewise we took some sips of lemonade, because she'd become thirsty.
>
> "Isn't that delicious?" I asked.
>
> "Yes," she said, "But now it's my turn to show you something."
>
> At that very moment I felt the wind seize the dress fabric. Then I was lifted upwards, as if by an invisible hand. I floated freely in the air. We sat there like this and waved our legs. We enjoyed the view, and the toffee, which was very hard, while the clouds floated past.

Ulf's decision to cross-dress is an act of selflessness for his sister. Despite his youth, Ulf is able to see beyond his own selfhood and perceive the otherness of his sister—and in doing so is perfectly willing to discard his own self in order for his sister to experience briefly the wonders of life as he sees them. In contrast to the texts discussed previously, the simple and beautiful message of *Min Syster är en Ängel* is that gender is no impediment to Ulf's intersubjective desires. It is possible for him to embrace his sister's feminine subjectivity without negating his own masculine subjectivity, indicated by the use of the word "we" to describe their actions. While it might be possible to assert that Ulf's seemingly altruistic gesture of "taking on" his sister's feminine subjectivity is, in fact, an act that unconsciously reasserts his own agency as a masculine subject, the text adopts strategies to refute and limit this interpretive outcome. For instance, the cover illustration depicts Ulf and his sister holding hands with each other—a behavioral stance that signals their mutually beneficial and cooperative relationship. And although the narrative is focalized through the character of Ulf, and his cross-dressing behavior is primarily motivated by a desire to show his sister the things on Earth that she is unable to experience for herself while in Heaven, his cross-dressing actually permits her to experience a certain degree of agency—as when she says to him, "But now it's my turn to show you something," and allows him to feel what it is like to "fly," as she is accustomed to doing in her world. It is also Ulf's sister who makes the decision to put an end to his cross-dressing, despite the joy it has given them both:

> "What's up?" I asked.
>
> "I have to leave now," she said.
>
> "Why is that?"
>
> "I have other things to do, you know."
>
> "Will we meet again soon?" I asked.
>
> "I don't think so," she said. "You will gradually forget me."
>
> "I will never do that," I said. "Where are you going?"
>
> "Just away with the wind," she said.
>
> She winked with one eye.

Ulf's sister's decision to stop their experimental adventure similarly attests to her agential power and the fact that her subjectivity has not been usurped by Ulf during this time, but has existed alongside it in a happy gender accord. That it is her choice to end it fulfills the arc of their collaboration, as the initial gesture (to begin the cross-dressing) was made by Ulf.

In an effort to incorporate an element of realism, Ulf's behavior does encounter some hostility. One friend's reaction to his cross-dressing is a little like Marty's in *Princess Max*, in that he says, "I think you're completely crazy." He is also questioned by his father about wearing the dress but, importantly, Ulf continues to wear it unperturbed:

> Tomorrow all of Stureby will have heard that I had walked around in a dress. But I couldn't care less about that. I had to do what was best for my sister!

Min Syster är en Ängel's progressive gender ideology—which encourages children to experiment with different gender roles, despite the fact that such experimentation is not always socially condoned—does not seem to have permeated English-language, male cross-dressing literature for children. Instead, children's books written in English can probably be summarized best by the following assertion:

She cross-dresses because she wants to be taken seriously; he generally cross-dresses because he doesn't.

(Kris Kirk and Ed Heath, *Men in Frocks,* 1984, 9)

The representation of male cross-dressing fares badly in comparison with the more sophisticated and critical gender discourse within the female paradigm. Rather than using cross-dressing as a catalyst for examining the socially constructed nature of gender, male cross-dressing narratives typically use cross-dressing to reinforce conventional gender stereotypes. Humor plays an integral role in the construction of male cross-dressing, and the amusing spectacle of a male character wearing a dress, inadequately struggling to come to terms with his newly acquired feminine identity, concurs with Bakhtin's idea of the carnival as a temporary suspension of the normal social codes which prescribe gendered behavior. However, the gender inversion which occurs in male cross-dressing narratives does not serve the same subversive function as Bakhtin's theory of the carnivalesque. Instead of challenging the traditional concepts of masculinity or femininity, the male paradigm uses cross-dressing to reinscribe them. Cross-dressing is deployed as a strategy to belittle femininity. The assumption of a feminine identity constitutes a loss of agency for masculine subjects, thus confirming the superiority of hegemonic masculinity. Books such as *Marvin Redpost: Is He a Girl?* and *Princess Max* provide notable improvements to this paradigm, yet their success in promoting a more fluid and empathetic concept of gender is overshadowed by their stereotypical construction of femininity. Only *Min Syster är en Ängel* escapes the conventional and conservative representations of gender that characterize the male paradigm. *Min Syster är en Ängel* offers an extraordinary depiction of cross-dressing, which does not revolve around the differences between masculinity and femininity but instead emphasizes an intersubjective state of gendered harmony.

The discrepancies in the representations of male and female cross-dressing are cause for much concern. While young readers are actively encouraged to embrace gender-bending heroines, children's texts are much more reluctant to endorse male cross-dressing as valid. For male characters, cross-dressing is either horrifying or humiliating, or involves a feminine gender performance based on an outmoded and limited concept of femininity. Until this incongruity is redressed more effectively, cross-dressing (like conventional concepts of gender) will continue to be constructed in a binaristic fashion, meaning one thing for girls and something different for boys. The real dilemma here is that while female characters (and hence female readers) will perceive cross-dressing as an effective strategy for challenging established gender concepts, male characters (and consequently male readers) will be actively discouraged from similar forms of gender evaluation. The sophisticated reading and interpretive skills needed to identify this ideological distinction are often lacking in inexperienced child readers, thereby establishing an ominous gender precedent. As an article published recently in *The Guardian* by Marina Cantacuzino explains, the prohibition of gender play for young boys can only have a detrimental effect:

> If your son wants to dress up as a queen, why shouldn't he? You would probably be happy to let your daughter dress up as a cowboy....
>
> If you try to make the child stick to the "right" sex, you deprive him or her of half the world (2001).

6

(MIS)PERFORMING GENDER THROUGH A LENS
Cross-Dressing in Children's Cinema

While today we may take for granted the subversive possibilities of drag, it nevertheless remains true that actual representations of drag in film have reinforced conventional ideas of gender more often than they have challenged them.

Andrew Grossman

It's official: men in dresses are funny!

Joal Ryan

INTRODUCTION

Hollywood has long been fascinated with men wearing dresses. A variety of filmmakers since the 1950s have sought to capitalize on audiences' appetites for the comic effect of a man (struggling) to wear a dress, creating an established history of adult male cross-dressing in Western cinema. Films within this adult tradition, which include *Some Like It Hot* [1959], *Tootsie* [1982], *Nuns on the Run* [1990], and *White Chicks* [2004], feature male protagonists who cross-dress not out of desire but rather out of necessity, and whose heterosexualized cross-dressing is constructed as harmless fun. This paradigmatic structure is not unlike the manner in which male cross-dressing is presented within literature aimed at much younger readers. Since the 1990s a similar cinematic tradition of male cross-dressing has transpired in films produced for young, particularly teenage, audiences. (In contrast to the literary trend, representations of female cross-dressing in children's films are extremely limited. Cinematic representations of male cross-dressing occur much more regularly.) Male cross-dressing films replicate the general cultural construction of male cross-dressing as an amusing joke (evident in both the adult cinematic and children's literary contexts). There are, however, some key differences between the construction of male cross-dressing in children's literature and in film. For the most part, cross-dressing films for children and teenagers replicate the model of male cross-dressing found in children's literature—the protagonist is male, his cross-dressing is rarely voluntary, and his antics while cross-dressed are humorous because of his inability to master a convincing feminine performance. However, the portrayal of cross-dressing in children's films augments, and at times diverges from, the literary paradigm due to the increased significance placed on the cross-dressers' physical appearance and the introduction of issues pertaining to the relationship between cross-dressing and sexual identity. Cross-dressing films are generally aimed at adolescents, whereas the age of the implied reader/viewer from the male cross-dressing model in picture books and junior fiction suggests a much younger, preteen audience. Cross-dressing films directed at teenagers typically feature teenage or adult characters, and the increased age of the cross-dresser ensures that issues associated with adulthood, such as sexual identity, are much more prevalent in cross-dressing films than in the male literary cross-dressing model. The film portrayal of cross-dressing is consequently more complex than literary representations of male cross-dressing because it overtly transgresses the boundaries that demarcate the adult world of transgender from the "acceptable" version of cross-dressing traditionally presented to children in books.

The visibility of sexuality in cross-dressing films for teenagers does not necessarily facilitate a more progressive or tolerant exploration of transgendered subjectivity. Instead, cross-dressing is generally associated in film with deviant sexuality (i.e., homosexuality), a departure from the prescribed norms of hegemonic masculinity which has potentially dire consequences. Thus cross-dressing films not only naturalize the relationship between sex and gender, but also explicitly negate any form of sexual identity other than heterosexuality. The relationship between cross-dressing and sexual identity (or, to be more precise, the negative association of male cross-dressing with homosexuality) is on occasion addressed by children's books; however, this correlation is always implicit rather than explicit. Cross-dressing films for adolescent audiences are distinctive because they unambiguously refer to the relationship between cross-dressing and homosexuality, but at the same time they vehemently seek to deny the existence of such a relationship with respect to their male protagonists. This denial of "othered" sexuality, accompanied with exaggerated assertions of the authenticity of the protagonist's masculinity, obliterates the potential for gender critique which cross-dressing can provide in other contexts. On the other hand, the overt introduction of sexuality as an issue related to the phenomenon of cross-dressing (regardless of eventual outcome) engages with the sexually oriented, adult world of cross-dressing which has traditionally been excluded from representations of cross-dressing in literature for children.

The blurring of the distinction between adult- and child-oriented cross-dressing which occurs in cross-dressing films for teenage viewers—a dichotomy which is heavily policed in children's books—generates an interesting dilemma in terms of the relationship between cross-dressing representation and its social reality. Although teen films engage with the adult discourse of cross-dressing, they do so by engaging with the discourse produced by other films. This chapter will focus primarily on three mainstream American films that target child and adolescent viewers: *Sorority Boys* [2002], *Mrs. Doubtfire* [1993], and *Ace Ventura: Pet Detective* (1994). Each of these engages with a view of cross-dressing from the mainstream, heterosexual center, rather than from the culturally marginalized position of the cross-dresser in a realistic social sense.

Andrew Grossman argues that the Hollywood-style slapstick treatment of adult male cross-dressing has created what he calls the "transvestite plot," "wherein a heterosexual character must temporarily cross-dress in accordance with a narrative contrivance, only to be happily unmasked at the conclusion" (2002). The thematic function of cross-dressing within adult films, such as *Some Like It Hot* or *Tootsie*, is to enable the male protagonist(s) to "become a better heterosexual by discovering his 'inner' femininity" (Grossman 2002). While this construction of male cross-dressing remains visible in contemporary adult cinema (*White Chicks*, released in 2004, is the most recent example), alternative depictions have emerged that redress the traditional marginalization of the cross-dressing subject. Grossman suggests that "Semi-commercial cult films such as Richard Benner's *Outrageous!* (1977) gradually pushed sympathetic (and gay) transvestite characters into a mainstream cinema that would in the 1980s embrace Hector Babenco's *Kiss of the Spider Woman* (1985), [and] writer Harvey Fierstein's *Torch Song Trilogy* (1988)..." (ibid). More recent films such as Pedro Almodovar's *All About My Mother* (1999) and Kimberly Pierce's *Boys*

Don't Cry (1999) have further contributed to this trend, featuring male-to-female and female-to-male cross-dressing characters, respectively, whose transgendered subjectivities are centralized within the narrative and sympathetically constructed.

Films for children and adolescents, however, have clung to the type of cross-dressing representation that emerged in the 1950s, rarely deviating from it. Reproducing the form of cross-dressing popularized in successful films such as *Some Like It Hot* and *Tootsie*, films for younger viewers predictably favor a construction of male cross-dressing as humorous entertainment, with the added benefit that it prompts male subjects to reevaluate their attitudes toward femininity. The problem with this type of representation is that the "humorous" element of the cross-dressing performance is the male cross-dresser's inability to step out of his masculine identity. The comedy of these adult cross-dressing films is patriarchal in nature because cross-dressing is used as a strategy to confirm hegemonic masculinity. Peter Lehman's contentions in relation to the representational strategies used to construct masculinity within comic films offer much insight into the humorous and carnivalesque portrayal of male cross-dressing in both adult and children's films. He argues that "Central male figures who literally and symbolically lack phallic power fear ridicule; laughter plays an important part in their actions….Indeed, the linkage of humor and lack of masculinity might even account for some central elements of the comedy film genre tradition" (1993, 105). Obviously a man wearing a dress or other signifying feminine attire is the ultimate embodiment of a male who "literally and symbolically lack[s] phallic power." Male cross-dressing is constructed in films as humorous because, aside from the visual incongruity, the act of putting on feminine clothing is the definitive signification of powerlessness. Although only a simple gesture, cross-dressing (temporarily) deprives them of their masculinity. As Lehman comments: "Because men were supposed to be powerful and active—that is, in absolute control of their bodies—images of male bodies out of control, physically marked as powerless, or both, sharply contrasted with cultural expectations [of hegemonic masculinity]" (106).

Elaine Showalter (as cited by Garber [1992] 1993, 6) argues that the comic success of *Tootsie*, a film in which an out-of-work male actor cross-dresses in order to obtain a woman's role (and gains considerable success while disguised as Dorothy Michaels), stems

> …from the masculine power disguised and veiled by the feminine costume….Dorothy's "feminist" speeches are less a response

to the oppression of women than an instinctive situational male reaction to being treated like a woman.

Showalter's analysis encapsulates the patriarchal ideology that implicitly underlies popular cinematic representations of cross-dressing, and is applicable almost verbatim to teen comedies such as *Sorority Boys* and *Mrs. Doubtfire*. The inherent misogyny that habitually underscores books containing male cross-dressing becomes more fully articulated in the medium of film. This has much to do with the genre and implied teenage audience of these cross-dressing films. Sharyn Pearce's discussion of the manner in which other recent high school "gross out" comedies such as *American Pie* [1999] have been received is equally applicable to cross-dressing films such as *Sorority Boys* and *Ace Ventura: Pet Detective* ("*Ace Ventura*"). She writes that they have typically "outraged propriety and good manners, ...[and have been] portrayed as risqué and reprehensible, featuring degrading, coarse material, out-of-control libidos and reliant upon crass humour as a way of appealing to a dumbed-down market" (2003, 69). This repudiation of political correctness partly explains the negative construction of cross-dressing as an emasculating experience for male subjects. The discourse of teenage masculinity perpetuated by "gross out" comedies such as *Sorority Boys* and *Ace Ventura* constructs adolescence not as a time for experimenting with identity, but as a period of development which demands conformity with normative identity categories. Transgression of these codes is presented as catastrophic, particularly in relation to peer perception and social institutions such as the law. The hegemonic construction of masculinity within these films views homosexuality as a threat to masculine identity, and because of the cultural association of cross-dressing with homosexuality, the simple act of a male putting on a dress is accordingly treated with panic and suspicion. The male cross-dressers' exaggeratedly inadequate attempts to master the finer points of feminine grooming and apparel (such as makeup, wigs, and short skirts that are uncomfortable and require constant groin adjustments in order to hide the penis), accompanied by exasperation at the pain induced by high heels, are presented as the ultimate masculine humiliation. The emphasis placed on the physical difficulty associated with being feminine in films such as *Sorority Boys* and *Mrs. Doubtfire*, as viewed from the perspective of the male character (and the gaze of the implied male viewer), is reliant upon a patriarchal representation of femininity as inferior to masculinity, monstrous and unnatural. (Homosexuality is similarly constructed as an undesirable deviation from hegemonic masculinity.)

Cross-dressing films for teenage/child audiences are therefore situated in the matrix of a variety of different ideological currents generated by both adult and children's cross-dressing discourses. Cross-dressing is primarily presented as comic entertainment in teen films, as is evident from the persistent crotch-grabbing humor of films such as *Sorority Boys, Ace Ventura,* and *Mrs. Doubtfire.* Each film heavily utilizes the bawdy and politically incorrect comedy that characterizes teen films as a genre, but the crassness used to present cross-dressing to the teenage viewer is underpinned by the ideological message that wearing a dress is emasculating and perverse behavior, and the necessary denial of femininity as a valid subject position. This is accompanied by a sinister "moral" undertone, which intertextually alludes to male cross-dressing as the preserve of sociopaths. The result is that these cross-dressing films for child/teenage audiences occupy a complex ideological space. They construct cross-dressing as funny and amusing (when practiced by heterosexual males), and also as a strategy for promoting intersubjective gender relations, demonstrated by the cross-dressers' newfound respect for women after their experience dressed as one. However, this "positive" portrayal is underscored by a mode of construction that degrades women and condemns cross-dressing as psychotic behavior. Uncomfortably straddling the divide between the adult and children's discourses of cross-dressing, these films produce a disturbing discourse of their own—a discourse which both trivializes and demonizes any gender and sexual identity which diverges from the cultural and social definition of hegemonic masculinity.

MALE CROSS-DRESSING AND THE GROTESQUE

Characterized by "exaggeration, hyperbolism, excessiveness" (Bakhtin, 305) and based on a playful opposition to formal and official culture, the carnivalesque mode is ideally suitable for male cross-dressing narratives which seek to invert the patriarchal gender binary by revealing what occurs when a man is made to wear a dress and experience femininity. Harking back to the carnivalized construction of male cross-dressing established in Hollywood classics such as *Some Like It Hot,* films for adolescents and teenagers similarly use a carnival environment as their preferred mode. Cross-dressing provides a "time-out" from the hierarchical gender structures of the real world (and of reality as it is constructed within the text), and is established as a democratizing form of play that enables male characters to experience feminine subjectivity temporarily.

Children's literature commonly uses the carnivalesque mode to present male cross-dressing, but the evocation of carnival is more pronounced in films for children and teenagers due to the heightened focus on the cross-dressed body. Cross-dressing films for teenagers, such as *Sorority Boys* and *Ace Ventura*, emphasize the "material bodily lower stratum" (Bakhtin, 370) as the greatest source of laughter and comedy, containing an outpouring of visual and verbal jokes that revolve around genitals, and bodily functions and fluids. The emphasis which cross-dressing films place on the male cross-dresser's body reveal it to be a physical entity that is both transgressive and "grotesque" (in the Bahktinian sense of the word). Literary representations of male cross-dressing produced for children focus less specifically on the body, grounding their construction of male cross-dressing on a more experiential and situational basis. Male cross-dressing characters react to the behavior that their gender disguise provokes in others, often becoming distressed at the loss of gendered status caused by adopting feminine clothing. Gender is symbolically associated with physical items of clothing in these narratives, but on an ideological level it is more closely associated with behavior and identity than with a particular type of body. This changes, however, in the visual medium of film. Ross Murfin and Supriya Ray suggest that "the humorous aspect of the grotesque is often grounded in an extreme physicality and a concern with sexuality" (1997, 150), a comment that is illustrated by the depiction of male cross-dressing in films for children and teenagers. The cross-dresser's physical body becomes the locus of all attention in film; with the question of whether the male protagonist can cross-dress successfully largely dependent upon his mastery of physical femininity (breasts, hips, hair, cosmetics, high heels, hairlessness, etc.). The implied teenage viewer also ensures that the topic of sexuality is regularly addressed, in contrast to literary examples of male cross-dressing where the subject of sexuality is directly avoided. *Sorority Boys, Mrs. Doubtfire,* and *Ace Ventura* openly associate cross-dressing with transgressive sexual identities (transsexual, transvestite, and, most commonly, homosexual), yet such a correlation is vehemently denied by the male protagonists in these films, whose gender identities are founded upon a patriarchal concept of masculinity that rejects anything but heterosexuality. Transgressive sexual identities are to be avoided at all costs, but because cross-dressing is popularly perceived as an indicator of "othered" sexuality, male cross-dressers must actively and constantly define their gender and sexual identities against transsexualism, transvestism, and homosexuality. This act of defining one's identity against transgressive sexuality ensures that sexuality is a perpetual and predominant theme in cross-dressing films.

Within the tradition of the carnivalesque body, Bahktin termed the distortion of the natural into ugliness or caricature "grotesque realism." Bakhtin's conceptualization of the grotesque is particularly relevant to the representation of the cross-dressed male body in films for teenagers and children, which is typically depicted as a monstrous amalgamation of masculinity and femininity. Bakhtin proposes that "the grotesque image ignores the closed, smooth, and impenetrable surface of the body" (317), presenting "another, newly conceived body" (318). The cross-dressed male body in children's films is similarly situated, violating its physical borders and boundaries in the emulation of femininity. The normal physical codes of masculinity are disrupted and subverted: the protrusion that signifies masculinity, the phallus, must be disguised; the feminine protuberances, the breasts, have to be artificially constructed. The grotesque body of the cross-dresser "outgrows its own self, transgressing its own body" (Bakhtin, 317) in its assumption of feminine physicality. The convergence of the "natural" qualities of the masculine body (body hair, facial hair), which are considered ugly within a feminine physical context, and the adornments associated with femininity (makeup, high heels, accessories) create an image that is grotesque because it is predicated on a doubling of the body, combining the physical signifiers of both masculinity and femininity. The cross-dressed body is presented to viewers as an amusing, and often quite hideous, permutation of masculine and feminine attributes, made more entertaining by the cross-dresser's overt and indelicate attempts to achieve and maintain his feminine physical appearance. He does this by wrestling with fake breasts, as occurs in a scene in *Mrs. Doubtfire* when the cross-dressed Daniel sets fire to his false breasts while trying to cook a meal in the unfamiliar domestic territory of the kitchen. Or by exaggeratedly adjusting his groin, which the male characters of *Sorority Boys* do repeatedly, grimacing all the while and suggesting that feminine clothing is representative of physical pain and suffering. This emphasis on the male cross-dresser's genitalia concurs with Bakhtin's argument that the "material bodily lower stratum" is a key strategic principle of the carnivalesque. Parts of the body such as the genitals and buttocks assume primary significance in cross-dressing films for teenage audiences, as male cross-dressers attempt to transform their masculine bodies into feminine ones.

Nevertheless, within Bakhtin's theorizing of carnival, the emphasis on the material bodily lower stratum results in instances of rebirth and rejuvenation. The grotesque body produces possibility and positivity.

Cross-dressing films can indeed be read in this way, as both *Sorority Boys* and *Mrs. Doubtfire* present cross-dressing as responsible for changing the male protagonist's attitude to women and facilitating a more intersubjective perspective of gender. Yet, as is the case with literary constructions of male cross-dressing, such positive interpretations of gender relations within the text are counteracted by a more compelling ideological discourse that treats femininity with hostility and contempt. The grotesque nature of the cross-dressed male body is a consequence of the indignities it has to suffer to achieve femininity. In effect, it is femininity that is responsible for rendering the masculine body grotesque. Femininity is deconstructed into protuberant body parts (breasts) and painful and artificial embellishments (high heels, makeup), made abject through the cross-dresser's antagonistic attitude. Despite their feminine "disguises," the cross-dressers of *Sorority Boys* and *Mrs. Doubtfire* are seldom convincing. They maintain their masculine subjectivity (and masculine physicality and behavior) while cross-dressed, unable to achieve any genuine insight into femininity. The doubling of the body, therefore, only occurs as a superficial reality because, in truth, the cross-dresser's masculinity retains primacy. It is never effectively hidden or discarded, and it retains ideological superiority over femininity. Stallybrass and White contend that "the grotesque is formed through a process of hybridisation or inmixing of binary opposites" (1986, 44), but the presentation of the male cross-dresser's body in film is not a genuinely hybridized form of masculinity and femininity. As Michaelsen argues, "Hybridity cannot really be hybridity—cannot really be a mixture and confusion of categories, types, bodies—if it is still possible, in the end, to identify the individual elements that compose the hybrid" (1998). The individual elements of masculinity and femininity are exposed and contrasted against each other within the cross-dresser (a skirt hem against a hairy knee; gauche, thick legs fumbling in high heels), but his gender identity is always primarily masculine, rather than a heterogeneous combination of masculinity and femininity. The potential for gender ambiguity that cross-dressing raises is silenced, transforming itself into a definite and concrete reassertion of hegemonic masculinity. The subversive possibilities of the cross-dressed body are never fully realized, affirming Paul Allen Miller's assertion that "any form of grotesque degradation that does not include a strong restorative element within it represents not the fulfilment of carnival but its loss" (Miller 1998, 257).

SEEING MALE CROSS-DRESSING

The most significant difference between cinematic and literary explorations of cross-dressing is, self-evidently, the emphasis that is placed on the visual aspects of gender performance in film. In film, the visual presentation of the cross-dressed subject is granted a status equal to, if not more important than, that of his behavioral performance. In literary texts this is not usually the case, because the visual appearance of the cross-dresser is something that a reader must imagine, relying on the narrator's comments and the judgment of other characters in an estimation of the cross-dresser's success. Indeed, it is characteristic of female-to-male cross-dressing narratives to focus only momentarily on the visual presentation of the female cross-dresser, leaving readers to assume that the cross-dressing protagonist's physical appearance is convincing and beyond suspicion. In cinema, however, the question of whether a cross-dresser can successfully project a gendered persona that is different from his or her biological origin is of primary importance. This operates as a double-edged sword in most cross-dressing films, both adult and children's. If the cross-dresser does not immediately look convincing, his behavioral performance is inevitably compromised, regardless of its actual quality. This is the case in *Mrs. Doubtfire*, as Daniel's feminine disguise is definitely questionable, to say the least. The result of this situation is problematic because the viewer (although complicit in the cross-dressing) must accept that Daniel's wife and children are blind to the similarity between their new housekeeper and their husband/father. In other instances, however, the male cross-dresser's inability even to look convincingly feminine, never mind behave appropriately, is employed as a deliberate strategy. *Sorority Boys* relies heavily on this tactic. Unable to look the part, and certainly unable to act it, the male cross-dressers' consummate failure to discard their own masculinity and replicate an authentic feminine identity contributes to the construction of their cross-dressing as humorous for the viewer, particularly when other, more gullible, characters are deceived by it. Contributing to the misogynistic depiction of femininity in these films is the fact that the characters most frequently deceived by poor male cross-dressing performances are women. The masculine subjectivities of male cross-dressers are rarely compromised by their feminine disguises, and their rendition of femininity is always parodic because it exaggeratedly reduces feminine subjectivity to a pastiche of demeaning behaviors and discourses. Their cross-dressing performances construct femininity as a subject position that is characterized by, among other things, an obsession with physical appearance; sexual passivity;

an ancillary position within the gender hierarchy; and being firmly rooted within a domestic context. The wretched, abject nature of femininity is confirmed by the male characters' universal dismay at the very notion of cross-dressing, their continually expressed shock at the way they are perceived and treated when dressed as females, and their relief at finally abandoning their disguise. Cyrino argues that "The female costume can serve to camouflage, cover, protect, and thereby ultimately reinforce the power of the male hero" (1998, 209), which is exactly what male cross-dressing achieves in films for children and adolescents.

MISOGYNY DISGUISED: MALE CROSS-DRESSING IN *SORORITY BOYS*

Aimed firmly at the teen market, as evidenced from its lowbrow humor and setting on an American college campus, *Sorority Boys* has a paradigmatic structure that replicates most elements of the literary male cross-dressing model. The three leading male characters of the film, Dave, Adam, and Doofer, cross-dress out of dire necessity. The boys are unjustly thrown out of their fraternity for misappropriating social funds—and decide that dressing as girls and pledging with a nearby sorority is their best chance of infiltrating the fraternity and exposing the real thief. They are not particularly happy about the plan but see it as their only chance to exonerate themselves. Like their literary counterparts, the male cross-dressers of *Sorority Boys* are initially unwilling, and often very wary, of putting on women's clothing—afraid of the emasculating power of feminine attire. The film's surface ideology mirrors the explicit ideology found in literary texts such as *Bill's New Frock* and *Marvin Redpost: Is He a Girl?*, using cross-dressing to promote harmonious gender relations between males and females. However, although they are cross-dressed as women, the male characters of the film learn little of value about femininity. Cross-dressing is essentially a strategy for meeting women, thus reinforcing traditional gender stereotypes through the depiction of mischievous males on a quest for sexual relations with women who are naïve to their "good-natured" duplicity.

None of the cross-dressing male characters of *Sorority Boys* is effective at emulating feminine behavior. They make little or no attempt to modify their masculine behavior, as is illustrated in a scene in which they sit down to a meal in their new sorority. Each cross-dressed boy eats with his mouth wide open and one burps intermittently, in an exaggerated display of the stereotypical teenage male's disregard for table etiquette. A more extreme example occurs when Doofer (aka Robert), is asked to join his sorority sisters in a group bonding session and share something personal about her(him)self. He pauses for a moment while considering an appropriate response, then excitedly replies, "Well, my name is Roberta, I'm addicted to porn, and I masturbate constantly. Pillow fight! Pillow fight!" His feminine incompetence is ridiculous, indicating his prevailing desire to use his female disguise for the purpose of sexual arousal and gratification. Yet, the fact that the sorority girls remain blind to his (un)disguised masculinity reflects very poorly on their own abilities to detect such an obvious gender fraud in their midst, not to mention their intelligence, powers of observation, and sensitivity.

The male characters' disregard for presenting an authentic feminine physical appearance performs an additional function in *Sorority Boys*, which is to dissociate the heterosexual male cross-dresser from any homosexual overtones. The strategy suggests that if the male cross-dressers looked in any way convincing, then doubt might arise about the authenticity of their masculinity—because of course the masculinity of any man who looks passable as a woman would subsequently be compromised, according to conventional gender/sexual stereotypes. The teen stars of *Sorority Boys* therefore play their feminine roles badly, but the extent of their failure is remarkable in itself, as film critic Roger Ebert comments:

> What is unusual about "Sorority Boys" is how it caves in to the homophobia of the audience by not even trying to make its cross-dressing heroes look like halfway, even one-tenth-of-the-way, plausible girls. They look like college boys wearing cheap wigs and dresses they bought at Goodwill. They usually need a shave. One keeps his retro forward-thrusting sideburns and just combs a couple of locks of his wig forward to "cover" them. They look as feminine as the sailors wearing coconut brassieres in "South Pacific." (2002)

Ebert's reference to the homophobic presentation of cross-dressing in *Sorority Boys* is also applicable to *Ace Ventura*, which espouses a similar (although perhaps more blatant) form of homophobia. The presence of homophobia in male cross-dressing cinema is particularly overt—much more so than in comparable children's literature. This is primarily because of the age of the target audience, as films featuring cross-dressing are directed at an older (teenage) viewer, who is presumably sophisticated enough to appreciate the wider significance of cross-dressing in an adult context, and thus equates it (in accordance with the views of mainstream popular culture) with homosexuality. Within the regime of compulsory heterosexuality that characterizes most aspects of mainstream modern culture, homosexuality is treated with fear and hostility. As Butler argues, "Since anal and oral sex among men clearly establishes certain kinds of bodily permeabilities unsanctioned by the hegemonic order, male homosexuality would, within such a hegemonic point of view, constitute a site of danger and pollution ..." (1999, 168). This kind of homophobic panic is plainly evident in *Sorority Boys* and *Ace Ventura*, and its presence assists in constructing the male subjects in accordance with the traditionalist values that characterize hegemonic masculinity, as recognized by Butler, who argues that "disavowed male homosexuality culminates in a heightened or consolidated masculinity, one which maintains the feminine as the unthinkable and unnameable" (89).

The strategic use of cross-dressing to heighten and consolidate hegemonic masculinity is particularly overt in *Sorority Boys*, which is blatantly misogynistic on multiple levels. The film's closure ostensibly promotes harmonious gender relations, depicting cross-dressing as an instrument that enables each boy to develop a more intersubjective appreciation of femininity. They find companionship among the sorority sisters in the face of alienation from their own fraternity house, discover the degrading treatment to which women are commonly subjected at the hands of men on their college campus, and are suitably appalled. They also develop meaningful romantic relationships with women they had previously dismissed because of their failure to conform to the culturally prescribed notions of feminine beauty. However, this narrative resolution is compromised by the carnivalesque comic mode that characterizes the progression of the narrative and which relies upon the construction of femininity as ugly and repulsive.

The carnivalized construction of male cross-dressing as grotesque is achieved primarily through the character of Adam. Adam is the most unwilling participant in the cross-dressing, and his reluctance is contrasted with the attitudes of Dave and Doofer, both of whom derive some pleasure from being invited into the secret world of women. Adam's experience of femininity is inherently negative because he can only conceive of women in objectified, physical terms. When dressed as Adina (he is even incapable of thinking up a plausible feminine name for himself), Adam engages with femininity as dictated by hegemonic masculinity: physical beauty is paramount. His obsession with replicating a pretty feminine appearance (which is somewhat ironic, considering all the boys' failure in this regard) is carnivalized into a comic routine of the exaggerated traumas he suffers as a result. The gender hierarchy is inverted as Adam becomes increasingly bitter about his inability to make himself as attractive a female as his cross-dressed friend Dave. He immediately defines himself according to the patriarchal ideologies which demand that a feminine subject's worth is entirely dependent upon her physical appearance. Adam's humiliation at his less-than-perfect female body, conveyed by his constant gripes about having a "fat ass," is exacerbated by the physical suffering he endures in the pursuit of beauty. He develops horrendous ingrown hairs on his legs from shaving, his bra rubs him raw around the chest area, and he repeatedly twists his ankles by falling over in high heels, which causes him to hobble painfully. Adam's cross-dressed body is grotesque, a transgressive doubling of both masculine and feminine features. His cross-dressed body inverts the patriarchal concept of masculinity as physically assertive and in control, and simultaneously inverts the traditional concept of femininity as aesthetically beautiful. Adam's out-of-control physical body induces laughter, but the degradation of the body that occurs throughout the cross-dressing experience also inspires fear in terms of the loss of agency it entails for Adam as a masculine subject. The reversal of the gender hierarchy occasioned by his cross-dressing, which places Adam on the receiving end of inappropriate sexual gestures and public abuse from other college boys because of his "ugly" feminine appearance, makes him increasingly irritable and edgy. Adam's bitterness and anger (he repeatedly begs the boys to give up the cross-dressing charade) therefore contradicts the "deeply positive" nature of the grotesque body, according to Bakhtin's conceptualization of it (19). *Sorority Boys* borrows the carnivalesque notion of the grotesque body not to transgress or subvert the traditional gender hierarchy, but to reinforce the dominant gender hegemony and assert the superiority of patriarchal masculinity.

The experiences of Dave and Doofer while cross-dressed are sharply contrasted with Adam's. Adam is arguably more conventionally attractive than either Dave or Doofer, both of whom look nothing short of ridiculous, but Dave and Doofer's approach to cross-dressing is different in that they attempt to interact and socialize with the girls of the D.O.G. sorority. Yet their attempts at socializing with their new female housemates have a single motivation: sexual desire. Instead of reevaluating their own phallocentric and voyeuristic male gaze in relation to the spectacle of women, Dave and Doofer use their cross-dressing as an opportunity to invade private feminine spaces and objectify women as sexual playthings from a closer vantage point. One such scene takes place in the communal shower at the sorority, where Dave is interrupted by the conveniently sight-impaired Leah. They are both shown frolicking among bubbles and steam, reproducing a common male fantasy about girls displaying lesbian tendencies within private feminine spaces. Dave's masculinity disrupts this fantasy, but it also places him firmly within it, as Leah genuinely believes he is female. The camera lingers on Leah's breasts, presenting the viewer with Dave's perspective and the way his gaze objectifies her body. He instantly becomes aroused, prompting the almost blind Leah to playfully chastise him (and his erection) by saying, "Daisy, stop poking me in the butt!"

Gender stereotypes abound in college campus films, and *Sorority Boys* is no exception. The less than subtle acronyms of the featured fraternity and sorority are K.O.K. and D.O.G., respectively. The fraternity, K.O.K., is representative of typical college masculinity. Its members party hard, drink and smoke to excess, and are obsessed with "getting laid." Their favorite pastime is playing pranks on unsuspecting females, best illustrated by their game of "dog catcher," which involves throwing a net over any ugly girls found within the frat house during a party, wrapping them up in the net, and ejecting them, accompanied by enthusiastic chants of support. Their favorite victims are the members of the D.O.G. sorority house, a direct reference to the popular derogatory term for unattractive women. The members of D.O.G. are a stereotypical assembly of socially marginalized femininity—a giant, a French exchange student with excessive body hair, a girl whose shrill and piercing voice frightens all who encounter her, and the natural leader of the group, Leah, whose blonde hair and attractive face would usually accord with the conventional definition of feminine beauty. However, her glasses and feminist refusal to be objectified by men place her firmly on the margins of femininity as decreed by the college environment of the film.

The movie settles into a carnivalesque comic mode as soon as the cross-dressed boys enter the sorority house, where exaggerated chaos ensues. The humorous construction of their cross-dressing experience is dependent not only on their poor feminine disguise, but also on horrible secrets of femininity which are revealed to them during their invasion of private feminine space. Within *Sorority Boys* it is not only the male cross-dressed body that is constructed as grotesque, but also the female bodies of the boys' new sorority sisters. In effect, it is femininity and the feminine body that are grotesque in both instances, whereas the male body is only so when inadequately disguised as female. The female body is presented as monstrous and uncontrollable, and aspects of its physical form are excessively and hysterically emphasized. One such scene occurs when Doofer is informed by the girls that it is his turn to clean the bathroom. The grotesque construction of the feminine body is revealed when Doofer turns to the task of unblocking the sink, whereupon he pulls out an excessively long and revolting plug of hair. He immediately commences a Chewbacca impression with the handful of bedraggled hair,[1] which serves to equate female hair with animalistic and inhuman qualities in a grotesque blurring of the distinction between human and animal. Doofer then comments to himself, "Chicks are disgusting!," which inverts the prevailing construction of women as beautiful objects of erotic stimulation. This scene is preceded by one in which menstrual blood is exaggeratedly constructed as grotesque. The giant-sized girl of the sorority bursts into the cross-dressed boys' bedroom on one occasion and pleadingly asks them, "Do any of you girls have any Heavy-Flow Maxi Pads I could borrow? 'Cos I soaked through an entire box this morning and had to use a roll of toilet paper...." The horrified looks on the faces of Adam, Dave, and Doofer are more effective than words at conveying their discomfort, illustrating that "the grotesque necessarily evolves out of humorous representations of a world familiar to the reader [or viewer], resulting both in alienation from that world and an unwilling participation in it" (Murfin and Ray, 151). Adam's dismay and fear at being confronted with the idea of excessive menstrual blood is the most pronounced, causing him to make an impassioned speech to Dave and Doofer:

> Do you have any idea what this is going to do to us? We're not supposed to know about makeup or periods or self-esteem issues! We're not supposed to see behind the curtain!

Adam's exhortation is a telling comment on the film's construction of femininity as horrific and grotesque when viewed from the perspective of hegemonic masculinity, but it is also significant because it betrays the film's superficial use of the grotesque to confirm rather than subvert dominant gender ideologies. Despite a resolution that implies the boys have learned a valuable lesson from their cross-dressing, the question this trite ending begs turns on what truths each boy has actually discovered about women. The answer is practically nothing, bar the fact that it's wrong to harass the female sex by throwing dildos through the windows of their sorority house or ejecting them from parties in a dog catcher's net—hardly an insightful masculine response to femininity.

The film's all-pervading misogynistic ideology is perhaps most distressing during the scene where it is suggested that Adina is raped by Jimmy, another member of the K.O.K. fraternity. The scene is unambiguously constructed as a comedy routine, with both boys trying to persuade each other to drink a drug-laced beverage so that they can fulfill their separate agendas. (Adam needs to find the incriminating video that will exonerate him and his friends from the misdemeanor of which they are accused; Jimmy wants to lose his virginity.) Each resorts to physical violence in order to force the other to comply (in a stereotypical display of masculine power, which results in them throwing each other around the room). Before a resolution has been reached, the scene ends. In the next shot it is morning, and the two boys are revealed lying in bed with their arms around each other. Horrified, Adam sneaks out of the room.

Curiously, the issue of what happened between Adam and Jimmy is raised again in the film's closure, after the boys' sex has been publicly revealed. Adam and Jimmy are having lunch together in a diner when Adam nervously says to Jimmy, "Nothing happened...did it?" The two boys exchange knowing glances, confirming that something definitely did happen, but after hesitating for a second, Jimmy replies, "No." His answer is a lie, confirmed by a quick flashback to the night in question which clearly reveals Jimmy standing above Adam's unconscious body with a devilish grin on his face. That Adam was assaulted seems perfectly clear, but the film constructs Adam's failure to remember the incident as humorous (the viewer becomes a coconspirator with Jimmy in hiding the details from Adam). This sidelining of the issue is symptomatic of the film's conservative construction of gender, which rejects (or ignores) the notion of a male rape victim, as this would involve an acknowledgment of homosexual identity. The construction of masculinity propagated by *Sorority Boys* invalidates homosexuality as a legitimate sexual identity through the cross-dressed boys' repeated protestations that their behavior is not indicative of transgressive sexual desires or identities. Hence, within this masculine framework there is no room for a logically coherent explanation of Adam and Jimmy's behavior. The solution to this dilemma is to turn what would usually be considered a serious and criminal act into a tasteless and offensive joke, confirming the implicit misogyny and homophobia which underlie the film's outwardly progressive gender agenda.

While the inherently conservative and patriarchal ideological construction of gender in *Sorority Boys* is of concern, the film is indicative of the general manner in which male cross-dressing is used to confirm hegemonic masculine values. *Sorority Boys* does attempt to promote a limited form of intersubjective gender relations between its male and female characters in its conclusion, but it is hindered by its teen/college campus genre which is underpinned by overtly patriarchal gender constructions. After publicly revealing their masculinity, the film ends with the three cross-dressers happily ensconced once again in their old fraternity house, with a frat party in full swing—during which it becomes apparent that Dave and Doofer have succeeded in initiating romances with two of the girls from the sorority house. This conclusion suggests that Dave and Doofer have learned to appreciate and respect femininity while inside the sorority house, and is also emblematic of their acceptance of feminine identities which fail to fulfill patriarchal expectations (the boys previously considered D.O.G. members to be emblematic of feminine failure).

The implication that cross-dressing has facilitated intersubjective gender relations is undercut by the misogynistic ideologies which perpetuate the film's closure. At the frat party Doofer is depicted sitting on a lounge chair, where he is being fed by the female French exchange student. Her conventionally submissive gesture, accompanied by Doofer's demeanour of sexual excitement, reinforces the boys' use of cross-dressing as a strategy for meeting women. His romantic conquest implies that he has been sexually rewarded for invading the private space of women. Leah, on the other hand, initially expresses feelings of shocked disbelief and betrayal when she discovers Dave's betrayal. Yet ultimately she forgives him. This conclusion confirms Dave's status as a hegemonic male, because not only does he get his girl, but he also heroically saves her from becoming a lesbian (Leah's homosexual attraction to the cross-dressed Daisy is redirected into a conventional heterosexual romance with Dave). The emasculating potentialities of cross-dressing (most of which are experienced by Adam, who is noticeably left without a romantic match) are discharged in relation to Dave and Doofer, whose masculine identities remain intact after cross-dressing. Rather than compromising their masculinity in any way, their cross-dressing reasserts their heterosexual masculine status through their successful reintegration into the fraternity and the suggestion of new romances.

VEILED MASCULINITY: CROSS-DRESSING IN *MRS. DOUBTFIRE*

The conservative and implicitly patriarchal construction of cross-dressing that occurs in *Sorority Boys* is also evident in *Mrs. Doubtfire*, but Chris Columbus's cross-dressing film differentiates itself from the teen-oriented *Sorority Boys* because it is aimed at a considerably younger age group. *Mrs. Doubtfire* received a PG rating from the Office of Film and Literature Classification (OFLC) when first released in Australia, meaning that it is not restricted to adults, but parental guidance is recommended for audiences under fifteen years old. Given that this classification signifies that the film is suitable for child viewers, it is surprising that *Mrs. Doubtfire* arguably offers a more enlightened representation of cross-dressing than either *Sorority Boys* or *Ace Ventura*, which were restricted to audiences over fifteen years of age. However, the more progressive treatment of cross-dressing in *Mrs. Doubtfire* remains couched in the conservative and often misogynistic ideological values typical of cross-dressing films for teenagers, resulting in an underlying tension and ideological ambivalence between the film's implicit and explicit thematic significance.

The depiction of cross-dressing in *Mrs. Doubtfire* offers a number of conflicting interpretive possibilities, each providing a differing construction of cross-dressing. On a simplistic level, *Mrs. Doubtfire* uses cross-dressing to promote progressive masculine identity formation and intersubjective gender relations in much the same way that *Sorority Boys* does. While playing the role of Mrs. Doubtfire, Daniel learns to be a more responsible parent. He is exposed to the daily tasks that society unquestioningly expects a woman and mother to perform, including domestic chores, cooking, and the supervision of young children (the last includes elements of education and entertainment, such as reading at bedtime and outings to parks), and discipline (ensuring that homework and household tasks are completed). Daniel's introduction to the traditionally feminine realm of housekeeping and child-rearing is fraught with difficulty. His struggle to perform femininity deconstructs the conventional social requirements of the role of the mother, presenting motherhood as both complex and challenging. The intrinsic value of motherhood is also emphatically validated, as Daniel's cross-dressing prompts his development into a more capable and responsible parent. By the film's end, Daniel has regained custody of the children, gotten a job at which he is successful, and partially reconciled with his wife, Miranda (they do not reunite, but are able to remain friends). Like *Sorority Boys*, *Mrs. Doubtfire* uses cross-dressing as a strategy for developing male empathy for feminine subjectivity. *Mrs. Doubtfire* is arguably more successful in promoting intersubjective gender relations because Daniel is not situated in a position of hegemonic masculinity from the outset, as is the case with the male cross-dressers of *Sorority Boys*. His development into a responsible parent and more sensitive male, facilitated by his exposure to the role of motherhood through cross-dressing, is more convincing than the similar transformations of Dave, Adam, and Doofer in *Sorority Boys* because Daniel's maturation is the result of a demonstrated process. He engages in feminine tasks and learns to master them (unlike *Sorority Boys*, where femininity is related to physical appearance rather than behavior). Through cross-dressing, Daniel gains a better understanding of his children by learning that discipline is as integral as pleasure and entertainment in child-rearing, and he also develops an appreciation of the fact that children need a stable home environment, reflected in his more responsible attitude to his employment and apartment. The lessons he learns about life and parenting are material, and the film directly attributes Daniel's development to the feminine perspective he gains from cross-dressing.

Mrs. Doubtfire also invites a contrary reading, however, which positions the film in the schematic framework typical of literary occurrences of male cross-dressing. In this alternative reading, Daniel's cross-dressing does not constitute a negotiation of feminine subjectivity by a male subject, but instead reasserts conventional masculinity, convincingly demonstrating that while cross-dressed as Mrs. Doubtfire, Daniel makes a better woman and mother than the biologically female Miranda. Daniel's rather poor cross-dressing disguise and feminine performance concur with literary examples of ineffective male cross-dressing such as *The Wind in the Willows*. Daniel's inability to perform femininity is used to humorous effect as a carnivalesque comedy routine that overturns the dominant gender hegemony, but the subversive and transformative potential of the carnivalesque mode is sacrificed for a conservative finale. Daniel's cross-dressing reinstates the superiority of masculinity over femininity because it enables him to prove, irrefutably, that he is a more effective parent than Miranda.

The choice of Robin Williams to portray the male-to-female cross-dresser in *Mrs. Doubtfire* encourages an interpretation of this nature. An actor with a considerable profile in the film industry, he is not exactly an obvious choice for a gender-bending role. His appearance is definitively masculine—to the point that his hirsutism is commented upon in an episode of *The Simpsons*, where the newsreader Kent Brockman warns his viewers that a hole in the ozone layer above the fictional American suburb of Springfield poses a danger to all, except those with a "Robin Williams level of hair coverage" ("Gift of the Magi," Episode 9, Season 11, 1999). Nevertheless, Daniel takes great effort with his feminine disguise. Unlike Adam, Dave, and Doofer in *Sorority Boys*, whose attempts at re-creating a convincing feminine appearance are abysmal, Daniel's disguise is painstakingly created with the aid of a mask, a wig, body padding, and heavy makeup. As is the case with most adult cross-dressing in a realistic context, visual appearance is made the key element of Daniel's cross-dressing success. This emphasis is interesting in itself because it creates a parallel with the realities of cross-dressing in an adult context, where the idea of visually "passing" as a woman is of paramount importance.[2] The arduous process of creating a convincing feminine "look" for Daniel, during which several different female disguises are unsuccessfully experimented with by his gay makeup artist brother, is the only precursor to his interview for the position of nanny.[3] The significant issue of behavioral transformation, which is equally (if not more) crucial to the cross-dresser's success, is never genuinely raised within the film. The only aspect of femininity which Daniel actually "performs" very effectively is in relation to Mrs. Doubtfire's voice. Her voice —which sounds genuinely elderly and feminine, with just the slightest lisp—is practically faultless. However, perhaps signaling the film's lack of serious engagement with the idea of gender performativity, Daniel's uncanny ability to sound exactly like a sixty-year-old woman is downplayed. After all, his profession as a voice-over actor is vividly brought to viewers' attention in the film's first scene, enabling Daniel's capacity to mimic a feminine voice to be constructed and interpreted within the framework of the numerous other silly voices which he employs at different points throughout the film.

Mrs. Doubtfire consistently uses a carnivalesque mode to present Daniel's cross-dressing as an inversion of the established gender hierarchy, employing the type of slapstick humor easily accessible to younger viewers. Yet, as is the case with *Sorority Boys* and other literary texts which present male cross-dressing in a carnivalized fashion, *Mrs. Doubtfire* selectively uses the carnivalesque purely to create an atmosphere of gender chaos rather than for the purpose of interrogating socially prescribed gender categories. Daniel's cross-dressing does turn the traditional gender hierarchy upside down, so to speak, but his inability to discard his primary masculine identity prevents him from experiencing femininity in a meaningful way and similarly inhibits the primary function of the carnivalesque. The carnivalized nature of Daniel's cross-dressing serves only to reinforce, rather than challenge, his status as a masculine subject.

The carnival's undermining of hierarchy, emphasis on the physical body, and playful nature is best exemplified in a montage of scenes which show Daniel performing his duties while disguised as Mrs. Doubtfire. This montage contrasts with the construction of Adam's cross-dressing in *Sorority Boys*, which is presented to viewers as an ordeal that is in every respect humiliating and unpleasant. Daniel/Mrs. Doubtfire, on the other hand, is portrayed as joyously exuberant in several scenes where he is shown playing with his children and engaging in domestic duties such as vacuuming and sweeping. These scenes represent Daniel's cross-dressing success, revealing his triumphant mastery of femininity—but in actuality they are a testament to his (perhaps masterful) refusal to abandon any of his conventionally masculine behaviors in favor of temporarily experimenting with feminine subjectivity. Mrs.

Doubtfire appears in one scene in a park with the children, playing soccer energetically (which is of course entertaining, since she is a white-haired woman of elderly appearance); in another he/she looks down from a window disapprovingly while Miranda and her love interest share a quick kiss, waves when the man looks up at her, then quickly turns his/her hand around and sticks his/her middle finger up in a gesture of derision; in the next scene, Mrs. Doubtfire is attacked by a mugger, with whom he/she fiercely wrestles and yells, "Back off, asshole!" in a loud, deep masculine voice. These scenes display the countless ways in which Daniel manages to retain his masculine identity, despite the illusion of elderly femininity that his appearance suggests. The musical soundtrack used in this montage complements this conservative reading of Daniel's behavior, as his actions in each scene are accompanied by the brash sounds of Aerosmith's song about transgressive gender identity, "Dude (Looks like a Lady)." (Much like The Kinks' song "Lola," the lyrics of "Dude (Looks like a Lady)" recount an experience in which a man is sexually attracted to a woman whom he later discovers is male.) The use of this song makes the notion of successful gender disguise obsolete. It is explicitly about cross-dressing, but unlike "Lola," in which The Kinks always refer to the male cross-dresser by her feminine name (a gesture that implicitly legitimizes the success of her feminine performance), Aerosmith's cross-dresser remains nameless. He is simply a "dude," which calls attention to his biological sex and thwarts the possibility of successful gender disguise. *Mrs. Doubtfire* uses the song for the same purpose, as it is the soundtrack to a medley of scenes which incongruously show the feminine-looking Mrs. Doubtfire behaving in a stereotypically masculine way. The music loudly directs the audience not to be confused by Daniel's appearance. He may look like a woman, but his behavior clearly indicates that he is not. Daniel is first and foremost a "dude" who just happens to "look like a lady."

Bakhtin's notion of the grotesque body as the human embodiment of carnival is an idea that is embraced in *Mrs. Doubtfire*, although, as with *Sorority Boys*, the construction of the male cross-dresser's body as grotesque does not prompt a rethinking of normative gender categories. Instead, the use of this aspect of the carnivalesque is illustrative of the way male cross-dressing narratives for children only use the notion of the carnival to facilitate a brief escape from reality, afterward returning contentedly to the same hierarchical gender structures. The depiction of Daniel's cross-dressed body as an ugly and unnatural distortion of masculinity and femininity is a concept that is developed more acutely in *Mrs. Doubtfire* than in *Sorority Boys* because prosthetic aids are introduced to assist Daniel with his feminine disguise. These "unnatural" components (breasts, body stocking, and silicon face mask) render Daniel's cross-dressed body grotesque not only by transgressing the distinction between masculine and feminine, but also by subverting the distinction between natural and artificial. The parts of the disguise that make Daniel appear more "naturally" feminine are in fact artificial, causing a reevaluation of "nature" and how it applies as a category to gendered bodies.

The type of camera shots used to display Daniel's body assist in constructing it as grotesque. Ironically, the male gaze to which female bodies are conventionally subjected to in Western cinema (Mulvey, 1975) is replicated here, the camera dissecting Daniel's body into fragmented parts and limbs. The camera focuses on individual elements of his body rather than presenting a coherent whole. This constitutes a fascinating, if not bizarre, spectacle for the benefit of the viewer. However, rather than exciting viewer pleasure as shots of passive feminine bodies are conventionally designed to do, this emphasis on body parts conversely generates repulsion and disgust, emotions which are fundamental to Bakhtin's notion of the grotesque. Daniel's "Mrs. Doubtfire costume" comprises a padded body stocking, designed to create the illusion of large breasts and a softly-rounded, elderly female body. Viewed on its own, the rolls of padded, beige fabric hanging in generous folds around Daniel's abdomen are oddly gruesome, particularly when contrasted with the plentiful dark hair on his arms and legs. The monstrous qualities of the body stocking are enhanced by the silicon mask (carefully constructed by his make-up artist brother), which Daniel wears over his face while disguised. Bakhtin suggests that the role of the mask in carnival is "related to transition, metamorphoses, the violation of natural boundaries" (1984, 40), all of which are functions that the mask performs within *Mrs. Doubtfire*. The mask represents the most delicate and labor-intensive part of Daniel's disguise (his brother is outraged when he has to remake it after Daniel carelessly loses it), and is worn because it gives Daniel's face the appearance of fine, elderly, female skin as well as concealing the true shape of his large, masculine-looking nose. The mask also represents a bridge to the world of femininity, as it directly transforms Daniel's masculine face into a convincingly feminine one. Daniel keeps the peculiar piece of silicon on a dummy's head in his apartment. The eyeless mask, made from material that realistically mimics the qualities of human skin, is grotesque in that it is an "impossible and improbable" (Bakhtin, 305) image—the face of a woman, but lacking both eyes and a body.

Bakhtin contends that the "essence of the grotesque is precisely to present a contradictory and double-faced fullness of life. Negation and

destruction (death of the old) are included as an essential phase, inseparable from affirmation, from the birth of something new and better"
(62). The representation of the cross-dressed male body in *Mrs. Doubtfire*, however, contains none of the positive or rejuvenative potential
so fundamental to Bakhtin's conceptualization of the grotesque. The
grotesque doubleness of Daniel's cross-dressed body destabilizes the
distinctions between concepts such as man/woman and natural/arti-
ficial, but this destabilization is temporary and ineffectual. The visual
success of Daniel's cross-dressing is undermined by his behavioral failure, which in turn negates the carnivalesque possibility of any genuine
subversion or transgression of established gender codes.

CROSS-DRESSING CONDEMNATION AND VALIDATION: TWO ALTERNATIVE READINGS OF *MRS. DOUBTFIRE*

The concluding events of *Mrs. Doubtfire* both challenge and reinstate the
conservatism inherent in the construction of Daniel's cross-dressing as
a means through which to reinscribe traditional gender categories. This
conclusion enables the film to be read in two contradictory ways, both
of which depart from the paradigm of cross-dressing established in
Sorority Boys, and also from the general portrayal of male cross-dressing in children's books. The first explicitly equates cross-dressing with
the traditional and widespread social (i.e., "adult") assumption that it is
immoral. This correlation destroys the film's previously established construction of cross-dressing as harmless fun, acknowledging the negative
social reactions that adult transvestism frequently engenders in mainstream circles—and at the same time subverts the tendency of children's
texts to reconceptualize cross-dressing as behavior that is playful but
not deviant. When Miranda finally discovers Mrs. Doubtfire's "secret,"
the film quickly diverts to a court scene where the final stage of Daniel's
custody battle for his children is played out. Although the judge finds
that Daniel is suitably employed and lives in a place fit to house three
young children, he awards sole custody to Miranda. This is purely due
to the judge's knowledge of Daniel's cross-dressing, and he makes his
views on cross-dressing as abhorrent behavior perfectly clear to Daniel
when he addresses him thus:

> Your lifestyle over the past three months has been very unortho-
> dox and I refuse to further subject three innocent children to your
> peculiar and potentially harmful behavior.

The judge's perception of Daniel's cross-dressing as degenerate and perverse brings the film's underlying conservatism to the fore, but his statement also highlights the complexity of Daniel's cross-dressing representation because it brings an array of conflicting ideological messages to the viewer's attention. In using cross-dressing as the reason for rejecting Daniel's custody application, *Mrs. Doubtfire* crosses over into the more adult-oriented territory of transgender politics. Cross-dressing is not overtly denounced as a criminal act, but the judge categorizes it as harmful and immoral behavior that is indicative of psychological abnormality, evident from his recommendation that Daniel undergo "a period of psychological testing and perhaps treatment." The film's previous representation of cross-dressing as playful and humorous is overshadowed by these events, which position cross-dressing as socially unacceptable.

Mrs. Doubtfire is a unique example of male cross-dressing cinema, however, because it provides an alternative subject position from which to interpret and interrogate these conservative attitudes to transgressive gender identities. This occurs in relation to the subject positions made available to the viewer from which to interpret the events of the film. *Mrs. Doubtfire* explicitly aligns the viewer with the character of Daniel (it is impossible to feel sympathy for Miranda, who seems to be a cardboard cutout of a tough career woman),[4] creating a positive picture of cross-dressing because it is viewed in the context of Daniel's morality and appeal as a character. The film's earlier presentation of cross-dressing as harmless play is challenged by the judge's harsh condemnation of Daniel's cross-dressing, but not completely vitiated because of the viewer empathy created by Daniel's devastation at being forcibly separated from his children. Peculiarly (within the context of a children's film), this scene can also be read as an objection to the discriminatory way in which the legal system treats transgendered individuals as if they are psychologically deficient or disturbed.

The gravity and negativity of the court scene in *Mrs. Doubtfire* is superseded by the progression of the subplot, which is instrumental to the unusually positive and socially realistic depiction of transgenderism available in this film. When not employed by Miranda as Mrs. Doubtfire, Daniel works as a shipping clerk at a television company. After catching the eye of one of the senior executives, who is intrigued and entertained by his comic acting ability, he is asked to revamp and host a children's television program—which he does as Mrs. Doubtfire. The success of the program parallels the children's misery at losing their nanny. Seeing him appear on television, Miranda (who also sorely misses the assistance of Mrs. Doubtfire) is prompted to approach Daniel and ask him to return as the children's caregiver.

Daniel's employment as a cross-dressing children's television host (and a successful one at that) subverts the court's ruling and revalidates cross-dressing as positive and beneficial. Cross-dressing ultimately reunites Daniel with his family, who reassess his parenting abilities based upon his success as Mrs. Doubtfire. These incidents undermine the conservatism of the court scene, but it is the continuance of Daniel's cross-dressing at the conclusion of *Mrs. Doubtfire* that marks the most significant transgression from prevailing constructions of male cross-dressing in children's literature and film. In most other cases of children's literature and film, male cross-dressing is definitively impermanent. The cessation of the cross-dressing at some point prior to the end of the narrative is a necessity in order for its ideological construction to remain removed from the (homo)sexualized adult concept of transvestism. Rather than conforming to this established pattern, Daniel's cross-dressing is presented as ongoing at the end of the film because of his new television role. *Mrs. Doubtfire* thus implicitly incorporates an adult transvestite dialogue into its treatment of cross-dressing, because its depiction of a heterosexual adult male who occasionally engages in, and enjoys, cross-dressing successfully encapsulates the reality of transvestism for most male-to-female cross-dressers. This is an impressive feat for a film that is basically a lightweight comedy. Admittedly, the film predominantly favors a conservative and at times misogynistic interpretation of male cross-dressing, but its conclusion offers a more tolerant and progressive alternative that challenges viewers to perceive cross-dressing as subversive behavior that is not necessarily immoral or deviant.

TRANSSEXUALISM VERSUS HEGEMONIC MASCULINITY IN *ACE VENTURA: PET DETECTIVE*

Ace Ventura: Pet Detective departs significantly from the model of cross-dressing available in either *Sorority Boys* or *Mrs. Doubtfire*. This is, first, because it presents a transsexual rather than transvestite character and, second, because the narrative is not focalized through this transgendered character. Instead, *Ace Ventura* uses cross-dressing to establish the hegemonic masculine status of the hero through strategic contrasts (i.e., Ace Ventura's masculinity is constructed in opposition to the gender and sexual identity of the cross-dressing character). A third element that distinguishes *Ace Ventura* is the way in which it constructs, and consequently demeans, its cross-dressing character. *Ace Ventura* places considerable focus on the issue of sexuality (or, more specifically, "othered" sexuality) as a means through which to contrast and assert the superiority of hegemonic masculinity and its regime of compulsory heterosexuality. The comedic taunts that regularly punctuate *Ace Ventura* are therefore more direct and openly hostile (and perhaps also more sinister) than those found in a film like *Sorority Boys* because they are aimed largely at homosexual/transgendered subjects rather than women, an already marginalized social group. The film is particularly vehement in its efforts to malign its transgendered character, making parodic reference to films such as *Psycho* and *The Silence of the Lambs* in an attempt to construct cross-dressing as the preserve of the criminally deranged.

Like *Sorority Boys* and *Mrs. Doubtfire*, *Ace Ventura* employs a carnivalesque style of comedy, relying on exaggeratedly puerile humor and visual gags to construct a comic world (and the character of Ace Ventura) as a kind of time-out from normal social and cultural conventions. It presents an often hilarious world within which the character of Ace looms large, a man whose behavior falls completely outside the normal range of propriety. Jim Carrey plays the role of Ace, his first starring role in a major film, and generated cult success for the film among adolescent male viewers. *Ace Ventura* was simply a vehicle for Carrey and his unique brand of face-pulling comedy—as its plot is absurd and mostly illogical. Carrey plays Ace Ventura, a "pet detective" whose services are called upon to find the kidnapped mascot of the Miami Dolphins (an American football team), a dolphin named Snowflake. Ace discovers that the culprit is an ex-Dolphins player named Ray Finkle, who disgraced the team in the 1984 Super Bowl by missing the games's crucial conversion kick. In tracking down the now mentally–disturbed Finkle, Ace discovers that "he" is actually now a "she" who, having assumed the identity of a missing female hiker, is now living as a female police officer named Lois Einhorn, who just so happens to be Ace's archrival.

The depiction of the transgendered Einhorn is heavy-handed and insensitive, and she is marked from the start as oppositional to the unconventional, yet immediately likable, Ace (with whom the implied viewer is immediately aligned). Lieutenant Einhorn is the villain—a nasty, venomous woman hell-bent on ridiculing and discrediting the extroverted, but obviously clever, Ace Ventura. She and Ace are both working on the same case, but it is he who picks up the vital clues. The film employs an interesting gender strategy in its choice of actor for the transgendered character of Einhorn. Although Einhorn is biologically male, she is played by Sean Young, a female actress (despite her conventionally masculine name) who is fine-featured and physically petite.

This strategy cleverly circumvents the problems which cross-dressing poses for the protagonists of *Sorority Boys* or for Robin Williams in *Mrs. Doubtfire*, as Einhorn does appear convincingly feminine. However, while Young is not masculine-looking in any way, she performs the role according to masculine behavioral codes—she talks aggressively, often places her hands on her hips in a manner that commands a larger spatial area than feminine physical gestures traditionally do, and maintains a certain masculine swagger when she moves.

The film therefore implicitly acknowledges the issue of gender as performative in a very subtle manner by playing up to a certain public perception that men simply cannot give an authentic feminine gender performance, as is evident from Einhorn's exaggerated masculine posturings. However, the film simultaneously engages with the literary discourse of female cross-dressing, as it is equally apparent that Young as an actress is aware of certain masculine behaviors and the need for her to replicate these in order for the unraveling of the mystery of her identity to seem believable. Hence *Ace Ventura* provides a more sophisticated (de)construction of gender, albeit in a very understated way, than films such as *Sorority Boys* and *Mrs. Doubtfire,* in which male cross-dressing characters are unable to discard their masculine identities and behaviors, resulting in feeble cross-dressing performances.

CROSS-DRESSING AS INTERTEXTUAL PARODY

Einhorn is established as a loathsome character early in the film, and her continuing desire to thwart the likable Ace's investigation immediately pits the viewer against her. In its portrayal of Einhorn as a transgendered character, *Ace Ventura* is both vicious and cruel. As is the case in *Psycho* and *The Silence of the Lambs*, Einhorn's transsexualism is not constructed as a genuine psychological urge to become female, but rather as the result of a homicidal delusion. Einhorn becomes a transsexual purely to wreak revenge on the football team, from which (s)he was previously disgraced. *The Silence of the Lambs* is used explicitly as an intertext in the film, with Ace equating Einhorn's transsexualism with the psychotic behavior of the cross-dressing serial killer in that film, Jame Gumb. *The Silence of the Lambs* deliberately constructs its villain's transsexuality as nonauthentic, a fact revealed to its FBI agent protagonist by the murderer's equally psychotic psychiatarist, Dr. Hannibal Lecter. Ace makes specific reference to both Gumb and Lecter when he reveals Einhorn's transsexuality to the men on her police force, characterizing and comically belittling it as a severe form of mental illness: "We're talking paranoid delusional psychosis. Cozy—if you're Hannibal Lecter!"

Ace Ventura is less than subtle in its self-conscious parodying of other films that feature transgendered characters. Immediately prior to Ace discovering that Einhorn is actually a biological male, he confronts her in her office and theatrically kisses her. When he realizes, a short time later, that she is a transsexual, the film lampoons *The Crying Game* (1992), re-creating the scenario in which that film's protagonist realizes that the woman he is in love with, and whom he has just kissed, is actually male. His horrified reaction to this knowledge is a violent bout of vomiting, which Ace also performs, but in a thoroughly more exaggerated manner. The film falls victim to the same overt homophobia that informs the cross-dressing ideology of films such as *Sorority Boys*, unflinchingly presenting homosexuality as repulsive to heterosexual masculinity.

The public revelation of Einhorn's transsexuality, which occurs in the film's penultimate scene, is similarly lacking in taste and sensitivity. Ace corners Einhorn in the abandoned warehouse where s/he has been hiding Snowflake the dolphin, and then proceeds to reveal her/his true identity in full view of the male officers s/he commands in her police unit. The revelation takes some time, however, as each time Ace tries to claim victory—by trying to rip off her "wig," which he soon discovers is real hair, or by exposing her breasts, which are similarly real—he is unable to find a genuine signifier of maleness. Finally, however, when Einhorn has been publicly stripped of everything but her underwear, Ace suddenly notices something that he had previously missed, and gleefully yells to the surrounding police officers:

> ... if the Lieutenant is indeed a woman as she claims to be, then, my friends, she is suffering from the worst case of hemorrhoids I have ever seen. That is why Roger Podacter is dead—he found Captain Winkie!!!

Einhorn's awkwardly clenched legs hold between them a penis, the outline of which can be seen from the back of her underwear as it protrudes from under her bottom. The grotesque image of Einhorn's body, which merges feminine physical attributes with the distinctly male phallus, is reinforced by the reaction of her all-male police squadron, all of whom echo Ace's disgust by vomiting theatrically. This scene contains a multitude of grotesque possibilities, as represented by the humorous focus it places on the human body, "leaky" bodily functions, and Einhorn's transgressive gender identity within which sexuality is implicated, but any prospect of a restorative reconsideration of conventional gender and sexual boundaries is overshadowed by the repetitive intertextual allusion to *The Crying Game* which occurs here. The original incident in *The Crying Game* occurs when Fergus, the film's main character, realizes that the mysterious and enigmatic woman who has captivated him is actually a biological male. Fergus discovers this while trying to make love to her, and his violent reaction is shocking but understandable. The recurrence of this intertextual parody in *Ace Ventura*, however, must be interpreted differently, as none of the men shown vomiting have ever been physically intimate with Einhorn. Their disgust is simply the result of coming face to face with a transsexual, a predicament constructed by the film as totally abhorrent. The hysteria that so often informs representations of cross-dressing in literature and film, which typically results in overtly homophobic and misogynistic constructions of transvestites and transsexuals, is credited by Garber as arising from "a more general and pervasive fear of transvestism *as* a powerful agent of destabilization and change, the sign of the *un*ground-edness of identities on which social structures and hierarchies depend" (Garber [1992] 1993, 223).

Garber's assertion that cross-dressing identities can be viewed fearfully as powerful agents of destabilization is clearly apparent in *Ace Ventura*, particularly in relation to the ways in which masculinity and femininity are constructed within the film, and also in the construction of Einhorn as oppositional to Ace. As most of the other characters are only minor, masculinity is presented primarily through the character of Ace. Ace's gender identity is an interesting construction. It conforms almost totally to a traditional mode of patriarchal masculinity, but also incorporates certain elements of the more contemporary "sensitive new man" (J. Stephens 2002, 38–54) paradigm. In accordance with the traditional construction of masculinity, Ace is a detective by profession and dependent upon his analytical skills for a living; he is proactive and confidently assured in his pursuit of the kidnapped dolphin Snowflake (hence his lack of respect for Einhorn, the men in her force, and their use of conventional police methods to investigate crime). He is evidently a skillful detective, in spite of his unconventionality, as he constantly outwits Einhorn and her police task force; he is adept at avoiding trouble, regularly negotiating himself out of potentially threatening situations; a smart-ass who always gains the upper hand in verbal stoushes. He has a prodigious sexual appetite and is romantically successful; and he finds the concept of homosexuality repugnant. However, Ace simultaneously deviates from this model of masculinity in a variety of ways, resulting in a gender identity that is slightly irregular: in terms of physical appearance, Ace is tall but also lanky and goofy (especially in the context of the Miami Dolphins players, who are overtly muscular). Although he is a detective, he is a "pet detective," a profession subordinated by its application to animals rather than people. His affinity with animals also suggests that there is a gentler side to his flamboyant nature. Ace's profession constructs him as an outsider, alienated from the more established patriarchal masculinity of Einhorn's exclusively male police task force. They repeatedly ridicule him and his chosen area of work. Nevertheless, the revelation of Einhorn's transgendered identity in the latter part of the film acts to consolidate Ace's gender identity in accordance with a hegemonic masculine schema. His earlier deviance from the normative framework of masculinity becomes less important in the context of the film's construction of Einhorn's (trans)gender identity as abnormal and repugnant. As Einhorn humiliatingly and publicly "loses" her tough feminine gender status in the eyes of her police task force, Ace, and the implied (heterosexual male) viewer, Ace himself conversely gains a more coherent and patriarchal masculine identity—a process which also moves him conveniently from the role of underdog/antihero to a conventional model of masculine heroism premised on action, competitiveness, and aggression. This is clear from the film's conclusion, which shows Ace beating up the mascot of the Dolphins' opposing team at the Super Bowl.

Whereas *Ace Ventura* concludes by strengthening and confirming Ace's gender identity in accordance with hegemonic masculinity, Einhorn is simultaneously disempowered and dispossessed of her gender identity. Upon the public revelation of her transgendered subjectivity, she is reduced to a figure of ridicule and mockery. Dressed only in her underwear, and rendered speechless in the face of Ace's dismantling of her power and status, she is humiliatingly defeated and demonized as a psychotic, but now powerless, villain. The film is particularly vicious toward Einhorn, and is probably the most extreme vilification of a transgendered subject evident in contemporary films directed at child and teenage audiences.

The representation of male cross-dressing in both books and films for child and adolescent viewers is remarkably similar, each medium using male cross-dressing (frequently presented in carnivalesque mode) as a comic strategy to confirm hegemonic masculinity within a context that denigrates femininity, homosexuality, and transgendered subjectivity. While limited and negative constructions of femininity and homosexuality can and do appear in examples of male cross-dressing books for children, their appearance in male cross-dressing films produced for younger audiences seems to be much more entrenched. The assumption, then, is that male cross-dressing comedies for children/adults provide viewers with very conventional constructions of gender. However, films such as *Sorority Boys, Ace Ventura,* and *Mrs. Doubtfire* are simultaneously responsible for creating a dialogue (albeit in an embryonic stage) between cross-dressing in the context of children's literature and its reality in contemporary Western society. In engaging with the "real" world of adult cross-dressing, these films at least represent a starting point from which more progressive and tolerant representations of cross-dressing can occur in children's literature and film.

TRANSGENDERED SUBJECTIVITY: SOCIAL REALISM AND GENDER DECONSTRUCTION IN *MA VIE EN ROSE*

One film which substantially develops the nascent dialogue between the representation of male cross-dressing in films produced for child/adolescent viewers and the contemporary concept of transgender is *Ma Vie en Rose,* directed by Alain Berliner [1997]. In the context of adolescent literature (which will be discussed in greater detail in Chapter 7), a number of contemporary young adult novels have chosen to venture into the uncharted waters of transgendered subjectivity by featuring adolescent characters who display (or play with the idea of having) attributes and behaviors that breach the normative gender codes prescribed for their sex, and that can thus be identified as either transgendered or queer. *Ma Vie en Rose* is a film which has much in common with these novels, yet it also differs quite significantly because of the youthfulness of its transgendered protagonist, Ludovic (Ludo). Rather than reacting against his masculine gender identity or willfully choosing to subvert it, Ludo genuinely believes that he should have been born a girl. He is certain that God made a mistake while creating him, accidentally bestowing upon him the male Y chromosome. He confidently tells his friend Jerome:

My "X" for a girl fell in the trash.

I got a "Y" instead.

A scientific error!

Ludo also firmly believes that God's mistake will one day be corrected. When Ludovic's grandmother quizzically asks him about his relationship with his friend Jerome, he confidently replies that they are going to marry when "I'm not a boy," a statement which makes perfect sense to Ludo's own evaluation of what he is "meant" to be. Ludo's performance of femininity is highly conventional, constructed around

a definition of femininity based on traditional behaviors such as dancing and playing with dolls, and feminine fantasies that revolve around
romance and marriage. Despite Ludo's identification with this stereotypical construction of femininity, the film makes it clear that he is
aware of the behavioral elements requisite for a successful performance
of either masculinity or femininity. One delightful scene shows him
standing before his bedroom mirror, trying to perform masculinity by
shooting an imaginary gun and then overtly adjusting his groin. The
problem with Ludo's performance of masculinity (a direct inversion of
the situation which occurs in other male cross-dressing films) is that he
is unable to discard his primary identification with femininity. Trying
once more to appease his parents, he attempts to kiss a female classmate, but is roughly rebuked with the retort "I don't kiss girls!"

Ma Vie en Rose is significant because it explicitly and realistically
deals with transsexual identity in its portrayal of a young boy who
desires, above all else, to be a girl. Perhaps the most realistic aspect
of *Ma Vie en Rose*, however, is the rating that it received in the USA
from the Motion Picture Association of America: R, meaning that
viewing of the film was restricted and patrons 17 years and under had
to be accompanied by an adult. The film contains no sex or violence,
but the rating suggests that the idea of a young child grappling with
an unconventional gender identity is, ironically, something that only
adults can understand and appreciate. Such a rating also seems to be
based on the assumption that sexual and gender identity are one and
the same. Given this rating, it is difficult to suggest that this film is
indeed children's text. The great tragedy of the restricted rating which
Ma Vie en Rose received is that this is a film which offers a rare and
frequently beautiful exploration of socially constructed gender sexual
identities, using childish innocence to deconstruct the often irrational
limitations which are socially imposed upon individuals who dare to
be different. Alan Stone compares the film to Disney productions, presumably because its thematic exploration of a child's search for identity
and affirmation of the nuclear family unit resonates with contemporary
films produced for child viewers:

> By film industry standards, Scotta's audacity in producing the
> film is even more impressive. *Ma Vie en Rose* has no action, no
> violence, no romance, no aliens, no natural disasters—not even
> a recognizable star. It is certainly no comedy and, though it is
> a film about children, many conventional parents will not want
> their children to see it. In sum, it has no targeted audience. Yet in
> a world that genuinely prized and did not just tolerate difference,

this film would have been made by Disney. It marks a new, truthful departure in cinematic understanding of difference in human sexuality and gender identity in children.

An important element of Ludo's story, however, is that he lives in a world which lacks tolerance for individuals whose identity deviates from conventional identity categories. Ludo's innocent cross-dressing behavior (appearing at parties in his sister's dresses and mother's makeup; acting out a wedding and taking the part of the bride) is tragically misunderstood by the adults in his world, who have no comprehension as to how they should deal with him. Part of the problem is that Ludo's cross-dressing is immediately confused with homosexuality, which is viewed by his small French community as a sin of enormous proportions. Ludo is, however, only seven years old, and his appreciation of sexuality is accordingly limited. His cross-dressing is the product of a subversive gender identity, yet the adults around Ludo continually confuse gender transgression with sexual transgression.

Ludo's cross-dressing causes rifts in his small and socially conservative neighborhood. It prompts his parents to send him to a psychiatrist, in the hope that medical intervention will correct Ludo's feminine identification. His parents' marriage is fractured as they struggle inexpertly with the question of how to handle their son's "problem." Finally Ludo is expelled from school, with the principal coldly telling his parents that "Ludovic's behavior and tastes are too eccentric for this school." After soccer practice one afternoon, Ludo is cruelly attacked by his peers, a situation made all the more tragic by the fact that his two older brothers are passive bystanders to the beating. Soon afterward, the traumatized Ludo climbs into a freezer and goes to sleep. His attempted suicide conveys the impact and severity of his social and familial alienation. Without support from family or peers, and subjected to strident public opposition and medical interference, Ludo finds it impossible to continue living. Michael Schiavi (2004, 1) comments upon Ludo's abjection, arguing that his voice is systematically appropriated by others:

> The sadism propelling *Ma Vie en Rose* is less literal than taxonomic, the brutal process by which, Pat Califia notes, "differently-gendered" subjects are divested of the voice that makes them subjects: "To be differently gendered is to live within a discourse where other people are always investigating you, describing you, and speaking for you; and putting as much distance as possible between the expert speaker and the deviant and therefore deficient subject" (1997, 2). The "expert's" words take on particular force

when categorizing a boy whose behavior draws the notice of everyone around him but who, paradoxically, cannot speak for himself.

Ma Vie en Rose contributes to a discussion and analysis of cross-dressing in children's literature because it is operative on two distinctive levels, the child's world and the adult's world, revolving around the effects and repercussions that result when the two collide. *Ma Vie en Rose* is the ultimate precursor to the modern children's cross-dressing text, as it combines a childhood naiveté regarding cross-dressing, innocently dissociated from wider cultural connections with homosexuality, immorality, and perversion, with the popular adult-oriented concept of transsexuality, which negatively correlates transsexual individuals with a range of immoral (and/or psychotic) behaviors.

Although Ludo's search for identity is also a tale of the calamitous social and personal effects of his quest, his story ultimately has a happy ending. Driven out of their neighborhood, Ludo and his family move to a new community, where he meets Chris (Christine), a girl who similarly shuns the behavior and physical appearance conventional to her gender. At her birthday party, Christine jealously regards Ludo's cavalier costume and then forces him to swap clothes with her. Ludo's mother becomes hysterical when she initially sees him wearing Christine's blue party dress, but Ludo's terror at her reaction, coupled with Christine's hurried explanation that she is responsible, ultimately prompts his parents to reconsider their attitudes to their son's transgendered behavior. Confronted by a female child who displays correspondingly transgressive gender behavior, Ludo's parents are implicitly made aware of the gender inequity that characterizes the two children's search for an identity that lies outside of socially prescribed gender boundaries. While Chris's masculine appearance and behavior are socially and parentally condoned within a society that enthusiastically encourages girls to pursue masculine interests, the same encouragement is sadly replaced by vilification when a boy attempts to do the same. This realization propels Ludo's parents to accept him as he is, an acceptance that is symbolically represented by the film's final scene, which shows Ludo, attired in Christine's blue dress, playing happily with the other children at her party.

The social reality of this final scene is debatable, given the previously staunch social opposition to Ludo's cross-dressing, but it does offer narrative hope for Ludovic and transgendered subjectivity. Christine's birthday party functions figuratively as a space of childish playfulness and gaiety, and Ludo's presence and active involvement within that space signals an end to the oppressive, adult categorization of his identity. He has regained the power to exist as a child, and his wearing of Christine's blue dress indicates that he has negotiated this new and self-determining existence on his own transgendered terms.

Ma Vie en Rose signals a new approach to the representation of cross-dressing in children's literature and film, questioning the imposition of sexualized adult discourses upon a child's subjective development. At the same time, Berliner's film effectively interrogates masculine identity (and its concomitant requirement of compulsory heterosexuality), providing a compassionate portrayal of transgendered subjectivity that endorses self-determination and difference.

FEMALE CROSS-DRESSING IN FILMS FOR CHILDREN AND ADOLESCENTS

The carnivalesque characters which populate films such as *Sorority Boys, Mrs. Doubtfire,* and *Ace Ventura* are absent from *Ma Vie en Rose,* which instead offers a unique construction of male cross-dressing that sensitively deconstructs normative gender categories. Ludo's cross-dressing therefore has much in common with the typical representation of female cross-dressing in children's literature, where cross-dressing similarly functions to critique prevailing social attitudes to gender. Given the success of cross-dressing heroines (and their historical abundance), it is surprising that female cross-dressing is almost totally absent from films produced for child or teenage viewers. Although *Mulan* is an excellent example of cinematic female cross-dressing, it is an animated film—a genre which circumvents the issue of visual appearance because of its two-dimensional nature. Visual appearance is a key distinguishing factor between male cross-dressing literature and film, but because *Mulan's* low modality (i.e., lack of photographic realism) makes this issue considerably less significant, I have chosen to omit it from the discussion of female cross-dressing in film. The remaining possibilities for an examination of female cross-dressing are limited to the classic children's film *National Velvet* [1944] and the British television series *Harry Enfield Presents Kevin's Guide to Being a Teenager* [1999], which in turn inspired the recent film *Kevin and Perry Go Large* [2000]. This film and television series will only be addressed briefly, as cross-dressing does not have a thematic function in either. Instead, it functions only as a plot device in *National Velvet,* and in the case of *Kevin's Guide to Being a Teenager,* it is not raised at all; rather, it is the result of casting. It is therefore difficult to compare these texts particularly effectively with the films discussed previously.

Cross-dressing plays a very minor and insignificant role in *National Velvet*, in contrast to the typical presentation of female cross-dressing in children's books. Velvet, the young female protagonist, decides to enter her horse, Pi, into the Grand National championship race. Because the race is only open to male jockeys, Velvet must pretend that she is male in order to participate. Attired in the conventional jockey's outfit (which is now currently worn by both men and women), the only effort Velvet makes to disguise her femininity is to cut her long hair. She manages to avoid detection simply by keeping her head down and remaining silent—but is immediately recognized as female when she falls off her horse in a faint after winning the title (a gesture distinctively gendered as feminine within the era in which the film was produced). Velvet's cross-dressing is therefore a failure in most respects, as she manages to disguise her biological sex for only a matter of minutes before she is publicly exposed as a female.

Cross-dressing, if Velvet's momentary disguise can even be called that, has little thematic significance. Gender issues are implicitly relevant to *National Velvet*, due to the role Velvet's mother (the first woman to swim the English Channel) plays in supporting her head-strong daughter, but the film's gender ideology subtly encourages feminine ability rather than critiquing the attributes socially constructed as feminine. The cross-dressing which occurs in *Kevin's Guide to Being a Teenager*, however, is of a quite different nature. The premise of this comedy skit, which was produced as a series for BBC Television, is to parody the agonies of adolescence and satirize the issues associated with adolescent identity. The irony of the situation is that the characters of thirteen-year-old Kevin and his best friend, Perry, are played by the middle-aged adult comedians Harry Enfield and Kathy Burke, respectively. The comedy of the series is anything but understated, revolving around the two comedians' overtly teenage costumes (baggy clothes, pimply faces, unkempt hair) and dramatically exaggerated performance of adolescent male behavior.

Perry is never presented to viewers as a cross-dresser (and the issue of cross-dressing is not raised within the context of the narrative), but Burke's masculine performance is inherently successful because her true sex is largely undetectable. As Perry, she awkwardly postures and slouches like any adolescent male—and, in fact, she is much more successful at rendering an authentic teenage male performance than her biologically male costar Enfield, whose performance as Harry is so overacted that it becomes a caricature of adolescent masculinity rather than insightful satire. Robert Furze, in a review of the film *Kevin and*

Perry Go Large, which was based on the BBC series, comments specifically on the difference between Burke's and Enfield's performances:

Enfield, too, has apparently no idea about the changes needed for the cross-over to cinema, feeling that it is enough to stick his tongue out, wave his arms around and snort just as he does in the show. Unfortunately, the close-ups writ large of him doing this "teenage act" reveal a shallow, cynical method to his synthetic caricature. There is no presence to Kevin, only a vacuum where character should be. Burke, on the other hand, cross-dressing in baggy, trendy gear, does "get it." Whereas Kevin merely sags like a bag of expensive clothes, Perry is the perfect lampoon of teenage masculinity, all swagger and gesture, whilst also showing a degree of sentience. It would be stretching it to say Burke saves the film, but at the very least she drags it away from total disaster.

Burke's cross-dressing performance is analogous to Sean Young's in *Ace Ventura*, in the sense that both of these female actors attempt to evoke a masculine subjectivity by changing their behavior in order to approximate the actions, gestures, and other body language associated with being a man. Their success lies primarily in the way that they move and use their (now masculine) bodies, as each woman effectively replicates the way in which men have been traditionally conditioned to occupy physical space more freely than women. Burke is more successful in her achievement of a convincing portrayal of masculinity than Young, although Young arguably has a much harder role to perform (she is a female actress trying to act like a man would act if he were a woman). As Perry, Burke is almost unrecognizable as a woman.[5] Not only does she master the art of giving a masculine performance, in terms of the way she swaggers and gesticulates, but she also manages to capture the awkwardness of male adolescence. This is illustrated in her repeated interactions with Kevin's parents (she averts her eyes and speaks in monosyllabic grunts), and also, most particularly, in a scene where Perry encounters an attractive teenage girl. Burke's cross-dressed performance is the perfect combination of unease and eagerness to please.

The character of Perry is perhaps the most interesting of all the cinematic (or televised, in this case) cross-dressing roles discussed so far (both male and female), because Burke's performance successfully unites the significant issues of behavioral and physical transformation. Until now, cross-dressing performances in children's literature and film have been divided according to gender: for female-to-male cross-dressers, the behavioral performance of masculinity is the focus, while for male-to-female cross-dressers, the only concession to femininity is an often dubious adoption of feminine clothing, footwear, and makeup. Male cross-dressers seem genuinely unaware that to pass as feminine requires more than just a physical makeover. Burke, however, proves that she is capable of both looking *and* behaving like a male.

Kevin's Guide to Being a Teenager provides a revealing contrast and useful point of conclusion to my earlier discussion of male cross-dressing performances in films. *Sorority Boys* and *Mrs. Doubtfire* each use a carnivalesque mode to present grotesque male cross-dressing characters who maintain rather than subvert normative gender categories. They fail to recognize the performative aspects of femininity, relying only on visual disguises, and as such their cross-dressing is always superficial and easily detectable. The cross-dressers' simplistic summation of femininity is also indicative of the misogynistic construction of femininity within these films, a construction which is maintained by both the cross-dressers' attitudes to their unwilling adoption of feminine identity and the hostility and contempt with which biological females within the narrative are portrayed. The small inroads that *Mrs. Doubtfire* makes in relation to promoting transgressive gender behavior as a viable lifestyle choice are, however, a significant and progressive development of the general representation of cross-dressing in children's literature and film. The importance of *Mrs. Doubtfire's* tolerant portrayal of subversive gender identity is highlighted when considered with a much more conservative film such as *Ace Ventura*, which disturbingly follows the precedent set in adult films such as *Psycho* and *The Silence of the Lambs* by depicting transsexualism as a signifier of sociopathy and moral depravity.

Although *Kevin's Guide to Being a Teenager* does not address the issue of adult cross-dressing reality, it does indicate that it is possible for an individual of one sex to transform his or her gender identity in a convincing manner—on both a physical and a behavioral level. Notwithstanding the fact that "convincing" is a slippery term when applied to the notion of gender identity as it relates to a fictional character within a theatrical performance, owing to factors such as a prepared script and directorial guidance, Burke plays the part of Perry in a manner which compellingly reveals the distinction between natal sex and gender. Her masculine transformation is indeed a satire of adolescent subjectivity, but, as Butler writes, "The parodic repetition of gender exposes...the illusion of gender identity as an intractable depth and inner substance" (1999, 187). This is, in essence, what contemporary transgendered subjects are seeking to persuade the rest of society to accept.

Burke's performance is also similar, in some ways, to the construction of cross-dressing in *Ma Vie en Rose*. Unlike *Ma Vie en Rose*, *Kevin's Guide to Being a Teenager* is not about the importance of treating transgendered individuals with tolerance. However, this television series, which features an adult, female actress whose satirical performance of adolescent masculinity is a deliciously comic blend of exaggerated bravado and teenage angst, is equally effective at proving that cross-dressing can have an unsettling impact on societal evaluations of gender and its presumed relationship with natal sex. In distinctive ways, both Perry/Burke and Ludo use cross-dressing to challenge, destabilize, and subvert normative gender categories for the purpose of reevaluating their day-to-day construction and operation. Such a comparison collapses the contemporary categories of transsexual and transvestite, resulting in an amalgamated cross-dressing subject who problematizes the patriarchal gender binary by interrogating the cultural practices which regulate and inscribe gender on individual bodies. *Kevin's Guide to Being a Teenager* and *Ma Vie en Rose* stand as exemplary illustrations of cross-dressing's ability to strike at the foundations of established gender paradigms. To use an expression coined by Anne Bolin, each text reveals that cross-dressing is about "the disassembling of gender" (1994, 485). While the cross-dressed performances of Burke and Ludo re-create stereotypical images of masculinity and femininity, each nonetheless visually and linguistically discloses the way in which bodies are gendered through the repetition of certain behaviors and gestures. The disjunction between the actor's or character's gendered actions/language and natal sex in these particular texts repeatedly calls into question those masculine and feminine attributes which have traditionally been perceived as "natural." Burke and Ludo lay bare the constructedness of patriarchal gender categories by successfully performing the gender identity supposedly at odds with their biological sex. By doing so, each categorically proves, to use Bolin's words again, that the figure of the cross-dresser is "disquieting to the established gender system and unsettles the boundaries of bipolarity and opposition in the gender schema by suggesting a continuum of masculinity and femininity, renouncing gender as aligned with genitals, body, social status, and/or role" (447).

7

EMERGING IDENTITIES
Cross-Dressing and Sexuality in Adolescent Fiction

Heterosexual ideology, in combination with a potent ideology about gender and identity in maturation, therefore bears down in the heaviest and often deadliest way on those with the least resources to combat it: queer children and teens. In a culture dominated by talk of "family values," the outlook is grim for any hope that child-rearing institutions of home and state can become less oppressive.

Michael Warner
Fear of a Queer Plant

INTRODUCTION

The sexual identity of cross-dressing characters is a subject that is rarely raised in children's literature. Within the modern transgender context, however, where the term "transgender" has come to signify a political alliance between all people "who challenge the boundaries of sex and gender" (Feinberg 1996, preface), sexuality plays a highly significant role in determining whether or not an individual conforms to the socially prescribed concepts of masculinity and femininity. Sexual identity is inextricably linked with gender identity in our society, and therefore adult cross-dressing functions not only as an expression of gender transgression but can also be an indication of a nonnormative sexual identity. The relationship between cross-dressing and subversive sexualities (transvestite, transsexual, homosexual) remained unacknowledged in children's texts until only recently. The recent proliferation of literature directed at adolescents, however, has demonstrated an unprecedented willingness to embrace adult concepts previously considered off-limits to younger readers, and is responsible for sowing significant seeds of change in the depiction of cross-dressing in children's narratives. Deviating from the paradigms established in literature and films for younger audiences, an increasing number of young adult (YA) novels provide readers with a representation of cross-dressing that embraces the complexity of transgendered subjectivity. Rather than shying away from the issues of gender and sexual non-conformity as they relate to cross-dressing, these texts confront and explore such concerns, as well as acknowledging the social obstacles and discrimination that transgendered individuals often face within the wider community. Currently, very few texts can be classified within this third cross-dressing category, which I've chosen to name the transgender paradigm. The thematic outcome and resolution of this type of cross-dressing portrayal are varied, as there remains a disjunction between the representation of female and male experiences within this model. Irrespective of these differences, this particular group of novels shares an emerging tolerance toward transgendered subjectivity and an appreciation of how cross-dressing can signify a legitimate expression of nonconformist sexual and gender identities. Subverting the long-established tradition for cross-dressing representations in children's literature, which dissociate themselves from the adult world of transgender, these novels indicate a radical change in the way that cross-dressing is presented to preadult readers.

"The Mouse, the Thing and the Wand" and "The Counterfeit Marquise," two transgender stories discussed previously in Chapter 2, are unusual in that they are historical fairy tales, yet deal with the subject of cross-dressing in a progressive and tolerant fashion more commonly associated with contemporary novels. These fairy stories explicitly depict transsexual and transvestite characters, each of whom transgresses the general paradigmatic structures of female and male cross-dressing. They do this by virtue of their transgendered sexual identities and because their cross-dressing is not confined to a specific period but is a permanent facet of their subjectivities. However, these fairy tales offer highly symbolic or fantastic versions of transgender existence that bear only a limited relationship to contemporary social reality. "The Mouse, the Thing and the Wand," a story of female-to-male cross-dressing revolving around a transsexual protagonist who desperately desires a biological male body to accord with her masculine gender identity, resolves the dilemma between the heroine's sex and gender by magically granting her a penis in the narrative's closure. "The Counterfeit Marquise," a fairy tale that features male-to-female cross-dressing, employs a similarly fantastical strategy: on the marquise's wedding night, her bridegroom reveals that he, too, is a cross-dresser. The fairy tale conventions employed by both texts—such as the brevity of the actual narrative, the use of archetypal characters (kings, princesses, or other royalty) and plots (death of a parent), and a happy ending—necessarily restrict the portrayal of transgendered subjectivity to a simple, one-dimensional construction that fails to encompass the social complexity of transgendered identity. Notwithstanding the limitations imposed by the use of the fairy tale genre and form, "The Mouse, the Thing and the Wand" and "The Counterfeit Marquise" are to be admired for their compassionate representation of individuals whose gender identity fails to accord with their sex. These fairy tales are historical precursors to the group of contemporary novels that I have categorized as belonging to the transgender model.

Aside from these unique fairy tales, precious little children's literature or film over the past two centuries has sought to include characters who are transgendered. This situation has changed over recent years because a thriving genre of YA literature has materialized. Texts within this genre which deal specifically with themes pertaining to homosexual identity are particularly relevant, because cross-dressing is often constructed as a rite of passage for gay male subjectivity. YA fiction tends to focus primarily on images and constructions of selfhood. It is concerned with exploring the relationships between individual selves and the social and cultural forces and ideologies that influence their formation, as well as the relationship between individual selves and other selves. YA novels thus constitute an ideal site for the exploration of cross-dressing in a manner that integrates and harmonizes the issues that are raised by representations of cross-dressing in the two other cross-dressing paradigms. Within the female-to-male paradigm, cross-dressing is a strategy for deconstructing the socially established concepts of masculinity and femininity. The female cross-dresser is a facility through which to create a third, more liberating, category of gender. The abundant potential of cross-dressing as a narrative strategy to generate insightful gender criticism is not utilized in the male paradigm. Male cross-dressing representations are typically too preoccupied with distancing their protagonists from the perceived threat of adult cross-dressing sexuality—or, to be more precise, the threat of homosexuality and its possibility for emasculation. The transgender paradigm bridges these two representational models. Like the female paradigm, it offers a representation of cross-dressing that acknowledges cross-dressing's ability to destabilize conventional gender constructions. In addition, it simultaneously engages with a more adult and sexuality-oriented transgender discourse—a discourse that is implicit within the male-to-female paradigm (if only because the texts within this paradigm strive to reject such an insinuation). The transgender paradigm uses cross-dressing to critique socially constructed gender categorizations, but at the same time it recognizes that cross-dressing is not just an analytical tool. It acknowledges that, in reality, cross-dressing has implications that relate to sexuality and sexual/gender identities.

The recuperation of cross-dressing as a relevant theme for texts directed at adolescent readers is evident in its changing construction in the transgender paradigm. The presentation of cross-dressing in my chosen examples of young adult (YA) fiction is closely related to contemporary "adult" transgender concepts, embracing the subjective complexity that these notions encompass. The traditional dichotomy between cross-dressing in children's literature (playful, harmless, experimental) and adult cross-dressing (sexual, pleasurable, compulsive, psychological) is redressed in these texts. The result is a portrayal of cross-dressing that refuses to disengage itself from reality and involves itself in the previously deemed adults-only world of transgender. However, the socially transgressive nature of cross-dressing within this transgender paradigm still functions differently in relation to the gender of the cross-dresser. There remains a disparity between the experiences of male and female cross-dressers, although in this case it inverts the established divergence between female and male literary cross-dressers. Whereas female cross-dressing has traditionally provided a serious critique of socially contrived gender categories, and male cross-dressing is commonly trivialized into a comedy routine the transgender paradigm presents female cross-dressing in a more conservative and negative fashion. Conversely, it is the male cross-dressers within this model whose gender construction challenges gender stereotypes and seeks to redefine "masculinity" and "femininity."

THE FEMALE TRANSGENDER SUBJECT

Two novels that substantively challenge the traditional presentation of cross-dressing, offering a renewed perspective on issues relating to the act of transvestism, are *Touch Me* (2000) and *Johnny, My Friend* (1985). Peter Pohl's *Johnny, My Friend* is a Swedish coming-of-age mystery novel that offers a particularly unusual portrayal of female cross-dressing. Narrated in the first person by Chris, who begins the story when he is eleven years old, it is about his short-lived friendship with Johnny, a mysterious and peculiar boy who suddenly enters his life and becomes his best friend. At the close of the novel a tragedy unfolds, and Johnny's murdered body is discovered. Only after his death does Chris discover that Johnny is actually a girl—a trapeze artist from a traveling circus who, it is suggested, is killed because of her cross-dressing transgressions. *Touch Me*, by James Moloney, an Australian YA novel, revolves around the relationship between Xavier, a conventional teenage boy, and a rather unusual girl named Nuala. Nuala is a charismatic and vivacious young woman who is regarded as strange and enigmatic by her peers because of her unusual presentation: she dresses as a man. *Johnny, My Friend* and *Touch Me* uniquely address contemporary issues relating to transvestism and transsexualism.

Johnny, My Friend contains a representation of cross-dressing that compassionately acknowledges the alienation, psychological anguish, and social intolerance that are inseparable from contemporary transsexual identity, issues that are not usually broached in children's fiction. Johnny's death is indicative of the social consequences that can follow the subversion of established gender codes. The novel imbues the act of cross-dressing with a gravity that is lacking from most portrayals of female cross-dressing, where the heroine's cross-dressing is typically forgiven because of the admirable deeds she has performed while in disguise, which elevate her beyond reproach.

The depiction of cross-dressing in *Touch Me* also indicates a departure from the conventional portrayal of female cross-dressing in children's literature, particularly in relation to the issue of cross-dressing sexuality. When Xavier finds himself attracted to Nuala's unconventionality, his blossoming romance is not welcomed by his male friends, who seem unable to comprehend Nuala's disdain for "normal" feminine conventions. Her visual oddity is construed as an abnormality by these boys, and explained in terms of abnormal and "othered" sexuality. They believe that Nuala is a lesbian. Of course, this does not offer an explanation for Xavier's relationship with her. His friendship with Nuala is rationalized in similarly illogical terms: because Xavier is spending time with a girl of questionable sexual orientation who dresses as a boy, his friends interpret this behavior as an indication of his own homosexuality. *Touch Me* is not an exploration of homosexuality, however, but rather a voyage into the more unconventional area of transgendered sexuality. While Nuala, the cross-dressing protagonist of *Touch Me*, is not transsexual or homosexual, her transgender performance is effective in conveying to the reader the potentially problematic issue of sexuality as it relates to transgendered subjects.

The issue of sexuality is integral to *Touch Me*. Sex plays a primary role in Nuala's cross-dressing, differentiating it from the more common representations of female cross-dressing. It is born out of an incident that occurred before the commencement of the narrative, when Nuala first became aware of her emerging sexuality. Tired of always having to play a conventionally passive sexual role with her boyfriend Gavin, she admits to wanting to have sex as much as he does. When he decides to test her voracity for sex by asking another male friend to attempt to seduce her, she retaliates by ending the romance and publicly rebuking him. As punishment, Gavin enlists the help of his friends to destroy Nuala's reputation. They spread wild rumors about her sexual promiscuity and create digitally enhanced pornographic pictures of her, which they then display at her high school.[1] The public humiliation that she suffers as a consequence of this vindictive behavior leads to her decision to reconstruct her body as something other than an object of male sexual desire. Nuala angrily responds by ridding herself of any outward signifiers of femininity or feminine sexuality—cutting her long hair and disguising her hips in loose men's clothing. Dressed as a young man, she is liberated from the objectifying gaze of masculinity and the traditional sexual threat it poses to femininity. This is amply demonstrated by the hostile reaction her appearance provokes in Xavier's male friends.

The construction of cross-dressing as an escape is also evident in *Johnny, My Friend*. Johnny's motivation for disguising himself (I refer to Johnny with the masculine pronoun because this is the pronoun used to refer to him throughout the text) is never made explicit, although the novel implies that it is the result of a repressive and unforgiving environment. The decision to cross-dress as a boy can be interpreted as an attempt to dissociate himself completely from his other existence (as a female trapeze artist, forced to perform in a ballerina-like ensemble). The question of whether "Johnny" is simply the most effective hiding device available to an unhappy and daring young girl, or a deliberately constructed image of the boy she would rather be, is left open. The possibilities offered by Johnny's cross-dressing are cruelly closed by his death. This ending ultimately warns of the hostility that may accompany gender subversion in a realistic social context.

The destabilizing and subversive power of the cross-dresser, evident from the murderous reaction to Johnny's transgender behavior, is displayed very differently in *Touch Me*. Nuala's ability to unsettle those around her is constructed in subtler, yet no less confrontational, terms. Her cross-dressing and the conflicting sexual messages it sends to her peers are complicated by her own attitude to it. Although dressed convincingly as a man, she does not actually pretend to be male. Her cross-dressing pleasure is born out of the very gender confusion her projected persona creates. She identifies as female when interacting with people she knows, yet seeks to appear male to those outside her acquaintance. The visual dilemma Nuala presents to others is also problematized by the fact that her masculine clothing accompanies a face that is dramatically enhanced with cosmetics. She wears dark lipstick that makes "a cherry-colored slash across her face," and her eyebrows are plucked into "thin, coal-black lines that curved over gaudy eye shadow and teased-out lashes" (26). In short, Nuala is an embodiment of drag.

Esther Newton, whose analysis of drag is included in Butler's exploration of gender performativity (Butler [1990] 1999, 174), explains the way in which a drag artist deliberately plays with the masculine/feminine dichotomy:

> At its most complex, [drag] is a double inversion that says, "appearance is an illusion." Drag says "my 'outside' appearance is feminine, but my essence 'inside' is masculine." At the same time it symbolizes the opposite inversion: "my appearance 'outside' is masculine but my essence 'inside' myself is feminine."
>
> (*Mother Camp* 1972, 103)

Vern and Bonnie Bullough give a more generalized analysis (which is useful in Nuala's context because she is biologically female) suggesting that drag is a "confusion of costume whereby the illusion of assuming the opposite sex is not intended to convince the viewer of authenticity but to suggest ambiguity" (246). The function of drag as a form of gender duality is not lost on Nuala. She is acutely aware of the effects of her gender-bending: "She smiled contemptuously. 'They can't work out whether I'm a cross-dressing female or a boy with serious cosmetic dysfunction'" (28). Nuala is quick to learn that her cross-dressing has powerful potential. She treats it as a game, relishing the perplexity that she constantly engenders in people unable to read her scrambled gender messages. She particularly enjoys male reactions, conscious of the fact that she is the more powerful individual as long as she remains "unknowable" and inexplicable.

Gender is constructed in *Johnny, My Friend* and *Touch Me* as something transformable and subject to individual manipulation. Johnny and Nuala successfully subvert conventional gender constructions, although the path of subversion for these characters is not as easy as it is for cross-dressing heroines in more traditional female cross-dressing texts. Johnny and Nuala's gender subversion is less extraordinary, and although they present convincingly as males in some circumstances, their biological femininity is not always hidden from view. In Johnny's case, this is strikingly illustrated by Chris's first comparison of him with the female literary character Pippi Longstocking ([1985] 1991, 10). Chris's perception of Johnny as female is instantly problematized when the "girl" announces that her name is "Johnny," but situations in which Johnny's femininity becomes visible continue to arise. Chris's mother asks, "Who's the young lady?" (44) when Chris brings Johnny home for the first time, but afterward Johnny's masculine behavior convinces her that her initial impression was incorrect. According to Chris's narration, Johnny maintains a successful masculine subjectivity throughout the novel, but it is difficult to ascertain whether this is because Johnny's masculine performance is truly authentic or because Chris is forgiving of his friend's behavior. The most telling indication of Johnny's performative failure occurs just prior to his death, when he and Chris spend a night camping together. As they huddle together for warmth, Chris becomes sexually aroused as he presses his body against Johnny's: "I just lay in another world and couldn't care less that my dick was pressing up against him" (209). Chris is completely unself-conscious about his sexual attraction to Johnny. He continues to refer to Johnny with the masculine pronoun "him" when recounting his sexual excitement, but never expresses any concern or curiosity about his transgressive same-sex desire. The implication of Chris's silence is that he is somehow aware that Johnny's masculinity is not genuine.

Nuala's cross-dressing, in contrast, is successful only to those people not in her immediate circle of friends. From afar she presents as a male, but on closer inspection she is recognizable as female due to her feminine name and voice, and the fact that she does not hide her biology in the context of her school life and social interactions. This said, Nuala's attempts to subvert gender conventions are perhaps more significant than Johnny's. In presenting herself as a girl in drag, Nuala confuses and undermines the assumptions regarding gender that inform even the most basic levels of human interaction. As Freud argues, "When you meet a human being, the first distinction you make is "male or female?" and you are accustomed to make the distinction with unhesitating certainty" ([1933] 1964, Vol 2, 113). Nuala presents simultaneously as both male and female, causing a disturbance wherever she goes. She is a testament to the artificiality of traditional gender constructs, constantly demonstrating the ease with which such constructs can be challenged and rendered meaningless—all that is needed is the requisite clothing and a knowledge of gendered behaviors. Nonetheless, this success comes at a price. Nuala is perpetually misunderstood because of her gender rebellion, and alienated even from those people who attempt to see past the barriers she has erected around herself. Nuala's starring role in a school performance of George Bernard Shaw's play *Saint Joan* is used as a cross-dressing metaphor throughout the novel. Nuala's female peer group approves of her cross-dressing behavior (presumably because it demonstrates her assertiveness in the face of community opposition), and like the adoration which Joan of Arc inspired, the girls similarly believe that Nuala is "their champion" (91). The symbolic relationship between Nuala and Joan of Arc is potentially disquieting, however, as it accentuates the correlation between nonconformist gender behavior and tragedy. The image of a cross-dressed Joan, executed partly because of her refusal to abandon her masculine clothing, ominously looms over Nuala's head and prevents the reader from possibly interpreting gender transgression as anything other than socially ruinous.

In spite of these issues concerning the success of Johnny and Nuala's masculine performances, both novels construct gender as a complex and multifaceted concept. *Johnny, My Friend* and *Touch Me* clearly reveal the artificiality of traditional gender divisions through the portrayal of characters who successfully achieve a gendered persona at odds with their biological sex, albeit only temporarily. Whether or not a biological female can give a convincing performance of masculinity is not at issue here: both Johnny and Nuala clearly do. At stake is the social cost of such transgressive behavior.

The treatment of cross-dressing in *Johnny, My Friend* and *Touch Me* is progressive, though not radical. These novels sympathetically introduce the concept of gender transgression within a realistic social setting to younger audiences. However, Johnny and Nuala's transgendered identities are not depicted as symptomatic of a contemporary relaxation of limited gender roles. Gender is revealed as an artificial social construct in each novel, but its traditional significance in a wider cultural context is maintained, both thematically and through the use of narrative strategies that reinscribe the hierarchical superiority of masculinity. Neither Johnny nor Nuala are permitted to tell their own stories; instead they are presented to readers through the eyes of male focalizing characters. Reproducing mainstream culture's tendency to marginalize transgender identity, relegating it to the periphery, where it is always perceived as "other," Chris and Xavier appropriate Johnny and Nuala's stories and reframe them within their own masculine/heterosexual (and therefore normative) perspective and experience. *Touch Me* is more complicit in constructing transgendered subjectivity as abject because it employs a focalizing character, Xavier, whose masculinity is initially situated firmly within a hegemonic masculine discourse (football, and Xavier's passion for it, is used metonymically throughout the novel to symbolize patriarchal masculine values). The novel's closure hopefully suggests that Xavier's relationship with Nuala has enabled him to negotiate a more other-regarding and agential masculine subjectivity which recognizes the oppressive nature of patriarchal gender practices, but his final gift of a dress to Nuala is indicative of his enduring desire to coerce her into adopting a more conventional gender identity. Nuala's acceptance of the dress, in which her own subjective development is implicated, is intriguingly left unexplored. In making Xavier's point of view central, the novel does not attempt to give Nuala's character focalizing capabilities. An example of the way in which the novel distances itself from Nuala can be found in its curiously revealing prologue. Almost cinematic in construction, this passage details the exact moment in which Nuala explicitly rejects her former feminine identity in favor of a more ambiguously gendered subjectivity. Throughout this scene Nuala is never referred to by name, but simply as "the girl" (1). She remains a distant and inexplicable character throughout the narrative, and her attempts at gender confusion are ultimately thwarted by Xavier's desire to "rescue" her from social alienation and bring her back within the less troubling parameters of femininity and heterosexuality (regardless of Nuala's self-professed excitement at existing in the invisible but liberating space between these normative confines).

The resolution of *Touch Me* is less tragic than that of *Johnny, My Friend*, but Johnny's death is significant in that it allows him to retain his transgendered subjectivity, unlike Nuala, who must abandon it. As narrator, Chris's reaction upon learning the truth about Johnny is demonstrably less colonizing than Xavier's comparable need to transform Nuala. The ending of *Johnny, My Friend* is framed by Chris assisting the police with information about Johnny's murder. The novel experimentally combines the present tense of the dialogue between Chris and the police, which re-creates the last moments of Johnny's life, with Chris's experiential perception of the situation, formulated as a series of overlapping, stream-of-consciousness thoughts. Interwoven among these two levels of narration is Chris's internal, grief-stricken monologue to the now-dead Johnny. His elegy to Johnny conveys his anguish at the events that have unfolded, but most crucially this dialogue expresses his regret at not being able to see that Johnny needed protection:

> And even so I left you in tears, all alone up there against the wall. Forgive me, Johnny. I didn't understand at all, I got scared, can you forgive me, I got so scared and screamed that I was dying,

when I should have been listening. And you should have had a chance to explain....

Johnny! For God's sake, Johnny. Forgive me and come back! (252–253)

Chris's poignant repentance for not sheltering Johnny from a hostile world is a more empathetic response to transgendered identity than Xavier's, but it is too little too late. Johnny's societal alienation is completed by his death—which erases the possibility of ever being able to speak for himself and ensures his enduring cultural invisibility as a transgendered subject.

The focalizing strategies used to marginalize Johnny and Nuala's voices accord with by the thematic treatment of transgendered identity in each novel. Both *Touch Me* and *Johnny, My Friend* thematically caution readers about the viability of gender transgression. The repercussions of transgender behavior are serious and far-reaching in these novels, demonstrated by the hostile reactions that both Johnny and Nuala encounter. Gender is presented as an oppressive social construct that can potentially be challenged by individual perseverance, but such a challenge is carefully depicted as fraught with difficulty and the possibility of negative social impact. *Touch Me* and *Johnny, My Friend* use cross-dressing to reveal the artificiality of traditional gender constructs, presenting it as a means through which such constructs can be subverted, but the overriding message in both novels is overtly negative. The transgender paradigm as it applies to female cross-dressers thus reverses a number of the female paradigm's critical achievements, suggesting that a refusal to be interpellated by oppressive gender ideologies can negatively impact a subject's capacity for agency.

Despite these shortcomings, *Touch Me* and *Johnny, My Friend* offer a renewed representation of cross-dressing that is more reflective of contemporary reality than other examples of female cross-dressing. First, Nuala is a character who embodies many of the elements associated with adult transvestism: she is heterosexual rather than gay, but derives pleasure from expressing a gender identity different from the one supposedly aligned with her biological sex. Johnny is similarly distinct from most examples of female cross-dressing because his masculine gender identity is not part of a temporary performance but rather a conscious expression of preference, marking him as transsexual within an adult transgender framework. Nuala and Johnny's behavior can therefore be read in accordance with an adult transgender discourse, as opposed to the female cross-dressing paradigm, which stridently discourages such associations. Second, the political and social repression that characterizes transgender experience in *Touch Me* and *Johnny, My Friend* is not unrealistic, but rather an accurate depiction of the negative social attitudes that transgender identity typically attracts.

The willingness of *Touch Me* and *Johnny, My Friend* to explore the concept of cross-dressing in a socially realistic fashion aligned with the adult concepts of transvestism and transsexualism is indicative of a desire to present the complex social issue of transgender to adolescent readers. A significant problem that arises in these novels, however, is that the cross-dressing featured in *Touch Me* and *Johnny, My Friend* is not presented as ongoing at the close of each text. Nuala's acceptance of the dress from Xavier signifies that she is finally ready to reembrace conventional femininity. Johnny's death likewise closes the door on his cross-dressing. The finite construction of cross-dressing in these novels neatly resolves the issue of transgender identity, when in reality transgendered individuals must constantly renegotiate and redefine their subjectivities against a matrix of normative gender and sexual discourses that reject difference. By definition, transgender identity can never be resolved because it blurs and intersects the categorical boundaries of sexuality and gender. *Touch Me* and *Johnny, My Friend* revert to the type of cross-dressing representation favored by the female paradigm, where the heroine's cross-dressing ceases and normality is restored. The reproduction of this strategy in novels that have otherwise striven to explore the adult-oriented subject of transgender sympathetically and realistically undermines their political impact. They address and explore the issue of nonconformist gender behavior, but fail to endorse it as a legitimate form of gender protest.

QUEERING THE MASCULINE SUBJECT

While both *Touch Me* and *Johnny, My Friend* broach the subject of cross-dressing in a sensitive manner, neither text presents gender as a substantively fluid concept. The traditional gender binary is ultimately maintained in each—despite Nuala's deliberate attempts to subvert the conventional constructions of masculinity and femininity through her cross-dressing performance. It is therefore not possible to describe either *Touch Me* or *Johnny, My Friend* as possessing an ostensibly queer aesthetic in their construction of gender. Interestingly, the construction of gender as "queer" is becoming more apparent in a number of YA novels that feature male cross-dressing characters, notwithstanding the general conservatism with which male cross-dressing is addressed in literature and film for younger audiences. Queer Theory has emerged since the 1990s as a response to a number of different phenomena, including Judith Butler's important theorization of gender as performative, gay and lesbian studies, and the political and social crisis initiated by the AIDS epidemic of the 1980s. Queer Theory, writes Jonathan Culler, "takes as its own name and throws back at society the most common insult that homosexuals encounter, the epithet 'Queer!'" (1997, 101). Butler's work is particularly important to the Queer Theory project due to the way in which she problematized the notion of identity in *Gender Trouble*, particularly in relation to the notion of an essential feminine identity. Butler's central hypothesis regarding categories of identity such as gender and sexuality (and also, by extension, race) is that they are not universal, but formed by various cultural and social productions—that is, they are repetitively performed by individuals, a process which creates the illusion that they are "natural." These identity categories are therefore "more likely to be the *result* of political cooperation than its condition of possibility" (Culler, 102). It is this contention which Queer Theory adopts as its founding principle, politicizing the idea that identity is not fixed or stable, but fundamentally unconsolidated and fluid.

Queer Theory poses an alternative to traditional concepts of identity, deliberately disrupting prevailing cultural assumptions about how identity is constructed. Jagose clarifies the Queer Project's agenda, specifically in relation to how it disables heterosexuality as a primary category of identity:

> Broadly speaking, queer describes those gestures or analytical models which dramatise incoherencies in the allegedly stable relations between chromosomal sex, gender and sexual desire. Resisting that model of stability—which claims heterosexuality as its origin, when it is more properly its effect—queer focuses on mismatches between sex, gender and desire. (1996b)

Queer Theory seeks to understand and expose the "regulatory nature of all kinds of identity politics" (Pennell and Stephens 2002, 165). This has resulted in the rebirth of the term "queer," which is now used "to signify a position from which to contest such normative identity categories" (165) as gay/straight/transgender or even man/woman. Jagose eloquently suggests that queer is therefore "less an identity than a critique of identity" (1996a, 131).

In contrast to male cross-dressing literature and film aimed at younger readers, a number of YA male cross-dressing novels offer constructions of cross-dressing subjectivity that resist easy classification and challenge conventional assumptions about what it means to be masculine or feminine, or heterosexual or straight. In so doing, these YA novels adopt what can be termed a "queer" aesthetic, providing a representation of cross-dressing identity that questions and subverts conventional assumptions about both gender and sexuality. The various types of cross-dressing representations discussed in previous chapters have predominantly used cross-dressing as a catalyst for exploring socially constructed gender stereotypes. Other categories of identity are typically eradicated within these texts in favor of gender, which assumes a prime position in terms of constructing a character's subjectivity. It follows, therefore, that Queer Theory, which is dedicated to analyzing the intersection of a plurality of identity categories, did not offer an appropriate theoretical framework for the more specifically gender-focused arena of these textual depictions of cross-dressing. The female and male cross-dressing paradigms discussed thus far have used cross-dressing to interrogate dominant models of masculinity and femininity, destabilizing them to varying degrees of success in the context of characters who move between normative gender categories. YA cross-dressing novels, however, tend to use cross-dressing as a signifier of nonnormative identities. (It could be argued that female cross-dressing representations offer a similar construction of gender identity, but the trend within this paradigm is for the heroine to return to her previous position of feminine subjectivity. The heroine's resumption of a feminine subjectivity consequently precludes the continued interpretation of her gender identity as nonnormative.)

The most significant distinction between male cross-dressing in YA novels and other representations of cross-dressing subjectivity occurs in the way that these particular texts engage with the issue of sexual identity, directly addressing the intersecting relationships between gender and sexuality that cross-dressing occasions—which can be ambiguous at times, given that transvestism is popularly associated with homosexuality, but practiced most commonly by heterosexual males. A similar ambiguity exists when tracing the relationship between Queer Theory and gay and lesbian studies, because although the two critical movements are linked, they are not totally analogous. Same-sex desire provides an obvious starting point for Queer Theory because it indicates a paradigm of sexuality outside of the normative heterosexual framework. Queer Theory differs, however, from gay and lesbian studies because it is more interested in cresting identity confusion then forging an alliance between certain groups of individuals based on sexuality, gender, or race. Hence, Queer Theory's political agenda provides an apposite theoretical stance from which to approach transgendered cross-dressing representations—precisely because this group of texts uses cross-dressing to signify a variety of nonnormative categories of identity. In some cases cross-dressing is practiced by boys who engage in heterosexual sex but consider their gender identity to be at variance with hegemonic masculinity; in other cases homosexual boys engage in cross-dressing as a response to their socially perceived failure to live up to patriarchal male stereotypes or because of a desire to experiment and play with different gender identities. It is relevant to point out at this stage that although the intersection of gender and sexuality is raised as a concern in *Touch Me* (when Nuala's cross-dressing is mistaken as a signifier of homosexuality), the structure of the novel precludes a queer reading of Nuala's identity. This is because Nuala's heterosexuality is never truly in doubt, as the narrative is framed around her romance with Xavier (and events in which she is involved are conveyed to readers from Xavier's normative masculine perspective). Presentations of male cross-dressing in YA literature, however, construct the gender and sexual identities of their protagonists in a much more complex fashion, challenging readers to reconsider what cross-dressing typically signifies within our society and to look at it as a valid form of expression for those individuals who do not (or choose not to) fit into traditional categories of identity.

The novels *Zazie in the Metro* (1959), *Postcards from No Man's Land* (1999), *Boy Overboard* (1997), *Funny Boy* (1994), and *Sky Legs* (2003) are all examples of YA fiction which depict male cross-dressing in a manner that deviates from the typical modes of representation addressed in previous chapters. Although not all of these novels engage in an actively queer construction of cross-dressing subjectivity, each acknowledges the way in which cross-dressing behavior has implications for both sexual and gender identity. (Indeed, a number of these texts also recognize that an individual's sexual and gender identities might not be intimately connected or constructed in accordance with dominant paradigms of identity.) This particular subset of transgendered YA novels is indicative of a remarkable transformation in the portrayal of cross-dressing because the novels expressly engage with the adult notion of cross-dressing, providing a representation of cross-dressing identity that pivots around issues of sexuality, considering the intersecting relationship between an individual's gender and sexual identities. These novels are also highly unusual because they represent male cross-dressing as a transgressive act that can have positive (or at least not wholly negative) repercussions for the masculine subject.

Bakhtin's theory of the carnivalesque plays a significant role in the construction of queered cross-dressing subjectivities within these novels. Cross-dressing is carnivalized to varying degrees, constituting a form of gender play that has a rejuvenative effect on the unconventional gender identity of the male cross-dressing protagonist. The subversive function of carnival is abundantly evident in YA male cross-dressing representations—much more so than within the general male cross-dressing paradigm, which initiates a carnival atmosphere but conservatively shies away from the transgressive potential that the carnivalesque offers. YA depictions of male cross-dressing, on the other hand, employ the carnivalesque specifically to harness its subversive powers. The male characters of these novels cross-dress in various contexts as part of elaborate games or ritualized forms of play (in *Zazie in the Metro* and *Sky Legs* the male characters cross-dress while on stage). Their cross-dressing constitutes a joyous form of "time-out" (J. Stephens 1992, 121) from the gender restrictions of society, creating a carnivalized mode of gender transgression from which to critique normative gender categories.

Whereas the female cross-dressers of *Touch Me* and *Johnny, My Friend* experience reactions of hostility and even violence to their transgressive cross-dressing behavior, the transgressiveness of the male characters' cross-dressing is generally constructed in redemptive terms, having a positive effect on the gender identity of the cross-dresser. The carnivalized form of cross-dressing that these male characters perform provides a playful representation of cross-dressing, in contrast to the more dire consequences which Nuala and Johnny endure. They find cross-dressing to be pleasurable and exciting, and also effective at twisting and mutating the standard social definitions of masculinity (most of which do not readily apply to them). The cross-dressing success of these male characters is manifested in the continuance of their cross-dressing at the close of each novel, accompanied by their steadfast refusal to be confined within the stifling and restrictive boundaries of hegemonic masculinity.

The transgender paradigm completely reverses the situation of unprecedented female success and almost total male failure in the other cross-dressing paradigms, but possible explanations for this gender discrepancy are rather unclear. Perhaps it is because females masquerading as males pose more of a threat to established patriarchal gender hierarchies, and are thus less socially acceptable. Or, on the other hand, maybe YA texts which feature male cross-dressers offer more positive representations of cross-dressing subjectivities because of the association with homosexuality, a subject that has been presented with increasing tolerance over recent years in books for young adult readers. Whatever the explanation, feminine and masculine cross-dressing identities are constructed very differently in the transgender paradigm. This difference is most evident in the construction of the male cross-dresser's subjectivity and perspective of his own behavior. The more common use of first-person narration importantly creates a more direct and intimate alignment with the reader, situating the reader alongside the cross-dresser as a subject who sits outside normative gender categories. *Touch Me* and *Johnny, My Friend* represent nonconformist gender behavior through narrators or focalizing characters whose own experience of gender is conventional, hence necessitating that the transgender behavior of its female characters is always presented as different and "othered." Male cross-dressing representations overturn this situation, inviting the reader to share the position of outsider. The language used to construct cross-dressing behavior also shifts, immediately becoming more sensual and emotional because it is personally applied to an "I" instead of a "you."

Narrative voice is a crucial aspect of any depiction of transgendered subjectivity. The majority of representations of cross-dressing in children's literature (even those within the female-to-male paradigm) use the third-person narrative voice. This accords with the way in which transgendered people have traditionally been marginalized and denied a voice of their own within contemporary Western culture, and also perhaps signifies the unwillingness of children's literature to delve too deeply inside the mind of the cross-dresser—demonstrated by the peripheral construction of female transgendered characters.

Zazie in the Metro and *Postcards from No Man's Land* are examples of male cross-dressing literature within the transgender paradigm also use the more traditional style of third-person narrative voice. The cross-dressing characters of these novels are not the main protagonists or focalizers of the story, but play secondary roles. They are viewed through the eyes of the principal focalizing character, and presented to the reader through a more conventional gender lens that serves to position them as "other." At the same time, however, the construction of cross-dressing within these texts departs from the more established paradigm of male cross-dressing because of its acknowledgment of the role of sexual identity in relation to cross-dressing subjectivity. *Zazie in the Metro* can be distinguished from other texts within the transgender paradigm because it was first published in 1959, providing a representation of male adult cross-dressing that is remarkable because it appeared forty years before the publication of other texts which offer a similar portrayal of transgendered characters. *Zazie in the Metro* is a novel that resists easy classification. It is the story of Zazie, a young girl who comes to Paris, briefly, to visit her Uncle Gabriel. The text is primarily focalized through the character of Zazie, but is polyphonic in nature— a variety of eccentric characters interrupt Zazie's narration with their own perceptions and points of view. The novel is a carnivalesque celebration of the city of Paris, depicting an exotic and chaotic world that is liberated from the constraints which normally govern society. While visiting her uncle, and freed from her usual parental constraints, Zazie discovers a city which comes alive at night, filled with odd inhabitants who shout, argue, and gesticulate wildly with little regard for the niceties of polite society. Much to Zazie's amusement, she soon finds herself experiencing life within a raucous community of likable eccentrics.

The novel is constructed almost entirely from dialogue, and is episodic in structure. Language assumes a starring role in *Zazie in the Metro*, reflecting the linguistic playfulness that characterizes the carnivalesque. Narrated in a free-flowing, conversational style, and peppered with colloquialisms and idiomatic expressions, the novel irreverently plays with linguistic conventions in a uniquely energetic manner. This style is epitomized in the novel's opening sentences: "Howcanaystinksotho, wondered Gabriel, exasperated. Ts incredible, they never clean themselves" ([1959] 2001, 3). The colorful and inventive language of the book contributes to the carnival atmosphere, neglecting the usual grammatical and syntactical rules in favor of free expression and a celebratory attitude to the phonetic qualities of particular words. This linguistic free-for-all is warmly embraced by each of the characters, demonstrating a lively communal disregard for the proper rules and structures of the English language. Bakhtin emphasizes that the spirit of the carnivalesque is particularly collective in nature, and this is manifested in Queneau's portrayal of Paris. Bakhtin argues that "Carnival is not a spectacle seen by the people; they live in it, and everyone participates because its very idea embraces all the people" ([1968] 1984, 7). Queneau's Paris embraces this idea of communality, and the frenzied, exhilarating world in which Zazie finds herself is very much the product of its inhabitants' wild and nonsensical antics.

Zazie in the Metro is ultimately a quirky homage to the city of Paris and its enigmatic underbelly, within which Gabriel plays a pivotal role. Gabriel is a female impersonator, and his eclectic assortment of companions forms a pseudo family for the displaced yet eminently independent and curious Zazie. Gabriel's occupation is revealed to the reader in the same nonchalant manner that Zazie discovers it for herself, but at the same time its construction is endowed with significance—more as an element of the oddity of Zazie's new home than as anything more sinister. This is evident from the exchange between Gabriel and his wife shortly after Zazie arrives, which first foreshadows his cross-dressing:

But Marceline has seen an object left lying about on a chest of drawers, she picks it up, runs to open the door, leans over the banisters and calls gently:

"Gabriel, Gabriel."

"What? What is it?"

"You've forgotten your lipstick." (21)

The complicity of Gabriel's wife in his cross-dressing signals another deviation from the established female and male cross-dressing paradigms. In both the female-to-male and male-to-female models, cross-dressing is usually an alienating and isolating experience. Yet within the transgender paradigm, it is constructed in more intersubjective terms. It is behavior that is both condoned and assisted by other characters (although only in its masculine form, as the contrasting experiences of Nuala and Johnny illustrate). This support is evident in Marceline's reminder of the forgotten lipstick, and her desire for Gabriel to be cross-dressed "properly" (i.e., wearing all of the requisite elements of his feminine disguise). A similar phenomenon occurs, to varying degrees, in the other male cross-dressing novels within the transgender paradigm, where the cross-dressers are aided in their cross-dressing by other characters who are tolerant and supportive of their gender transgression.

Gabriel's friends are also aware and supportive of his cross-dressing, but since Zazie is permitted a larger focalizing role within the novel, it is with her character that the reader is predominantly aligned. To Zazie, her uncle's cross-dressing is initially strange. Her reaction is one of uncertainty upon first learning of his choice of profession. She accepts that it is what he does for a living, but is concerned about how to define his identity in relation to it. Gabriel is rendered problematic to her because she assumes, in accordance with the prevailing popular assumption still in existence today, that he must therefore be gay. The heterosexual and happily married Gabriel is then forced to defend himself against such presumptions, and attempts to convince Zazie and other characters that being a drag queen does not necessarily equate to being homosexual—an act of persuasion during which homosexuality is initially figured negatively. For example, the following exchange takes place between Gridoux, a friend of Gabriel's, and a passer-by. The stranger's comment that Gabriel is a "seductress," a sexual and feminine term indicative of Gabriel's behavioral deviation from hegemonic masculine values, is interpreted by Gridoux as a slur on Gabriel's sexuality. Gridoux responds furiously, defending Gabriel from the suggestion of homosexuality even though the stranger has never directly raised the subject:

> "Gabriel," stated Gridoux solemnly, "Gabriel is a respectable citizen, a respectable and honourable citizen. What's more, everyone around these parts likes him."
>
> "He's a seductress."
>
> "You really make me vomit, you do indeed, you and your superior airs. I tell you, Gabriel is not a queer, have you got that, yes or no?" (62–63)

Zazie is similarly confused upon hearing that her uncle is a "fairy," innocently asking, "What exactly is it, a fairy?...A pansy? A queen? A pederast? A hormosessual? Are there little differences?" (106). Her questions remain unanswered, and the conflation of cross-dressing with homosexuality, and of deviant sexual behavior such as pedophilia, is unresolved. The text's repetition of the historically abusive word "queer" (63, 69) and Zazie's mispronounced version of "homosexual"— "hormosessual" (68, 106)—which she understands is a negative concept, mean that Gabriel's cross-dressing is unfavorably compared with homosexuality. However, a noticeable shift in Zazie's point of view occurs, resulting in the gradual acceptance of her uncle's transgendered identity. Her need to define his identity, precisely because it transgresses conventional gender and sexual boundaries, becomes less important, resulting in Zazie's tolerance of, and even pride in, Gabriel's cross-dressing:

> "Afterwards, we're going to see him dance."
>
> "Dance? Who?"
>
> "My unkoo."
>
> "Does he dance, that elephant?"
>
> "And in a tutu, what's more," retorted Zazie proudly. (103)

The carnivalized nature of Gabriel's cross-dressing assists Zazie's acceptance of it as an unusual, but nevertheless acceptable, form of behavior. Gabriel's cross-dressing performances are constructed as playful spectacles that delight his appreciative audiences. In true carnival style, his theatrical routine blends both high and popular culture, as it involves Gabriel performing a ballet dance while dressed in a tutu and wearing makeup. The paradoxical combination of ballet and drag mocks the notion of ballet as a high-culture art form. Gabriel's "suppleness" is also incongruous with his colossal size and improbable attire, creating a subversive medley of behaviors and visual effects that challenges traditional concepts of art and gender:

> And, springing to his feet with a suppleness as singular as it was unexpected, the colossus performed several entrechats, flapping his hands up and down behind his shoulder-blades in imitation of the flight of the butterfly.

> The glimpse of his talent created considerable enthusiasm among the travellers. (125)

Perhaps most importantly, the carnivalization of Gabriel's cross-dressing highlights the joy and energy that he brings to his performance, and to which the audience enthusiastically responds in kind. Zazie instantly becomes involved in the festive escape from normal societal rules which Gabriel's dance offers, and once she is able to appreciate this, she, too, becomes delighted by it.

Zazie in the Metro offers a positive and playful portrayal of adult male cross-dressing that successfully integrates the adult transgender domain into the realm of children's literature. The carnivalesque mode employed in the theatrical construction of Gabriel's cross-dressed dance performances disrupts dominant social and gender boundaries through his simultaneous violation of and adherence to acceptable codes relating to masculine behavior. The enthusiasm with which he dons a tutu to dance in front of an audience is contrasted with the traditional masculine aggression he displays while protecting Zazie and his friends from the angry mob in the novel's climax. The depiction of Gabriel as an adult heterosexual male who cross-dresses out of personal choice is highly significant because it reflects the reality of adult cross-dressing—a reality that is mostly ignored in, or actively rejected by, children's literature. Nevertheless, Gabriel's cross-dressing is not particularly effective in challenging the conventional constructions of masculinity or femininity. The structure of the novel is partly responsible, because its polyphonic nature makes it difficult for the reader to gain much insight into the interiority of any of its characters. It is driven by events and dialogue, offering little in the way of meaningful characterization. The reader's limited access to Gabriel's own thoughts about his cross-dressing override its transgressive potential, and his gender identity remains framed in accordance with a very traditional version of masculinity: he is a devoted husband, the economic provider for the family, and readily performers the role of father figure to Zazie. Gabriel's fervent renunciation of homosexuality confirms his situation within a patriarchal mode of masculinity. However, the relationship between homosexuality and cross-dressing is clearly articulated within the text, and is therefore illustrative of Roberta Seelinger Trites's observation that many YA novels demonstrate the limits of homosexual discourse (a discourse in which transgendered sexuality can be included because it also deviates from normative heterosexuality) because "As a group they show how a genre can become more self-aware of a social issue without necessarily providing the reader with progressively transformative experiences" (1997, 104).

Seelinger Trites's argument about the problematic representation of characters with marginalized sexual identities in adolescent fiction is equally relevant to Aidan Chambers's *Postcards from No Man's Land*. Like *Zazie in the Metro*, this novel contains a peripheral cross-dressing character, here named Ton. He plays a minor role in the narrative, but is relatively unusual in children's literature because he is transgendered in the contemporary sense of this word. Ton is biologically male but masquerades as a female, delighting in the gender confusion his appearance creates. It is noteworthy to mention that Ton does not cross-dress but wears the typically androgynous uniform of today's adolescents—jeans, white T-shirt, and leather jacket. The construction of his transgendered subjectivity is symptomatic of the way in which transgendered individuals have been represented in much mainstream adult literature and film. Ton's presence within the narrative is limited, and he functions primarily as an enigma for Jacob, the text's protagonist, epitomizing all that is strange and confusing about the new country in which Jacob finds himself.

Postcards from No Man's Land, like *Zazie in the Metro*, experiments with a variety of narrative styles. The story focuses on Jacob, who is English, and his experiences in Amsterdam. These are presented in the third person, but are heavily focalized through Jacob's eyes. His main reason for coming to Amsterdam is to visit his dying grandmother, and as he discovers more about her past, his narrative is interrupted with fragments from her life during World War II, which are given a sense of immediacy through the use of first-person narration. The novel is, however, primarily Jacob's story, and since Ton's transgendered identity confuses and unsettles Jacob quite dramatically, the reader only gains glimpses of Ton through Jacob's bewildered eyes. Jacob first meets Ton in a café. Feeling unsure of himself in his strange new surroundings, he is approached by Ton, whom he assumes is an attractive young girl. Ton exploits this mistake, kissing the startled Jacob while simultaneously revealing his true sex, and then disappearing. Ton's sexually provocative behavior perplexes the innocent Jacob: "Ton's lips placing fleetingly on his the ghost of a kiss. And her hand pressing his hand deep in to her crotch, where he felt the swell of a compact set of penis and balls" (11). Ton produces a range of reactions in Jacob throughout the novel, all of which are represented in terms that indicate his presence simultaneously excites and alarms Jacob. After their first encounter, Jacob responds in an "ensuing daze" (11), and on subsequent occasions his reaction varies from feeling "mischievous" (292) around Ton, to "blushing" (301) because of the uncertainty Ton's presence occasions. Ton's role within the text is slight, and his construction as marginalized "other" conforms to the traditional representation of transgendered characters in Western literature. His purpose is to confuse and unsettle Jacob, serving to defamiliarize the new world in which Jacob finds himself. Ton's behavior is carnivalized to a certain extent, as his gender performance—which is ostensibly feminine, yet revels in the simultaneous revelation of his biological masculinity—is a festive display of sexual provocation and desire. He successfully confounds and perplexes Jacob, but as the narrative does not allow him to focalize any of its events, it also prevents any authentic insight into his character. Ton therefore remains an enigma to both Jacob and the reader, and his transgendered subjectivity is the principal reason for his unfathomability.

Postcards from No Man's Land attempts to portray Ton in a more sensitive light, alluding to Queer Theory's endeavor to provide a position "from which to contest...normative identity categories" (J. Stephens 2002, 165). Jacob's cousin, Daan, describes his relationship with Ton in a manner that similarly resists conventional sex/gender/sexuality categorizations:

> Ton never sleeps with women. That's the way he is. Simone only sleeps with me. That's the way she is. I sleep with them both. That's the way I am. They both want to sleep with me. That's how we are. That's how we want it.... All the stuff about gender, male, female, queer, bi, feminist, new man, whatever—it's meaningless. As out of date as marriage forever. I'm tired of hearing about it. We're beyond that now. (299)

Daan's challenging statement, however, is treated with caution by the more conformist Jacob, whose response illustrates the prevailing, and rather more conservative, ideological framework of the text: "'You are, maybe,' Jacob said. 'Not all of us, though. Not most of us probably. Not where I come from anyway'" (299). Jacob's repeated application of the word "not" to Ton and Daan's unconventional sexual behavior clearly conveys his negative perception of it, ideologically separating his view of the world from theirs. Jacob's comment suggests that queer or transgender sexuality should be treated as strange, a problematic deviation from more acceptable standards of (hetero)sexuality. As a foreigner in a strange city whose cultural codes he does not fully understand, Jacob is quick to position Daan and Ton as "other" to himself, to the extent that he perceives their liberal views on sexuality and gender as alien to his own British cultural identity. Daan and Ton's unconventional sexual lifestyles and attitudes are a mystery to Jacob, and he is hesitant or unwilling to try to understand the complexity of them. Instead, they form part of the enigma that is Amsterdam, a city where he is but a temporary visitor and witness to myriad things that confound him. Jacob's initial encounter with Ton, during which Jacob was clearly sexually attracted to him, is left behind in favor of his blossoming heterosexual romance with Hille. As the primary focalizer of events, Jacob's slightly bewildered perspective of Daan and Ton's transgressive sexual mores creates a restrictive subject position for the reader. Neither Daan nor Ton focalize any part of the narrative, so the reader is only provided insight into their subjectivities through dialogue. This access is then tempered by the fact that the story is related from Jacob's viewpoint, so his uncertainty and skepticism toward such fluid concepts of sexuality and gender take precedence within the story. Jacob's propensity to treat Ton, and to a lesser extent Daan, as people who are essentially unfathomable and foreign is aided by the novel's construction of Daan and Ton as less than likable characters. They are not welcoming to Jacob when he first arrives in Amsterdam—Ton's behavior is deliberately suggestive and potentially insensitive—and this ensures that the reader is unequivocally aligned with the more sympathetic Jacob. The novel consequently privileges Jacob's more traditional attitude toward sexuality—with its concomitant resistance to deviation from socially acceptable norms. Indeed, as Kerry Mallan argues, "Ton prepares Jacob for the costs of transgressive sexuality and disruption of the phallocentric order when he relates his own exiling from his home by his homophobic father who has "never forgiven himself for breeding a 'queer,' and who can only survive as long as he does not see his son" (2002, 159).

At the close of the novel, Daan and Ton are constructed (through Jacob's eyes) as characters whose lifestyles seem questionable, with their happiness presented as precarious at best. Jacob's evolution as an agential subject, in contrast, is legitimized in much more positive terms. His subjectivity develops in response to the discovery of his family history, a process which assists him to rationalize his own place within his family and the world, and also enables him to feel less alienated within the Dutch culture. Jacob's burgeoning confidence within himself is awakened by Geertrui's retelling of her life story, which subsequently provides Jacob with a historical context for his own existence. The novel's teleology privileges monogamous heterosexuality, using Geertrui's relationship with Jacob's grandfather to anchor Jacob's presence within the context of his family's history. Geertrui's story, unlike Jacob's, is intimately narrated in the first person, and its eventual revelation to Jacob is imbued with gravitas because she is now on her deathbed. Jacob perceives her relationship with his grandfather as beautiful, passionate, and intensely tragic, an epic love story of "Romeo and Juliet" proportions which he relates to so personally that he refigures himself as a participant in it: "While episodes from her story played in his head like scenes from a film. Making it more disturbing, young Geertrui was Hille, her Jacob was himself" (291).

Jacob's romance with Hille, a Dutch girl, mirrors and complements the historical love story told by Geertrui. Their contemporary romance is endowed with redemptive potential, as the novel suggests that it might rectify the tragic events of the past. In comparison with the almost mythic heterosexual romance between Geertrui and Jacob's grandfather, Daan and Ton's more carefree sexual attitudes and lack of commitment to monogamous relationships can only be viewed by both Jacob and the reader as lacking depth or emotional weight. Daan's pronouncement to Jacob regarding his refusal to be constrained by labels such as "gay," "straight," "man," or "woman" is therefore without resonance, sounding instead like hollow (or perhaps delusional) rhetoric. His and Ton's sexual transgression is firmly situated on the periphery of the novel's construction of sexuality. Kimberley Reynolds confirms this, contending that "Daan is doing more than posting a free love manifesto when he explains his way of life to Jacob, but the book does not follow through the logic of the position" (2002, 112). Daan's last-minute protestations about the validity of his sexual identity, his right to determine his own sexuality, and the freedom which this decision allows have little effect on Jacob's estimation of him and Ton. The representation of transgendered and queer subjectivities in *Postcards from No Man's Land* conforms in stereotypical fashion to the established tradition within Western culture of marginalizing characters whose sexual and gendered identities differ from the socially prescribed norms of "heterosexual," "man," and "woman." The transgressive behavior of both Daan and Ton effectively relegates them to a "no man's land" within the text, locating their socially rebellious identities within a place that is a chaotic and potentially dangerous wilderness, dislocated from reality.

MALE CROSS-DRESSING AS QUEER
AND CARNIVALIZED SPECTACLE

The failure of *Postcards from No Man's Land's* to escape the represen-tational strategies which have characterized the negative portrayal of transgendered/queer subjectivities in Western literature and film is regrettable. This is so especially in light of its specific attempts to theorize and validate, via Daan's speech to Jacob, each individual per-son's right to negotiate their own sexual and gender identities. Daan's progressive ideological statement is compromised by the narrative strategies used in the text, such as focalization and point of view, which heavy-handedly alienate the reader from both him and Ton, and pre-dispose an interpretation characterized by the more conservative atti-tude of Jacob.

The marginalized representation of transgendered/queer subjectivity is radically redressed, however, in three recently published YA novels from New Zealand, Australia, and Sri Lanka: *Boy Overboard*, by Peter Wells; *Funny Boy*, by Shyam Selvadurai; and *Sky Legs*, by Irini Savvides. These texts feature male cross-dressing characters whose gender and sexuality are constructed against social conventions, essentially exist-ing outside of them. The cross-dressing protagonists of these novels are allowed to speak for themselves, the first-person narrative style of each book permitting the reader direct access to their thoughts, emotional states, and interpretation of the world around them. As cross-dressers, these characters resist and even defy normative gender and sexuality categorizations, ultimately (re)creating their own gendered identities— which confuse and elude classification.

Jagose argues that "Queer marks a suspension of identity as some-thing fixed, coherent and natural" (1996a, 98). She emphasizes the lack of an acceptable definition for "queer," suggesting that "the inflection of queer that has proved most disruptive to received understandings of identity, community and politics is the one that problematises normative consolidations of sex, gender and sexuality—and that, consequently, is critical of all those versions of identity, community and politics that are believed to evolve 'naturally' from such consolidations. By refusing to crystallise in any specific form, queer maintains a relation of resistance to whatever constitutes the normal" (1996a, 99). *Boy Overboard*, *Funny Boy*, and *Sky Legs* adhere to this notion of queer in their representation of the subjectivity of their protagonists, using cross-dressing and the carnivalesque mode to interrogate the "incoherencies in the dual gen-der regime and the oppressive regulation of sexual desire and practice in a social order dominated by the metanarratives of hegemonic masculinity" (Pennell and Stephens 2002, 166).

The process of queering the male protagonist's subjectivity is facilitated in each of these novels by the carnivalized use of cross-dressing. Bakhtin argues that the Renaissance carnival culture involves the "temporary suspension of all hierarchic distinctions and barriers among men and of certain norms and prohibitions of usual life" (Bakhtin, 15). *Boy Overboard, Funny Boy,* and *Sky Legs* each employ cross-dressing for this purpose, constructing it as a theatrical performance that enables the masculine subject to escape the gendered behavioral codes socially imposed upon him. The temporary feminine disguise offered by cross-dressing is, in essence, a relaxation of the boundaries that define and police hegemonic masculinity. Cross-dressing is a ritualized escape, an opportunity to pass through the barriers that normally divide and separate masculinity from femininity.

Boy Overboard exemplifies a resistance of this nature in its exploration of the emerging queer subjectivity of its eleven-year-old narrator, Jamie. The narrative concludes with Jamie arriving at the school fancy dress ball, splendidly cross-dressed as Cleopatra, Queen of the Nile. The outfit has been designed and painstakingly created by his brother Matthew—homage to the boys' idealized notion of the iconic "golden years" of the Hollywood film industry. Jamie's cross-dressing is not, however, a simplistic re-creation of femininity. The inspiration for the costume is a publicity photograph for the film *The Ten Commandments* which features Yul Brynner. Jamie is rapturously enthralled by the picture:

> I gazed down at Yul Brynner, marvelling.
>
> He looked so fierce, so proud. He was the epitome of all that was manly.
>
> Yet I could see he was wearing a short skirt, what appeared to be a metal brassiere, jewellery and make-up. (168)

While Jamie intently examines the picture, a photograph of Kim Novak on the opposite page of the book becomes intrinsically interlaced with his view of Yul Brynner, resulting in an image that is erotic, inviting, and, most important, simultaneously masculine and feminine:

> ...as I gazed down intently, the photo of Kim slid across the page and hovered in superimposition, over Yul the King.
>
> I became lost in reverie, and it was as if Yul had opened up the hard vault of his chest and revealed inside it the hot invitations of a soft and yielding Kim, a vixen with sharpened fingernails

behind whose gleaming eyes lay, in turn, a metal hardness, a double-edged ambiguity, both masculine and feminine webbed together, inseparable and never to be apart. (168–169)

Jamie's cross-dressing is an assured success, his Cleopatra costume constituting "the first real garments I have ever worn...dressing me as I was always meant to be dressed" (180). While Jamie's assertion that wearing feminine clothing occasions his rebirth as an agential subject, freeing him from the prescriptive codes of hegemonic masculinity. His previous comments about the costume, simultaneously acting as a signifier of masculinity *and* femininity, suggest a collapse of normative categories of identity. His identity can thus be read as queer, as it is ambiguously constructed as a multiplicity of contrary gender identifications and sexual desires.

The location of Jamie's subjective awakening, a school dance, is also highly significant. In Foucaldian terms, a school dance is a heterotopic space—a place that is "outside of all places, even if it may be possible to indicate [its] location in reality" (Foucault 1986, 24). The school dance, as a heterotopia, is concurrently mythic and real, sacred and forbidden. It is a space in which the demarcation between the adult's and the child's world is blurred, where the "crisis" (to use Foucault's terminology) of adolescence takes place. Adult sexuality and illicit pleasure encroach upon childish innocence to create a space that is "other." The "unreal space" (Foucault, 24) of the school dance hence provides a legitimate site for the exploration of queer/transgender subjectivity, which likewise acts as a locus of (gender and sexual) displacement and resistance. Jamie's queer subjectivity is presented as "a state of mind and emerging sensibility" (Pennell and Stephens 2002, 172), defined as it is against the boundaries of the social conventions that construct male adolescence. Jamie's subjectivity is therefore fragmentary in many respects until the cross-dressing episode—which finally allows him to feel (if only temporarily) "whole":

Is this what I have been waiting for? For this movement, this motion towards being? Is this the climb which has silently been happening inside my blood? Flood? For one second I comprehend something: the M is joining to E, this is what is soundlessly happening during this dance, as the white light bounces round over our heads: yes, part is joined to part and a form of wholeness, hidden behind the choreography of costume, is happening. (**Boy Overboard**, 259)

The idea of carnival is implicit to the construction of Jamie's cross-dressing as a spectacle within the context of the novel. The process of costuming him, lovingly undertaken by Matthew, is ritualized through the application of makeup and construction of the garments that constitute the Cleopatra outfit, and also through the pleasure that Jamie derives from being dressed in this way. The emphasis that Bakhtin places on the plurality within the spirit of carnival is also manifested in Jamie's cross-dressing because he views himself as both masculine and feminine while wearing the costume. The spectacle of Jamie's cross-dressed appearance at the dance embodies the spirit of the carnivalesque, enabling him to "be" himself in a realm that exists outside the gendered and sexual boundaries of everyday life. His carnivalized cross-dressing functions as a resistance to these cultural codes, allowing their incoherencies and inconsistencies to be exposed in the freedom it creates for him as a subject. As Pennell and Stephens note, "The strong sense of subjective agency Jamie feels as he experiences a state of wholeness, the M joined to the E, functions as an expressive form of cultural critique" (2002, 176).

The queering of Jamie's subjectivity in *Boy Overboard* is also evident in Selvadurai's *Funny Boy*, despite the very different function which cross-dressing performs in relation to the evolving subjectivity of the young male protagonist. While Jamie's cross-dressing occurs toward the end of the narrative, signifying an epiphanous moment of joy in which he is able to conceive himself as a unified subject, the cross-dressing behavior of Arjie, the central character of *Funny Boy*, forms the basis of the first chapter (or episode) of the novel. It is presented as an activity in which seven-year-old Arjie has long been involved. Unlike Jamie, Arjie is not fully cognizant of the social or personal implications of his desire to wear feminine clothing. It is simply something that he enjoys doing. His youth makes him innocently unaware that such behavior is generally considered to be socially unacceptable. The novel is a realist coming-of-age memoir, narrated in the first person by Arjie, which details—in a series of vignettes rather than chronological chapters—his experience of growing up gay within the precarious political context of Sri Lanka in the 1970s and 1980s. The opening episode of *Funny Boy*, titled "Pigs Can't Fly," focuses on an incident in which Arjie's parents discover and then forbid his cross-dressing. This incident forms a crucial moment in the development of Arjie's queer subjectivity. His parents are unable to rationalize their strict prohibition of his wearing feminine clothing, and their seemingly illogical and extreme reaction marks the emergence of Arjie's determination to question and resist the restrictive cultural forces and ideologies which prevailed in Sri Lankan society at the time.

Like *Boy Overboard, Funny Boy* is a novel which provides a representation of queer subjectivity based on the fundamental principle of identity as never fixed but constantly changing and developing. Jagose's comment that queer is "less an identity than a critique of identity" is particularly relevant to the construction of Arjie's subjectivity. Resisting the paradigmatic structures and outcomes of the bildungsroman narrative genre (the novel of adolescent development that is predicated upon the male hero's alienation from, education in, and subsequent reentry into society). *Funny Boy* is premised upon Arjie's growing disillusionment with, and ultimate rejection of, the cultural and ideological values which construct his social environment. Pennell and Stephens argues that "The hallmark of entering queer space in *Funny Boy* is the valorization of pleasure, desire and sexual freedom as the means for critiquing heteronormativity" (2002, 176). Arjie's conscious transgression of the behavioral codes and cultural values which construct hegemonic masculinity, for the sake of sexual desire and gender freedom, is a gradual and ongoing process throughout the course of the narrative. It is his cross-dressing, however, which first causes him to become aware of the rigid and strictly enforced gender dualism of his society. The innocent pleasure which the seven-year-old Arjie derives from cross-dressing and the hostile reaction it subsequently provokes in his family are highly symbolic, functioning as a powerful critique of the patriarchal ideologies which police normative gender and sexuality identity politics (Pennell and Stephens 2002, 165).

Funny Boy is episodic in structure, containing six self-contained but interconnected stories. The first of these revolves around the family tradition of "spend-the-days," the one Sunday each month that Arjie's entire extended family spends at his grandparents' house. Spend-the-days were the days "most looked forward to by all of us, cousins, aunts, and uncles" ([1994] 1995, 1), but for Arjie they are particularly significant because of the elaborate game of "bride-bride" devised and played by him and his young female cousins. Although he is a boy, Arjie is permitted into the "territory of 'the girls,'" to which he is irresistibly attracted because it offers "the potential for the free play of fantasy" (3). The boys commandeer the larger area outside the house for games of cricket, but Arjie "gravitated naturally" to the girls' smaller area, which was "confined to the back garden and the kitchen porch" (3). There, he and his cousins reenact fairy stories together and Arjie is rewarded for his lively imagination by being made the leader of the group. This enables him always to play the heroine of the piece:

Of all our varied and fascinating games, bride-bride was my favourite. In it, I was able to combine many elements of the other games I loved, and with time bride-bride, which had taken a few hours to play initially, became an event that spread out over the whole day and was planned for weeks in advance. For me, the culmination of this game, and my ultimate moment of joy, was when I put on the clothes of the bride. (4)

The act of "re-creating" himself as a feminine subject is transformative for Arjie in much the same way that wearing the Cleopatra costume is for Jamie in *Boy Overboard*. Cross-dressing provides each with the opportunity to escape patriarchal masculinity and reenter the world as a glamorous female worshipped by men. (Ironically, both male characters desire a passive feminine subjectivity that is the sexual object of the male gaze.) Arjie and Jamie yearn to experience the type of "iconic" and glamorous feminine identity that is familiar to them from films, and through cross-dressing they are able to transcend their biological male sex and culturally prescribed masculinity to glimpse what it is like to exist within a feminine subjectivity. Arjie's cross-dressing is overtly carnivalized as a spectacle, constituting a form of role-playing game in which all of his female cousins eagerly participate. The process of attiring him in his bridal outfit is elaborate, involving "the sari being wrapped around my body, the veil being pinned to my head, the rouge put on my cheeks, lipstick on my lips, kohl around my eyes" (4). It exemplifies the carnivalesque agenda to invert the normal rules and conventions of society by appointing a boy as the bride, allowing him to assume the central role of interest (as passive object of the male gaze) throughout the ceremony. Despite the role of passivity traditionally assigned to women within the wedding ceremony, Arjie (like Jamie) experiences a jubilant feeling of wholeness when attired in his bridal regalia:

...I was able to leave the constraints of myself and ascend into another, more brilliant, more beautiful self, a self to whom this day was dedicated, and around whom the world...seemed to revolve. It was a self magnified, like the goddesses of the Sinhalese and Tamil cinema, larger than life....I was an icon, a graceful, benevolent, perfect being upon whom the adoring eyes of the world rested. (4–5)

Paradoxically, neither Jamie nor Arjie engage in any substantive behavioral performance of femininity while cross-dressed. Their desire to experience the type of iconic femininity that they have seen performed in films, which necessitates that the feminine subject adopt a passive role as the object of masculine sexual desire, does not extend beyond the visual representation of femininity. The cross-dressing in which Jamie and Arjie engage queers, rather than simply feminizes, their gender identities. Although both characters derive immense pleasure from cross-dressing, neither professes an actual desire to be feminine. In contrast, they enjoy being able to experience femininity as a masculine subject—delighting in the transgression of socially constructed gender codes which segregate the sexes and traditionally assign the role of sexual object to feminine individuals. This is illustrated most effectively in *Boy Overboard*, where both boys and girls are eager to dance with Jamie while he is dressed as Cleopatra at the school ball (258). The cross-dressing experiences of Jamie and Arjie can be marked as queer because they produce an amalgamation of masculinity and femininity within a single body, resulting in a gender identity that resists classification.

Arjie's experience of cross-dressing is fundamental to the later development of his subjectivity, despite its short-lived existence, because of the extreme reaction it provokes in his parents. Although usually the children are unseen by the adults while playing bride-bride, the arrival of Arjie's cousin Tanuja (nicknamed "Her Fatness" by the children) initiates a process which leads to the eventual discovery of Arjie's cross-dressing by the adult members of the family. Prevented from playing the role of the bride herself, Her Fatness retaliates against Arjie's primacy within the group by taunting him for his lack of masculinity. Although Arjie is only seven, the English-educated Tanuja is quick to associate his cross-dressing with homosexuality, calling him a "pansy," "faggot," and "sissy" (11). Tanuja then turns to her mother for support, which is when the cross-dressed Arjie is discovered by Kanthi Aunty. Brought to the attention of the adults, Arjie is stigmatized as "funny" (14) and severely punished for his unconventional behavior. Yet no rational explanation for the punishment is ever provided to Arjie, whose intelligent and questioning mind acutely perceives the injustice of his treatment:

> It was clear to me that I had done something wrong, but what it was I couldn't comprehend. I thought about what my father had said about turning out "funny." The word "funny" as I understood it meant either humorous or strange, as in the expression "that's funny." Neither of these fitted the sense in which my father had used the word, for there had been a hint of disgust in his tone. (17)

Despite Arjie's tender age, his father's prohibition of "bride-bride" is explicitly related to his association of cross-dressing with homosexuality. The homophobia which pervades Arjie's Sri Lankan culture is so potent that it regulates all male behavior, regardless of whether the masculine subject is a child, and therefore unaware of the significance of his actions. Pennell and Stephens suggest that homosexual desire is used in *Funny Boy* as the means through which "it offers its queer critique of the constant injustices that are sustained by the regulations of patriarchal societies" (176). Arjie's cross-dressing is instrumental in achieving this, as it forms the foundational basis for his questioning of the mores and normative values of his culture. Directly confronting his mother about why he is not permitted to play with the girls in the future (a question which also implicitly addresses the issue of why he can't dress in the bridal sari), Arjie receives an answer that openly acknowledges the often irrational nature of such behavioral regulation:

> "Why?" I asked, ignoring her gesture. "Why do I have to play with the boys?"
>
> "Why?" Amma said. "Because the sky is so high and pigs can't fly, that's why." (19)

Banished from the girls' territory, with his behavior now carefully monitored and supervised by his family, the subsequent episodes of the novel chart Arjie's journey toward adolescence and his increasing resistance to the repressive gender and sexual codes of Sri Lankan society. The prohibition of his childish cross-dressing game impacts greatly upon him, making him aware, for perhaps the first time, of his alienation from his family, peers, and culture. He sagely comments to the reader, "The future spend-the-days were no longer to be enjoyed, no longer to be looked forward to. And then there would be loneliness. I would be caught between the boys' and the girls' worlds, not belonging or wanted in either" (39). Michael Warner remarks that "Every person who comes to a queer self-understanding knows in one way or another that her stigmatisation is intricated with gender, with the family, with notions of individual freedom, the state…" (1993, 6). Arjie's dawning understanding of how his queer identity affects each facet of his existence arrives after the cross-dressing incident and informs his behavior thereafter, resulting in the self-acknowledgment of his difference and eventual (and overt) contestation of the regulatory social practices that seek to silence homosexuality. This occurs during his school's prize-giving night, when Arjie spectacularly subverts the institutional forces which have sought to constrain his sexual and gender freedom. He thwarts the headmaster's speech through his ruinous delivery of a poem that exalts the role of the conservative school system within the formation of masculine identity. The novel ends with Arjie's family fleeing the Sri Lankan political crisis between the Tamils and Sinha-lese, but undermines the conventional narrative closure associated with novels situated within the bildungsroman genre.

Arjie does not finish his story as a fully developed adult with a coherent and autonomous sense of self. His subjectivity is still evolv-ing, reflected in his attitude to leaving Sri Lanka: "We are going, not with the idea that something delightful awaits us, but rather with the knowledge that great difficulties lie ahead" (309). The ambivalence with which Arjie regards his future mirrors the ambiguous construction of his transgressive gender and sexual identities, engaging in the same type of definitional elasticity that Queer Theory itself employs. Yet in spite of this ambiguity surrounding Arjie, the reader is not left with the impression that he is incapable of surviving this next challenge. Arjie's ability to question, confront, and defy the regulatory social and insti-tutional forces of his Sri Lankan culture—initially demonstrated in his response to the prohibition of his cross-dressing as a child—provides hope for his successful negotiation of a new culture, as well as the antic-ipation that his queer subjectivity will continue to resist the pressure of oppressive cultural regimes.

The resistance of oppressive cultural and social regimes is an impor-tant thematic concern of Irini Savvides's recent novel for young adults, *Sky Legs*. The process and results of this resistance are, however, quite different from those of *Boy Overboard* and *Funny Boy*. The most sig-nificant difference between *Sky Legs* and these other novels is that cross-dressing is used metonymically to queer a male subject who is not homosexual. Although Pete, the cross-dressing character of *Sky Legs*, is not gay, his identity is constructed in adherence to the overarch-ing principles of Queer Theory—these being the potential to question seemingly fixed notions such as gender and sexuality, and even man and woman. It is in relation to this notion of queer as a "critique of iden-tity" (Jagose 1996a, 131) that *Sky Legs* differentiates itself from *Zazie in the Metro*, despite the apparent similarities between the heterosexual characters, Pete and Gabriel. Both are heterosexual male cross-dress-ers, but the construction of their subjectivities is vastly different. Where Gabriel lacks interiority, Pete does not. While Gabriel's cross-dressing is the only thing that contravenes a somewhat traditional masculine gender identity, Pete's gender and sexual identities are based on notions of "opposition and resistance to the 'pervasiveness of social regula-tion'" (H. L. Minton 1997, 349). In effect, Pete's heterosexual identity is queered in *Sky Legs*. Although he perceives himself as being straight, his cross-dressing interrogates normative understandings of (hetero)sexual identity. His gender identity remains ambiguous throughout the novel, corroborating Jagose's definition of queer as signifying something that is "necessarily indeterminate" (1996a, 97).

The principal narrator of *Sky Legs* is Eleni, a young girl who has recently lost her mother and has moved with her father to a new house in the Blue Mountains, near Sydney. Eleni is eager to relocate, mostly because of her attraction to a figure called the Winter Goddess, whom she had glimpsed during a Winter Magic parade on a previous visit to the mountains. The Winter Goddess is dressed in white satin and walks on stilts, beautiful and carefree; her presence excites Eleni, making her hopeful for magical possibilities in this unfamiliar place. But this first impression soon proves to be misguided, as the new town is much more politically conservative than Eleni's former community in bohemian inner Sydney. Unbeknownst to Eleni, however, the Winter Goddess is actually her male classmate Pete. Although Pete is not the principal character of *Sky Legs*, he is permitted a number of narrative intrusions in which episodes of the story are told from his perspective in the first person. His narration is brief, but it does allow the reader direct access to his thoughts and feelings, most of which revolve around questions relating to his own unconventional identity.

Like Jamie in *Boy Overboard* and Arjie in *Funny Boy*, Pete's identity is constructed against the social forces that define and maintain the notion of hegemonic masculinity. He is an outsider at school, partly through choice. He is also a born actor, a chameleon who takes particular pleasure in performing feminine roles. Yet he resists the identity that such behavior would usually confer:

> There I was, singing to myself as I put on my make-up for the role. He watched me and that was it.
>
> "You're just a fag! What do you think you're doing?"
>
> "I'm not a—." I couldn't use that word. It isn't that I hate gays or anything, but I think the word's ugly. And it's the truth—I'm not gay. Okay, I don't mind dressing up for a play, but I'm not gay.... Maybe it'd be easier if I was. But the truth is I like dressing up and the make-up's ok. And I like girls. Go figure. (167)

As with Jamie and Arjie, Pete feels a certain sense of "wholeness" when dressed in feminine clothing. His subjectivity is queered because of the way in which it defies categorization. He fails to live up to the expectations of conventional masculinity, preferring traditionally feminine activities such as sewing. And although he takes pleasure in wearing feminine clothing and makeup, he is not gay. Peter is simply a boy who enjoys dressing as a girl—a confusing anathema to those who seek to define him within the boundaries of masculinity and femininity, homosexuality and heterosexuality. Connell suggests that Queer Theory "celebrates the symbolic disruptions of gender categories" (1995, 59), a description which accurately articulates Pete's refusal to be circumscribed by normative identity categories. His identity maintains a "relation of resistance to whatever constitutes the normal," to use an expression of Jagose's (1996a, 99), existing ambiguously in the margins and peripheries of dominant gender and sexual paradigms.

Unlike Jamie, though, Pete engages in unconventional behavior that provokes a severe and hostile reaction in his peers, to the point where he is savagely attacked and beaten for daring to wear a dress to school. This event signifies an important transformation in Eleni's emerging sense of self and her perception of Pete. Rather than attempting to define, explain, or understand him, she learns instead to accept and appreciate the fact that he is different. She also assists him in coming to terms with his own difference, and is instrumental in helping him resist the pressure from those around him to conform. They then embark on what looks like a promising romance, based as it is on both Eleni's and Pete's recognition of the attributes that make each of them unique.

The queering of Pete's subjectivity suitably matches the mode of magical realism which Savvides uses in *Sky Legs*—evident most clearly in the character of Mihali, an angel whose mission is to guide Eleni through the trauma of losing her mother. "Magical realism" is the term given to the genre of fiction which blends the "strange, the uncanny, the eerie and the dreamlike" (Hawthorn 1994, 191) into what we consider to be consensus "reality." M. H. Abrams suggests that novels written in the magical realist mode "violate, in various ways, standard novelistic expectations by drastic—and sometimes highly effective—experiments with subject matter, form, style, temporal sequence, and fusions of the everyday, the fantastic, the mythical, and the nightmarish, in renderings that blur traditional distinctions between what is serious or trivial, horrible or ludicrous, tragic or comic" (1993, 135). Magical realism seeks to challenge and fuse opposites, and therefore shares a similar subversive objective with Queer Theory in its attempts to resist and destabilize established concepts. Like Queer Theory, magical realism is difficult to define. Its nature is experimental, illustrated by the unconventional narrative techniques used in *Sky Legs*. These include a polyphonic narrative style, the integration of literary and nonliterary genres (such as memos, letters, and diary entries), and the employment of the carnivalesque in the text's recurring clown motif. This magical realist frame facilitates the queering of Pete's subjectivity, as both magical realism and Queer Theory share a similar agenda. While the outcomes of these agendas may differ, their affinity lies in the use of "denaturalisation as a primary strategy" (Jagose 1996a, 98).

RECLAIMING (TRANS)GENDER

Sky Legs, Boy Overboard, and *Funny Boy* herald a new and promising future for the representation of cross-dressing and cross-dressers in children's literature. Each novel successfully uses cross-dressing as a strategy for interrogating conventional gender categories, and actively acknowledges the issue of sexual identity which cross-dressing necessarily invokes in an adult context. Both *Zazie in the Metro* and *Postcards from No Man's Land* introduce a male cross-dressing character to preadult audiences, but he is limited to playing a peripheral role and his unconventional behavior is focalized through another's eyes. *Sky Legs, Boy Overboard,* and *Funny Boy,* however, go further. Their use of first-person narration allows the interiority of their cross-dressing characters to be directly represented; hence their subjectivities are free of overt mediation. These novels redress the conventional marginalization of transvestite and transsexual characters in Western literature and film, inviting the reader to react to the repressive and regulatory function of normative gender categories from the perspective of individuals situated outside them.

These male cross-dressing novels also differentiate themselves from the representation of female cross-dressing which occurs within *Touch Me* and *Johnny, My Friend.* The construction of cross-dressing in these novels is distinct from the more conventional portrayal of female cross-dressing in children's literature. It addresses the issue of transgender in a context that is not dissociated from the contemporary Western cultural appreciation of cross-dressing. Instead, it delves into the area of cross-dressing sexuality and the negative ramifications which can accompany subversive gender behavior in a realistic social context. Each of these novels represents cross-dressing in a manner that admirably tries to tackle the issues which are relevant to such behavior in our culture, but they do so cautiously. They are hesitant to endorse cross-dressing as a legitimate behavioral practice, although each novel perceptively uses it to interrogate the established gender binary. The success they achieve in providing an insightful critique of normative gender categories is, however, moderated by the eventual cessation of the female protagonist's cross-dressing for reasons that reinforce, rather than subvert, the regulatory power of cultural and institutional forces in relation to adolescent gender and sexual identities.

The disjunction between male and female cross-dressing within the transgender paradigm is, curiously, also maintained in the two fairy tale precursors to the transgender model. "The Mouse, the Thing and the Wand" and "The Counterfeit Marquise" resolve the dilemma of the protagonist's cross-dressing in different ways according to sex: the female-to-male cross-dressing character of "The Mouse, the Thing and the Wand" finds happiness only when she magically acquires a biologically male body, thereby reinscribing the traditional relationship between sex and gender, while the male-to-female cross-dresser of "The Counterfeit Marquise" retires to a house in the country. There she happily remains a cross-dresser,[2] an ending which advocates the positive effects of gender subversion. The implication of these different narrative closures is that male cross-dressers are able to negotiate a less tenuous form of transgender identity than females, whose cross-dressing initially facilitates, but then denies, subjective agency.

The representation of male cross-dressing within the transgender paradigm defies the trend, established more broadly in children's literature, toward conservative depictions of male characters who dress in feminine clothing. Within the transgender paradigm it is male characters who use cross-dressing as an expression of resistance to the social forces which seek to monitor gender. *Sky Legs, Boy Overboard,* and *Funny Boy* all present cross-dressing as a valid behavioral practice and refuse to stigmatize it as abnormal or deviant. These novels address the complexity of what it means to be a transgendered individual and offer progressive representations of cross-dressing which embrace a queer aesthetic—presenting their cross-dressers' identities in a way that problematizes, confuses, and defies categorization. They present cross-dressing as a form of questioning of, or rebellion against, socially ingrained and constructed notions of masculinity and femininity. These characters cross-dress because of an inability to fulfill conventional gender expectations attached to their biology. In this they are actively involved in a critical reassessment of traditional constructions of gender and sexuality. Just as important, they provide readers with a compassionate representation of characters with unconventional sexual and gender identities. By using strategies such as first-person narration, these YA novels bring cross-dressing to the forefront of their narratives. They prompt us as readers to embrace their male cross-dressing characters and their social rebellion, in much the same way that Eleni finds herself doing with Pete:

One two three

He says

One two three one two three

I hear and move slowly to the wind's call

Happy I waltz on a mountain top

With a boy wearing a dress. (297)

Novels such as *Sky Legs, Boy Overboard,* and *Funny Boy* signal a considerable change in the portrayal of cross-dressing within narratives for children and adolescents. These books, which depart from the more established cross-dressing paradigms, confront the social reality of cross-dressing. They recognize that cross-dressing is a subversive behavior which directly challenges the status quo of the regulatory social regimes that police gender and sexuality within our culture. Whereas YA novels featuring female cross-dressers focus predominantly on the negative social ramifications of transvestism, male protagonists fare much better. Their experience of cross-dressing is gratifying and enjoyable, and although their behavior provokes hostility in some quarters, they do not let this deter them from expressing their unconventional gender identities. The male protagonists of *Sky Legs, Boy Overboard,* and *Funny Boy* defy normative gender and sexual categories, exemplified in each instance by the illicit pleasure they derive from transgressing the gender divide through cross-dressing. Pete, Jamie, and Arjie are actively involved in what Michael Warner terms a "thorough resistance to regimes of the normal" (1991, 16). They use cross-dressing (either explicitly or implicitly) as an expression of difference and defiance. This results in the affirmation of a queer subjectivity that problematizes concepts such as masculine and feminine, gay and straight. Marjorie Garber argues that "The difficulty, the challenge, and the interest posed by the complex interrelationship between transvestism and gay identity lie in simultaneously tracking the dissemination of the signifiers of sex and gender and in combating the oppressive effects of institutionalized binarity" ([1992] 1993, 161). *Sky Legs, Boy Overboard,* and *Funny Boy* play an important role in challenging the restrictive effects of "institutionalized binarity." These texts employ cross-dressing, in accordance with a queer framework, to destabilize and defy what is generally considered to be "normal" gender and sexual behavior.

CONCLUSION

Vern and Bonnie Bullough's *Cross Dressing, Sex and Gender* (1993) opens with a straightforward yet cogent statement: "Cross-dressing is a simple term for a complex set of phenomena" (vii). The complexity surrounding cross-dressing as a subject is demonstrated by the variety of cross-dressing representations evident in children's literature and film, which have a correspondingly divergent impact upon the ideological construction of gender. Representations of cross-dressing, aside from offering a revelatory perspective concerning the operation of masculine and feminine discourses within children's literature and film, also disclose a significant disjunction with regard to the way that transgressive gender behavior is treated according to the cross-dresser's sex. While female characters are encouraged to subvert traditional gender boundaries and cross the threshold into masculine gender territory, male characters regard the incursion of femininity (as signified by cross-dressing) with fear and hostility.

When female characters in children's literature cross-dress, they skillfully expose the inherently oppressive nature of normative gender categories. Cross-dressing principally enables the female protagonist to escape the confines of patriarchal femininity and experience masculine subjectivity. At the same time her triumphant performance of masculinity highlights the constructedness of socially prescribed gender norms by demonstrating that gender, as argued by Butler, is an "identity tenuously constituted in time, instituted in an exterior space through a stylized repetition of acts" ([1990] 1999, 179). Having mastered the art of a successful masculine performance, cross-dressing becomes the means through which gender stereotypes can be positively subverted and reappropriated by subjects to whom they do not holistically apply. The female cross-dresser's success hinges upon more than just the achieving of an authentic masculine identity: while cross-dressed, she gains public respect and commendation because she forges a new identity for herself which amalgamates and redefines conventionally masculine and feminine behaviors. The gender identity of female cross-dressing subjects takes an unprecedented form in that it becomes a "third" category against which "masculinity" and "femininity" are interwoven and dissected through the theatricality of performance.

Less successful instances of female cross-dressing are also evident, naturally, but their lack of effectiveness can be attributed to focalization strategies which limit the cross-dressing characters' interiority and prevent them from being introspective about their behavior. This lack of interiority removes the potential for cross-dressing to act as a strategy of gender criticism because the cross-dresser does not reflect on her cross-dressing behavior in relation to the modifications she needs to make to her conduct in order to be perceived as masculine. Retellings of Joan of Arc provide a particularly pertinent illustration of this point, as Joan's successful performance of masculinity in both a political and military context is not explored in fictional reconstructions of her subjectivity. The effectiveness of female cross-dressing representations is largely due to the association of cross-dressing with agency. However, by limiting the cross-dressing heroine's interiority, these examples of female cross-dressing literature do not sustain or develop cross-dressing as a theme for examining culturally produced gender categories. Nevertheless, less successful female cross-dressing narratives maintain cross-dressing as a legitimate behavior. Joan of Arc retellings, which demonstrate a reluctance to give her a fictional identity that differs greatly from documented historical evidence (and there is little evidence of her attitude to her contentious cross-dressing) still praise her courage in refusing to submit to the directions of the Inquisition when ordered to stop cross-dressing. Novels such as *Monstrous Regiment* and *Rose Daughter* similarly validate the behavior of their female cross-dressing characters by thematically interrogating dominant social paradigms, gendered or otherwise.

Female cross-dressing is constructed as transgressive gender behavior that can be engaged in without social or personal cost to the cross-dresser. Indeed, her social status is elevated by the public recognition awarded to her after her cross-dressing disguise is revealed (the public celebration of Joan of Arc is ongoing; the French people's exaltation of her heroism during her life persisting in the context of the enduring cultural legacy she left behind). For male cross-dressers, however, the situation could not be more different. Male cross-dressing is comically presented as a humiliating and panic-inducing experience for the masculine subject, behavior that lowers his gender status and symbolically divests him of subjective agency. Unlike female cross-dressing narratives, which use cross-dressing as a catalyst for examining the socially constructed nature of gender, male cross-dressing narratives conversely employ cross-dressing to reinforce conventional gender stereotypes. Humor is integral to the construction of male cross-dressing, and the amusing display of a male character wearing a dress, incompetently struggling to come to terms with feminine identity, coincides with Bakhtin's idea of the carnival as a temporary suspension of hierarchical codes—which in this case is the hierarchical structure of socially prescribed gender relations. However, the gender inversion that occurs in male cross-dressing narratives does not serve the same subversive function as Bakhtin's concept of the carnivalesque. Male cross-dressing literature and film does not explore or challenge traditional concepts of masculinity or femininity through the male character's (inept) performance of femininity. Instead, male-to-female cross-dressing marginalizes feminine subjectivity, the assumption of a feminine identity constituting a loss of agency that can only be restored when the cross-dresser resumes his former masculine identity. The implication of this is that femininity is an undesirable and inferior gender status that is abhorrent because it entails the surrender of subjective agency.

The construction of male cross-dressing inevitably results in the creation of an implied masculine reading position that requires female readers to identify against themselves due to the persistent devaluation of feminine subjectivity. The thematic construction of female cross-dressing as a legitimate and beneficial practice through which to encourage meaningful gender experimentation is denied by male cross-dressing narratives, which just as convincingly discourage male characters (and hence male readers) from following suit. The representation of gender binarism in male cross-dressing literature is further cemented in film, where male cross-dressing comedies such as *Sorority Boys*, *Mrs. Doubtfire*, and *Ace Ventura: Pet Detective* reproduce polarized cultural stereotypes of cross-dressing as harmless heterosexual male fun or as an ominous indication of psychosis. A misogynistic construction of femininity dominates the presentation of male cross-dressing in films for children and adolescents where feminine subjectivity (represented by the feminine identity which the male subject is forced to endure through his cross-dressing and also in relation to secondary female characters) is treated with ridicule and contempt. The depiction within these films of the cross-dressed body as grotesque, a hideous union of masculine and feminine physical traits, does not herald a potentially rejuvenative reevaluation of gender stereotypes, following Bakhtin's concept of grotesque realism as "deeply positive" in function ([1968] 1984, 19). The cross-dressing protagonist's refusal to relinquish his masculine identity entails that his cross-dressed body is only a superficial and illusory amalgamation of gendered bodies. His cross-dressed physical body is monstrous only because of his enforced adoption of femininity, an ideological standpoint that serves to render femininity abject.

Cross-dressing films for children and adults are also responsible for generating a nascent dialogue between the adult's and the child's perspectives of cross-dressing. These have hitherto been separated in children's literature as a consequence of the nonsexualized depiction of both male and female cross-dressing. The results of such a dialogue are not altogether promising, as the introduction of a sexualized, adult-oriented cross-dressing discourse in these films focuses mainly upon the perceived relationship between cross-dressing and homosexuality. Homosexuality represents a deviation from the compulsory heterosexuality required by hegemonic masculinity, and as such it is staunchly rejected within children's cross-dressing films that conservatively maintain masculinity as the only viable category of identity. A film such as *Mrs. Doubtfire* implicitly repositions cross-dressing as a legitimate form of gender playfulness. It rebukes the suggestion that transgressive gender behavior warrants criminal or moral censure. However, this more tolerant approach to transgendered subjectivity is compromised by the accompanying misogynistic feminine discourse which is familiar to most male cross-dressing literature. Only *Ma Vie en Rose* successfully escapes this conundrum, offering a sympathetic portrayal of transgressive gender identity that thought-provokingly champions the erasure of regulatory and oppressive gender regimes. The restrictive R(17+) rating that this film earned in the USA, however, separates it from other, considerably more conservative, examples of cross-dressing cinema freely available to children and teenage viewers.

Contemporary YA fiction redresses the predicament of the cross-dressing subject in the female and male paradigms by bridging the potential offered by both models. The transgender paradigm reverses the cultural marginalization of transvestite and transsexual characters. It creatively uses cross-dressing to interrogate regulatory gender regimes but is importantly anchored within social reality. The relationship between gender and sexuality is not repressed within these texts, which instead seek to include heterosexuality as a normative category of identity that can be successfully challenged by cross-dressing.

The significant achievements of the transgender paradigm are nevertheless frustrated by the maintenance of a gendered distinction with regard to the consequences of male and female transgender behavior. In contrast to the subversive and individualistic gender discourse traditionally employed in female cross-dressing literature, it is male cross-dressers who provocatively challenge established gender discourses within the transgender paradigm. These characters embrace cross-dressing as a legitimate expression of unconventional gender and sexual identities, and the resulting depiction of male transgendered subjectivity fulfills all the potentialities offered by cross-dressing in children's literature: it subverts stable categories of identity within a socially realistic environment and thematically champions individuality and resistance.

The queer interpretive aesthetic which readers are invited to apply to transgendered male subjectivity is unexpectedly absent from comparative portrayals of female transgendered subjectivity. Transgendered female characters are primarily represented in terms of their "otherness." The subjectivity of the female transgendered character remains closed off to readers. Her lack of accessibility within the narrative (she either does not focalize or is underfocalized) undermines her subjective complexity as she is always viewed through another's eyes. The transgendered female character's behavior is interpreted through and against the male focalizing character's own conventional gender and sexual identity, and she is consistently identified as deviant, disquieting, or dangerous. The pleasurable cross-dressing experiences of male transgendered characters are alien to comparable female characters, whose transgendered behavior incites serious, even fatal, social repercussions.

Children's literature acknowledges the transgressive potential of cross-dressing in varied and conflicting ways. Female cross-dressing literature embraces the possibility that cross-dressing offers in relation to destabilizing conventional gender boundaries, but male cross-dressing representations respond to the same possibilities with fear, renouncing them in favor of a conservative reassertion of gender and sexual stereotypes. Contemporary adolescent fiction uses transgendered subjectivity as the impetus for an interrogative and open-ended exploration of regulatory gender regimes, but the gender division that exists between the female and male cross-dressing paradigms is similarly maintained within this literary subgroup, albeit in opposite form. Cross-dressing, as it occurs in children's literature and the world at large, can play a highly significant role in the pursuit of social justice. We live in an environment where gender divisions are often rigidly enforced and policed, but the simple truth of the matter is that, as Bullough and Bullough remark, "inevitably, many individuals violate these socially defined norms" (ix). Cross-dressing functions as an important practice of resistance. When used effectively, cross-dressing can function critically without an inherent bias for either masculine or feminine discourses—exposing the socially constructed boundaries of each. Cross-dressing representations in children's literature, particularly those involving female or transgendered (male) characters, ingeniously expose the manner in which hierarchical gender structures and practices are culturally inscribed and reproduced. Depictions of male-to-female or female transgendered cross-dressing are much less successful at achieving this, but nonetheless provide a unique site from which to examine the ways in which cultural practices such as literature and film contribute to the gendering process.

Individuals who cross-dress enunciate the distinction between sex and gender. By going "into the closet" and reappearing in differently gendered attire they enrich and challenge the ways in which we perceive gender and sexuality, undermining so-called "natural" categories of identity. The cross-dresser's unique ability to reconceptualize traditional gender relations is both acknowledged and encouraged within a broad spectrum of children's and adolescent literature, but a large body of literary and cinematic texts directed at the same young audience is equally determined to dissuade its readers from participating in or responding compassionately to behavior that is resistant to normative gender and sexual discourses. Until gender and sexual experimentation are culturally condoned and openly encouraged, a process in an incipient stage within the literature and films for children and adolescents, oppressive gender ideologies which cast masculinity and femininity as "natural" and inherently oppositional concepts will continue to prevail.

> It is not gender which causes problems; rather, it is the imposition of a gender on an individual by another. When the imposition is removed, polarity of masculine and feminine may remain, but as personal preference rather than imposed imperative. Penises, breasts and vaginas will once again become body parts rather than regulators of behavior and identity. And we'll all breathe a little easier.
>
> **Transsexual activist Nancy Nangeroni**
> **as quoted in Fienberg,**
> ***Transgender Warriors:***
> ***Making History From Joan of Arc***
> ***to Dennis Rodman, 1996.***

NOTES

CHAPTER 2

1. All references to *Mulan* specifically relate to the Walt Disney film (1998), not the historical Chinese legend on which the film is based.

2. "The Subtle Princess" is a French fairy tale included in Marina Warner's anthology *Wonder Tales* (1996). Finessa is a truly admirable and wondrous woman who embodies perfection in every respect. Upon leaving for a journey, the king (her father) locks Finessa and her two sisters (both of whom are silly and selfish) in a tower, entrusting to each of them a magic glass bobbin that will break if they do anything dishonorable. A villainous prince breaks into the tower and tricks the two sisters into betraying themselves. Soon after, they each give birth to a son. Intent on revenge, Finessa cleverly disguises herself as a male doctor and outwits the crafty prince. Soon after she finds love in the arms of his younger brother, and is single-handedly responsible for preventing both of their deaths and ensuring their eternal happiness.

3. When considering the various cultural practices which discursively construct individual bodies, racial identity is a significant factor. Butler's concept of identity as performative, rather than fixed or stable, necessarily suggests that racial identity, like gender identity, is constructed out of the repetition of certain behaviors and actions. Racial performativity is a relevant concern when analyzing the construction of Mulan's identity, particularly in light of the fact that Chinese femininity is presented as interpellated and nonagential within the type of Western cultural framework that is privileged within Disney films. However, I have chosen to limit my discussion of performativity to gender in order to draw more effective comparisons with other female cross-dressing texts.

CHAPTER 3

1. Although Disney drew its inspiration for the film *Mulan* from a Chinese poem, the legend of Mulan is culturally specific to China and unknown to Western audiences, the implied viewers of the Disney film.
2. Windows have a particular symbolic function in picture books. A character that "looks out the window or stands in the door…is implicated in the unspoken meanings of thresholds" (Moebius 1986, 145). Joan is depicted in this particular illustration as standing on the threshold of her old (feminine) life, which she is about to leave in order to embrace a new (masculine) existence as a warrior for the French people.
3. Extracted from the transcripts of the trial of Joan of Arc. *Medieval Sourcebook: The Trial of Joan of Arc.* Accessed on September 30, 2005. http://www.fordham.edu/halsall/basis/joanofarc-trial.html.
4. Gabrielle refers to Joan of Arc as both Jeanne and Jeanette in Garden's *Dove and Sword*.

CHAPTER 4

1. After traveling to the city and establishing a male presence at the king's court, Wahda is chosen to be the king's bodyguard. One night the sound of a vampire is heard outside the king's chamber, and Wahda sets out to uncover its origin. She encounters the vampire attempting to suck blood from a newly crucified corpse and, in the struggle which ensues, manages to tear a piece of cloth from the ghoul's garments. When she presents this material to the king, his queen is so enamored with its beauty that she demands that the source of the cloth be discovered, in order for an entire suit of clothes to be made from it for her. Without hesitation, Wahda sets out on a journey to find the vampire. While on her travels she encounters many different monsters and people, all of whom accept the authenticity of her masculinity and never fail to be impressed by her wondrous behavior. When Wahda at last returns with the magical cloth, the king is so delighted that he promotes her to the position of Prime Minister. Using her newly acquired status, Wahda ingeniously forms a plan that reunites her with her family.
2. Sergeant Jackrum subverts the typical construction of female cross-dressing in *Monstrous Regiment*. Despite being the most stereotypical representation of masculinity in the novel, the conventionality of Jackrum's masculinity is tempered by the incorporation of more feminine attributes and behaviors which are demonstrated in relation to the maternal tendencies and compassion which she/he shows toward the cross-dressed members of the squad. Jackrum also proves herself/himself to be an astute observer of gender, illustrated by her/his immediate identification of the female sex of the squad members (she/he is aware that they are all cross-dressing long before they are aware of each other's

disguise), and she/he is also responsible for revealing the biological sex of the Borogravian army commanders. Jackrum's perceptive approach to gender corresponds to the construction of gender within the female-to-male cross-dressing paradigm, but again Jackrum diverges from this mold by maintaining a masculine disguise after retiring from the army.

3. Madame D'Aulnoy, a seventeenth-century French teller of fairy tales, often used variations of the "Beauty and the Beast" theme in her stories. Jack Zipes remarks that D'Aulnoy's many versions of "Beauty and the Beast" possess very specific allusions to gender and so-called "appropriate" masculine and feminine roles (specific to D'Aulnoy's historical context). Zipes argues that D'Aulnoy defines the different and oppositional genders of Beauty and her beast in the following archaic manner: "The woman must be constantly chastised for her curiosity, unreliability, and whimsy. True beauty depends on prudence and discretion which is figuratively depicted by the heroine either sacrificing herself to a male beast or submitting to his commands and wishes because he has a noble soul and civil manners. The hidden message in all these tales is a dictum which the women of D'Aulnoy's time including D'Aulnoy herself had to obey or face degradation and ostracism: control your natural inclinations and submit to the fate which male social standards decree" (Zipes 1983, 37).

CHAPTER 5

1. *Min Syster är en Ängel* is currently available only in Swedish.

CHAPTER 6

1. Chewbacca is a hairy and bearlike alien character featured in George Lucas's *Star Wars Trilogy* (1977-1983).
2. "Passing" is a term which is commonly used within the transgender community to refer to the feat of blending into the community as either a man or a woman (Grey 2002).
3. In relation to this point, it is pertinent to note that Daniel's brother is immediately recognizable as gay. His profession (makeup artist) is stereotypically effeminate, and therefore homosexual in orientation. His voice is highly camp, and he lives with his male lover. He is also played by the actor Harvey Fierstein, who is himself openly gay and a well-known gay rights activist. The use of an overtly gay man to effect a feminine transformation on a heterosexual male is significant, suggestive of the clichéd notion that homosexuality is to some extent harmonious with femininity, or otherwise lacking in genuine masculinity, and therefore is able to assist in the emasculation of a heterosexual biological male.

4. By asking viewers to align themselves with Daniel's viewpoint, it could also be argued that the implied viewing position which *Mrs. Doubtfire* offers is conventionally conservative because it requires female viewers to identify against themselves.
5. Burke does have an advantage in that she is much more androgynous-looking than the conventionally attractive Young, who is both petite and classically pretty.

CHAPTER 7

1. This information is revealed to the reader only in the latter stages of the text, when Nuala attempts to explain her behavior to Xavier.
2. The marquise's husband, a female-to-male cross-dresser, is similarly successful in achieving happiness. However, the narrative is focalized purely from the marquise's perspective and her husband's viewpoint is only implicitly addressed, confirming the notion that this fairy tale is a story of male, rather than female, cross-dressing success.

BIBLIOGRAPHY

PRIMARY SOURCES

Ace Ventura: Pet Detective. Directed by Tom Shadyac. Warner Brothers, 1994.

Aladdin. Directed by Ron Clements and John Musker. Walt Disney Pictures, 1992.

All About My Mother (Todo Sobre Mi Madre). Directed by Pedro Almodovar. Sony Pictures Classics, 1999.

American Pie. Directed by Paul Weitz. Universal Pictures, 1999.

Beauty and the Beast. Directed by Gary Trousdale and Kirk Wise. Walt Disney Pictures, 1991.

Blade Runner. Directed by Ridley Scott. Warner Bros, 1982.

Boys Don't Cry. Directed by Kimberley Peirce. Fox Searchlight, 1999.

Cinderella. Directed by Clyde Geronimi, Wilfred Jackson and Hamilton Luske. Walt Disney Pictures, 1950.

The Crying Game. Directed by Neil Jordan. Miramax, 1992.

Chambers, Aidan. *Postcards From No Man's Land.* London: Bodley Head, 1999.

Fine, Anne. *Bill's New Frock.* London: Mammoth Books, [1989] 1999.

———. *Alias Madame Doubtfire.* New York: Bantam Books, [1988] 1993.

Garden, Nancy. *Dove and Sword.* New York: Scholastic Inc, [1995] 1997.

Grahame, Kenneth. *The Wind in the Willows.* London: Methuen Children's Books, [1908] 1973.

Harry Enfield Presents Kevin's Guide to Being a Teenager. Directed by Clive Tulloh. Tiger Aspect Productions, 1999.

Husain, Sharukh. (Ed.), *Women Who Wear the Breeches – Delicious and Dangerous Tales.* London: Virago, 1995.

Jennings, Paul. *The Gizmo.* Ringwood: Penguin Books Australia Ltd, 1994.

Joan of Arc. Directed by Christian Duguay. Artisan Entertainment, 1999.

Kevin and Perry Go Large. Directed by Ed Bye. Fragile Films, 2000.

L'Héritier de Villandon, Marie-Jeanne. "The Subtle Princess" (translated by Gilbert Adair), 1695, as appears in Warner, Marina (Ed.), *Wonder Tales: Six Stories of Enchantment.* London: Vintage, 1996: 65–97.

The Little Mermaid. Ron Clements and John Musker. Walt Disney Pictures, 1989.

MacDonald, Ross. *Another Perfect Day*. Brookfield, Connecticut: Roaring Book Press, 2002.

Ma Vie En Rose. Directed by Alan Berliner. Sony Pictures Classics, 1997.

McKinley, Robin. *Rose Daughter*. New York: Ace, [1997] 2002.

The Messenger: The Story of Joan of Joan of Arc. Directed by Luc Besson. Columbia Pictures, 1999.

Moloney, James. *Touch Me*. Queensland: University of Queensland Press, 2000.

Morpurgo, Michael. *Joan of Arc*. San Diego, New York and London: Harcourt Brace and Company, [1998] 1999.

"The Mouse, the Thing and the Wand" as appears in Husain, Sharukh. (Ed.), *Women Who Wear the Breeches – Delicious and Dangerous Tales*. London: Virago, 1995:117–144.

Mrs Doubtfire. Directed by Chris Columbus. Twentieth Century Fox, 1993.

Mulan. Directed by Tony Bancroft and Barry Cook. Walt Disney Pictures, 1998.

National Velvet. Directed by Clarence Brown. Warner Studios, 1944.

Nuns on the Run. Directed by Jonathan Lyn. Twentieth Century Fox, 1992.

Perrault, Charles and François-Timoléon de Choisy. "The Counterfeit Marquise" (translated by Ranjit Bolt), 1695, as appears in Warner, Marina. (Ed.), *Wonder Tales: Six Stories of Enchantment*. London: Vintage, 1996: 123–147.

Pierce, Tamora. *Alanna – The First Adventure*. USA: Random House, [1983] 1997.

———. *In the Hand of the Goddess*. UK: Scholastic Children's Books, [1984] 1998.

Pohl, Peter (translated by Laurie Thompson). *Johnny, My Friend*. UK: Turton and Chambers, [1985] 1991.

Poole, Josephine. *Joan of Arc*. New York: Dragonfly Books, [1998] 2000.

Pratchett, Terry. *Monstrous Regiment*. London: Doubleday, 2003.

Psycho. Directed by Alfred Hitchcock. Universal, 1960.

"A Riddle for a King" as appears in Husain, Sharukh. (Ed.), *Women Who Wear the Breeches – Delicious and Dangerous Tales*. London: Virago, 1995:1–10.

Queneau, Raymond. *Zazie in the Metro*. New York: Penguin Books, [1959] 2001.

Sachar, Louis. *Marvin Redpost: Is He a Girl?* New York: Scholastic, 1993.

Savvides, Irini. *Sky Legs*. Sydney: Hodder Headline Australia, 2003.

Selvadurai, Shyam. *Funny Boy*. London: Vintage, [1994] 1995.

The Silence of the Lambs. Directed by Jonathan Demme, MGM, 1991.

The Simpsons, "Grift of the Magi" (Episode 9, Season 11). Created by Matt Groening. Twentieth Century Fox, 1999.

Snow White and the Seven Dwarfs. Directed by David Hand. Walt Disney Pictures, 1938.

Some Like it Hot. Directed by Billy Wilder. MGM, 1959.

Sorority Boys. Directed by Wally Wolodarsky. Touchstone Pictures, 2002.

South Pacific. Music by Richard Rodgers and lyrics by Oscar Hammerstein II, 1949.

Stark, Ulf. *Min Syster är en Ängel*. Sweden: Alfabeta. 1996.

Star Wars Trilogy. Directed by George Lucas. Twentieth Century Fox, 1977–1983.

Stiller, Laurie and Gregory Rogers. *Princess Max*. Sydney: Random House, 2001.

Tarzan. Directed by Chris Buck (II) and Kevin Lima. Walt Disney Pictures, 1999.

Tootsie. Directed by Sydney Pollack. Columbia Tristar, 1982.

To Wong Foo, Thanks for Everything! Julie Newmar. Directed by Beeban Kidron. Universal, 1995.

Twain, Mark. *The Adventures of Huckleberry Finn*. London: Penguin Books, [1884] 1966.

Warner, Marina (Ed.). *Wonder Tales*. UK: Vintage, 1996.

Wells, Peter. *Boy Overboard*. Auckland: Vintage, 1997.

"What Will Be Will Be" as appears in Husain, Sharukh. (Ed.), *Women Who Wear the Breeches – Delicious and Dangerous Tales*. London: Virago, 1995:195–230.

White Chicks. Directed by Keenan Ivory Wayans. Columbia Tristar, 2004.

SECONDARY SOURCES

Abrams, M. H. *A Glossary of Literary Terms*, 6th ed. Fort Worth, Texas: Harcourt, Brace Jovanovich, 1993.

Allen, J.J. *The Man in the Red Velvet Dress – Inside the World of Cross-Dressing.*
New York: Birch Lane Press, published by Carol Publishing Group, 1996.

Andrew, J. D., "The Theater of Irish Cinema." *Yale Journal of Criticism* 15.1 (2002) 23–58.

Bakhtin, Mikhail (trans by Helene Iswolsky). *Rabelais and His World*. USA: Indiana University Press, 1984 (1968).

Beemyn, Brett. "Cross-dressing." *glbtq: An Encyclopedia of Gay, Lesbian, Bisexual, Transgender, and Queer Culture*. Claude J. Summers (ed). December 28, 2004. Accessed March 31, 2005. <http://www.glbtq.com/social-sciences/cross_dressing_ssh.html>

Bolin, Anne. "Transcending and Transgendering: Male-to-Female Transsexuals, Dichotomy and Diversity" as appears in Herdt, Gilbert (Ed.). *Third Sex Third Gender: Beyond Sexual Dimorphism in Culture and History*. New York: Zone Books, 1994.

Bornstein, Kate. *Gender Outlaw*. New York: Vintage, 1995.

Brocklebank, Lisa. "Rebellious Voices: The Unofficial Discourse of Cross-dressing in d'Aulnoy, de Murat, and Perrault." ChLAQ 25 (3), 2000:127–136.

Bullough, Vern and Bonnie Bullough. *Cross Dressing, Sex and Gender*. Philadelphia: University of Pennsylvania Press, 1993.

Butler, Alban and Michael J. Walsh. *Butler's Lives of the Saints*. San Francisco: Harper & Row, 1985.

Butler, Judith. *Bodies That Matter: On the Discursive Limits of "Sex"*. New York: Routledge, 1993.

―――. *Gender Trouble: Feminism and the Subversion of Identity*. New York: Routledge, [1990] 1999.

―――."Performative Acts and Gender Constitution: An Essay in Phenomenology and Feminist Theory." Pp 270–282 in Case, Sue-Ellen (Ed.). *Performing Feminisms: Feminist Critical Theory and Theatre*. Baltimore: Johns Hopkins UP, 1990.

Cantacuzino, Marina. "My Son the Cross-Dresser." *The Guardian*. 4 July, 2001. Accessed September 30, 2005. <http://www.guardian.co.uk/parents/story/0,3605,516430,00.html>

Clark, Katerina, and Michael Holquist. *Mikhail Bakhtin*. Cambridge: Harvard University Press, 1984.

Connell, R. W. *Masculinities*. St Leonards: Allen and Unwin, 1995.

Culler, Jonathan. *Literary Theory: A Very Short Introduction*. Oxford: Oxford University Press, 1997.

Cyrino, M. S. "Heroes In D(u)ress: Transvestism and Power in the Myths of Herakles and Achilles." *Arethusa* 31.2 (1998) 207–241.

Danow, David. *The Spirit of the Carnival*. Lexington, Kentucky: The University Press of Kentucky, 1995.

Davis, Stephen J. "Crossed Texts, Crossed Sex: Intertextuality and Gender in Early Christian Legends of Holy Women Disguised as Men." *Journal of Early Christian Studies* 10.1 (2002) 1–36

Dekker, Rudolf M. and Lotte C. van de Pol. *The Tradition of Female Transvestism in Early Modern Europe*. New York: St Martin's Press, 1989.

Ebert, Roger. "Sorority Boys". *The Chicago Sun Times*, 22 Mar. 2002. (Accessed September 30, 2005: http://rogerebert.suntimes.com/apps/pbcs.dll/article?AID=/20020322/REVIEWS/203220305/1023)

Fienberg, Leslie. *Transgender Warriors: Making History from Joan of Arc to Dennis Rodman*. Boston: Beacon Press, 1996.

Foucault, Michel. "Of Other Spaces". *Diacritics*, 16:1 (1986): 22–27.

Freud, Sigmund. "Femininity", in *New Introductory Lectures on Psycho-Analysis: The Standard Edition of the Complete Psychological Works of Sigmund Freud*, edited by James Strachey. London: The Hogarth Press and The Institute for Psycho-Analysis, [1933] 1964.

Fuchs, Cynthia. "Robin Williams in a Dress." Film review of *Mrs Doubtfire*. Available from Film Reviews, Women's Studies Database, University of Maryland. Accessed on September 30, 2005. <http://www.inform.umd.edu/EdRes/Topic/Diversity/Specific/Sexual_Orientation/Books/mrs-doubtfire-fuchs>

Furze, Robert. Film review of *Kevin and Perry Go Large*. Available online from W.H.Smith. Accessed on November 24, 2004. <http://www.whsmith.co.uk/whs/go.asp?MENU=DVD_AND_Video&pagedef=/dvdvideo/reviews/show.htm&data =main_kevinperry>

Garber, Marjorie. *Vested Interests: Cross-dressing and Cultural Anxiety*. London: Penguin, [1992] 1993.

———. *Vice Versa: Bisexuality and the Eroticism of Everyday Life*. London: Penguin, 1997.

Gauntlett, David. "Judith Butler." 1998. Available online from *Theory.org.co.uk*. Accessed September 30, 2005. <http://www.theory.org.uk/ctr-butl.htm>

Grey, Michaela. "The Phallus in the Mirror: Narcissism and Transsexual Identity". 2002. Accessed September 27, 2005. <http://michaelagrey.com/cerebral/phallus.html>

Grimm, David E. "Toward a Theory of Gender: Transsexualism, Gender, Sexuality, and Relationships." *American Behavioral Scientist* 31, no. 1 (September/October 1987): 66–85.

Grossman, Andrew. "Transvestism in Film." *glbtq: An Encyclopedia of Gay, Lesbian, Bisexual, Transgender, and Queer Culture*. Claude J. Summers (Ed.), 2002. Accessed March 24, 2005. <http://www.glbtq.com/arts/transvestism_film.html>

Hawthorn, Jeremy. *A Glossary of Contemporary Literary Theory*. 2nd ed. UK: Edward Arnold (Hodder Headline), 1994.

Herdt, Gilbert (Ed.). *Third Sex Third Gender: Beyond Sexual Dimorphism in Culture and History*. New York: Zone Books, 1996.

Hixon, Martha P. "Tam Lin, Fair Janet, and the Sexual Revolution: Traditional Ballads, Fairy Tales, and Twentieth-Century Children's Literature." *Marvels & Tales* 18.1 (2004) 67–92.

Jagodzinski, J. "Women's Bodies of Performative Excess: Miming, Feigning, Refusing, and Rejecting the Phallus." *Journal for the Psychoanalysis of Culture and Society* 8.1 (2003) 23–41.

Jagose, Annamarie. *Queer Theory*. Carlton, Victoria: Melbourne University Press, 1996a.

———. "Queer Theory." *Australian Humanities Review*. Issue 4, December 1996b. Accessed October 6, 2005. <http://www.lib.latrobe.edu.au/AHR/archive/Issue-Dec-1996/jagose.html>

Kirk, Kris and Ed Heath. *Men in Frocks*. London, UK: GMP Publishers Ltd, 1984.

Kress, Gunther and Theo van Leeuwen. *The Grammar of Visual Design*. London and New York: Routledge, 1996.

Lacan, Jacques. *Écrits: A Selection*. Trans. Alan Sheridan. New York: W.W. Norton & Company, 1977.

Lehman, Peter. *Masculinity: Bodies, Movies, and Culture*. New York; London: Routledge, 2001.

———. *Running Scared: Masculinity and the Representation of the Male Body*. Philadelphia: Temple University Press, 1993.

Levine, Richard M. "Crossing the Line." Available online from Tri Ess. Accessed October 4, 2005. <http://www.geocities.com/WestHollywood/Heights/7396/rdrm/crossingtheline.html>

Macquarie Dictionary (3rd edition). Macquarie University, NSW: The Macquarie Library, 1999 (1981).

Mallan, Kerry. "Challenging the Phallic Fantasy in Young Adult Fiction". Stephens, John (Ed.). *Ways of Being Male*. New York: Routledge, 2002.

Matzner, Andrew. "Joan of Arc." *glbtq: An Encyclopedia of Gay, Lesbian, Bisexual, Transgender, and Queer Culture*. Claude J. Summers, (Ed.), 2004. Accessed March 1, 2005. <http://www.glbtq.com/social-sciences/joan_arc.html>

McCallum, Robyn, *Ideologies of Identity in Adolescent Fiction: The Dialogic Construction of Subjectivity*. New York and London: Garland Publishing, 1999.

Medieval Sourcebook: The Trial of Joan of Arc. Accessed September 30, 2005. <http://www.fordham.edu/halsall/basis/joanofarc-trial.html>

Merriam-Webster Online Dictionary available at Merriam-Webster Online, http://www.m-w.com/.

Meyerowitz, Joanne. "Sex Research at the Borders of Gender: Transvestites, Transsexuals, and Alfred C. Kinsey". *Bulletin of the History of Medicine* 75.1 (2000) 72–90:75.

Michaelsen, Scott. "Hybrid Bound." A review of José David Saldívar, Border Matters: Remapping American Cultural Studies. Berkeley: U of California P, 1997. *PMC* 8.3 (1998). Accessed June 10, 2007 http://www3.iath.virginia.edu/pmc/text-only/issue.598/8.3.r_michaelsen.txt.

Miller, Paul Allen. "The Bodily Grotesque in Roman Satire: Images of Sterility." *Arethusa* 31.3 (1998) 257–283.

Minton, H. L. "Queer Theory: Historical Roots and Implications for Psychology." *Theory and Psychology 7*, No. 3 (1997): 337–53.

Montrose, Louis. "Spenser and the Elizabethan Political Imaginary", *ELH* 69.4 (2002) 907–946.

Mulvey, Laura. "Visual Pleasure and Narrative Cinema." *Screen* 16(3) 1975: 6–18.

Murfin, Ross and Supryia M. Ray. *The Bedford Glossary of Critical and Literary Terms*. Boston: Bedford Books, 1997.

Moebius, William. "Introduction to Picturebook Codes". *Word and Image*, 2, 2 (1986): 141–51.

Nangeroni, Nancy. As quoted in Fienberg, Leslie. *Transgender Warriors: Making History from Joan of Arc to Dennis Rodman.* Boston: Beacon Press, 1996 (p.163).

Newton, Esther. *Mother Camp: Female Impersonators in America.* Chicago: University of Chicago Press, 1972.

Norton, Jody. "Transchildren and the Discipline of Children's Literature." *The Lion and the Unicorn* 23, no. 3 (1999): 414–36.

Ormand, K., "Oedipus the Queen: Cross-gendering without Drag." *Theatre Journal* 55.1 (2003) 1–28.

Osborne, Peter and Lynne Segal. *Gender as Performance: An Interview with Judith Butler. (*Published in *Radical Philosophy* Issue 67, Summer 1994*),* as appears online in extracted form at *Theory.org.uk.* Accessed September 30, 2005. <http://www.theory.org.uk>

Pearce, Sharyn, ""As Wholesome As…": American Pie as a New Millenium Sex Manual", Mallan, Kerry and Sharyn Pearce (Eds.), *Youth Cultures: Texts, Images, and Identities.* Westport, Connecticut: Praeger Publishers (Greenwood Publishing Group), 2003, 69–80.

Pennell, Beverley. "Redeeming Masculinity at the End of the Second Millennium." Stephens, John (Ed.). *Ways of Being Male.* New York: Routledge, 2002 (pp.55–77).

Pettitt, Annie. "Performative Pastiche: Judith Butler and Gender Subversion." *Colloquy,* Issue 3, 1999. Accessed September 30, 2005. <http://www.arts.monash.edu.au/others/colloquy/archives/IssueThree/Pettitt/Pettitt.html>

Piggford, George. " 'Who's That Girl?': Annie Lennox, Woolf's *Orlando* and Female Camp Androgyny." *Mosaic,* 30/3, September, 1997.

Ramet, Sabrina Petra (Ed.). *Gender Reversals and Gender Cultures: Anthropological and Historical Perspectives.* New York: Routledge, 1996.

Reynolds, Kimberley. "Come Lads and Ladettes." Stephens, John (Ed.). *Ways of Being Male.* New York: Routledge, 2002 (pp 96–115).

Ryan, Joal. "It's Official: Men in Dresses Are Funny!" (2000). Available online from Hollywood.com. Accessed September 30, 2005. <http://www.hollywood.com/news/detail/article/312501>

Schiavi, Michael R. "A "Girlboy's" Own Story: Non-Masculine Narrativity In Ma Vie en Rose." *College Literature* 31.3 (2004) 1–26.

Scott, A. O. "A College Course in Lowbrow Humor." *The New York Times,* March 22, 2003. Accessed July 16, 2004. <http://www.nytimes.com/2002/03/22/movies/22BOYS.html?ex=1051761600&en=da130e93faa86157&ei=5070>

Sedgwick, Eve Kosofsky. *Epistemology of the Closet.* Berkeley: University of California Press, 1990.

———. *Novel Gazing: Queer Readings in Fiction.* Durham, NC: Duke University Press, 1997.

———. *Performativity and Performance.* New York: Routledge, 1995.

Showalter, Elaine (Ed.). *Speaking of Gender.* New York and London: Routledge, 1989.

Smith, Paul. *Discerning the Subject.* Minneapolis: University of Minnesota Press, 1988.

Stallybrass, Peter and Allon White. *The Politics and Poetics of Transgression.* London: Methuen, 1986.

Stephens, John. *Language and Ideology in Children's Fiction.* London and New York: Longman, 1992.

――― (Ed.). *Ways of Being Male.* New York: Routledge, 2002.

―――. "Witch Figures in Recent Children's Fiction: The Subaltern and the Subversive." Lawson Lucas, Ann (Ed.). *The Presence of the Past in Children's Literature.* Westport, Connecticut and London: Praeger, 2003:195–202.

Stephens, John and Robyn McCallum. *Retelling Stories, Framing Culture – Traditional Story and Metanarratives in Children's Literature.* New York: Garland, 1998.

Stephens, John and Beverley Pennell. "Queering Heterotopic Spaces: Shyam Selvadurai's Funny Boy and Peter Wells' Boy Overboard." Pp 164–184 in John Stephens, (Ed.), *Ways of Being Male.* New York: Routledge, 2002.

Stephens, John and Rolf Romoren. "Representing Masculinities in Norwegian and Australian Young Adult Fiction." Stephens, John (Ed.). *Ways of Being Male.* New York: Routledge, 2002 (pp.216–33).

Stephens, Matthew. *Hannah Snell: The Secret Life of a Female Marine.* UK: Ship Street Press, 1997.

Stone, Allan. A. "Seeing Pink." *Boston Review.* Accessed September 30, 2005. <http://bostonreview.net/BR22.6/stone.html>

Stryker, Susan. "My Words to Victor Frankenstein Above the Village of Chamounix – Performing Transgender Rage." *GLQ* 1(3): 227–254, 1994.

―――. "Transgender". *glbtq: An Encyclopedia of Gay, Lesbian, Bisexual, Transgender, and Queer Culture.* Claude J. Summers (Ed.), 2005. Accessed March 24, 2005. <http://www.glbtq.com/social-sciences/transgender. html>

Taketani, Etsuko. "Spectacular Child Bodies: The Sexual Politics of Cross-Dressing and Calisthenics in the Writings of Eliza Leslie and Catherine Beecher." *The Lion and the Unicorn* 23, no. 3, (1999): 355–72.

Toll, Robert, C. *Blacking Up: The Minstrel Show in Nineteenth-Century America.* New York: Oxford University Press, 1974.

Trites, Roberta Seelinger. *Disturbing the Universe: Power and Repression in Adolescent Literature.* Iowa City: University of Iowa Press, 2000.

―――. *Waking Sleeping Beauty: Feminist Voices in Children's Novels.* Iowa City: University of Iowa Press, 1997.

―――. "Queer Discourse and the Young Adult Novel: Repression and Power in Gay Male Adolescent Literature." *Children's Literature Association Quarterly* 23, no. 3 (1998): 143–51.

Walsh, Michael (Ed.). *Butler's Lives of the Saints*. Tunbridge Wells, Kent: Burns and Oates, (1956) 1985.

Warner, Marina. *Joan of Arc: The Image of Female Heroism*. California: University of California Press, [1981] 2000.

——— (ed). *Wonder Tales: Six Stories of Enchantment*. London: Vintage, 1996.

Warner, Michael. "Introduction: Fear of a Queer Planet," *Social Text*, 9, 4 (1991): 3–17.

———. *Fear of a Queer Planet: Queer Politics and Social Theory*. Minneapolis: University of Minnesota Press, 1993.

Westin, Boel. "The Androgynous Female – (or Orlando inverted) examples from Gripe, Stark, Wahl, Pohl." Pastemak, L. (ed). *Gender in Children's Literature*. Stockholm: Baltic Centre for Writers and Translators, 1999.

Wixson, C. "Cross-Dressing and John Lyly's Gallathea." *SEL Studies in English Literature* 1500–1900 41.2 (2001) 241–256.

Woodhouse, Annie. *Fantastic Women – Sex, Gender and Transvestism*. Basingstoke: Macmillan Education, 1989.

Zipes, Jack. *Fairy Tales and The Art of Subversion*. London: Heinemann Educational Books, 1983.

NAME AND TITLE INDEX

SUBJECT INDEX